ILLUSTRATED COURSE GUIDES

Written Communication

THIRD EDITION

Jeff Butterfield

Cengage

Australia • Brazil • Canada • Mexico • Singapore • United Kingdom • United States

Cengage

***Written Communication*, 3rd Edition: Illustrated Course Guides**
Jeff Butterfield

Product Director: Kathleen McMahon

Associate Product Manager: Reed Curry

Associate Content Developer: Maria Garguilo

Marketing Director: Michele McTighe

Marketing Manager: Jeff Tousignant

Marketing Coordinator: Cassie Cloutier

Contributing Author: Lisa Ruffolo

Developmental Editor: Lisa Ruffolo

Content Project Manager: Jen Feltri-George

IP Analyst: Amber Hill

Senior IP Project Manager: Kathy Kucharek

Proofreader: Brandy Lilly

Indexer: Elizabeth Cunningham

Print Buyer: Fola Orekoya

Composition: Lumina Datamatics Inc.

Art Director: Diana Graham

Cover Template Designer: Lisa Kuhn, Curio Press, LLC www.curiopress.com

Text Designer: GEX Publishing Services

Library of Congress Control Number: 2016938489

ISBN-13: 978-1-337-11929-0

Cengage
200 Pier 4 Boulevard
Boston, MA 02210
USA

Printed in the United States of America
Print Number: 03 Print Year: 2023

About the Series

Students work hard to earn certificates and degrees to prepare for a particular career—but do they have the soft skills necessary to succeed in today's digital workplace? Can they communicate effectively? Present themselves professionally? Work in a team? Industry leaders agree there is a growing need for these essential soft skills; in fact, they are critical to a student's success in the workplace. Without them, students will struggle and even fail. However, students entering the workforce who can demonstrate strong soft skills have a huge competitive advantage.

The *Illustrated Course Guides—Soft Skills for a Digital Workplace* series is designed to help you teach these important skills, better preparing your students to enter a competitive marketplace. Here are some of the key elements you will find in each book in the series:

- **Focused content allows for flexibility:** Each book in the series is short and focused, covering only the most essential skills related to the topic. You can use the modular content in standalone courses or workshops or you can integrate it into existing courses.
- **Visual design keeps students engaged:** Our unique pedagogical design presents each skill on two facing pages, with key concepts and instructions on the left and illustrations on the right. This keeps students of all levels on track.
- **Varied activities put skills to the test:** Each book includes hands-on activities, team exercises, critical thinking questions, and scenario-based activities to allow students to put their skills to work and demonstrate their retention of the material.

Read the Preface for more details on the key pedagogical elements and features of this book. We hope the books in this series help your students gain the critical soft skills they need to succeed in whatever career they choose.

Advisory Board

We thank our Advisory Board who gave us their opinions and guided our decisions for the second editions. They are as follows:

Paulette Gannett – SUNY – Broome Community College
Sherry Sparrowk – Peninsula College
Audrey Styer – Morton College
Charlene West – Durham Technical Community College

Preface

Welcome to *Written Communication, Second Edition: Illustrated Course Guides*. If this is your first experience with the Illustrated Course Guides, you'll see that this book has a unique design: each skill is presented on two facing pages, with Essential Elements on the left and illustrations and examples pictured on the right. The layout makes it easy to learn a skill without having to read a lot of text and flip pages to see an illustration. The design also makes this a great reference after the course is over! See the illustration on the right to learn more about the pedagogical and design elements of a typical chapter.

Focused on the Essentials

Each two-page lesson presents only the most important information about the featured skill. The left page of the lesson presents about five key Essential Elements, which are the most important guidelines that a student needs to know about the skill. Absorbing and retaining a limited number of key ideas makes it more likely that students will retain and apply the skill in a real-life situation.

Hands-On Activities

Every Essential Elements lesson contains a You Try It exercise, where students demonstrate their understanding of the lesson skill by completing a task that relates to it. The steps in the You Try It exercises are often general, requiring that students use critical thinking to complete the task.

Real World Advice and Examples

To help put lesson skills in context, many lessons contain yellow shaded boxes that present real-world stories pulled from today's workplace. Some lessons also contain Do's and Don'ts tables, featuring key guidelines on what to do and not do in certain workplace situations relating to the lesson skill. The Technology @ Work lesson at the end of every part covers Web 2.0 tools and other technologies relating to the part.

Each two-page spread focuses on a single learning objective.

Short introduction reviews key lesson points and presents a real-world case study to engage students.

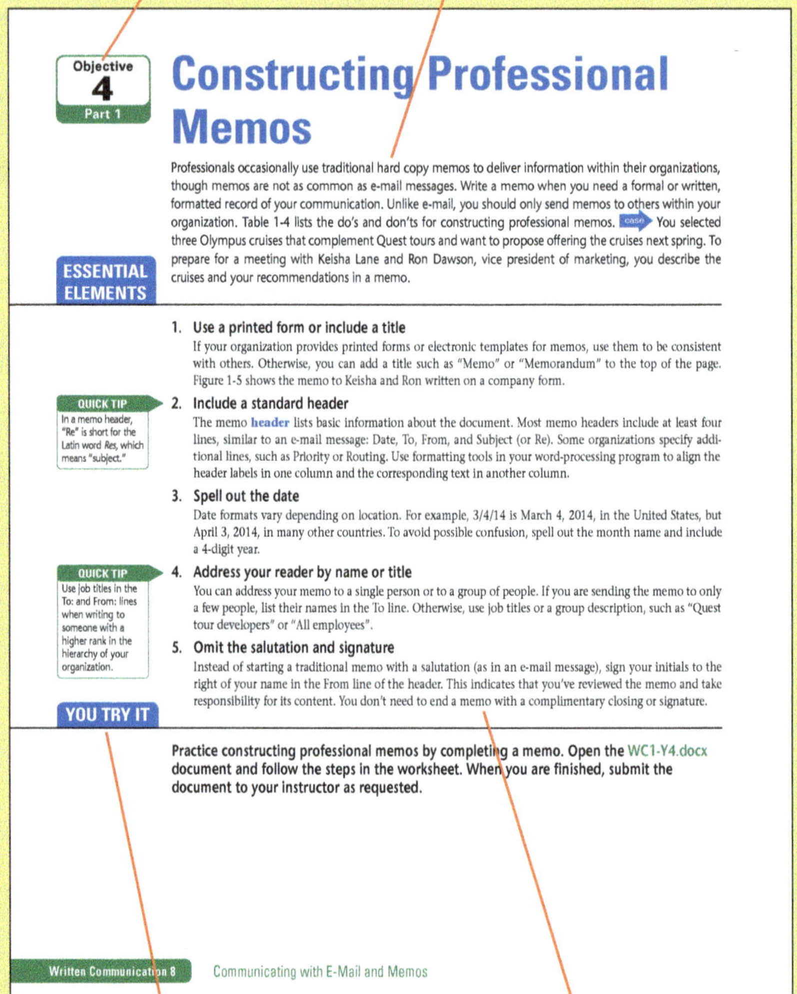

Objective 4 Part 1

Constructing Professional Memos

Professionals occasionally use traditional hard copy memos to deliver information within their organizations, though memos are not as common as e-mail messages. Write a memo when you need a formal or written, formatted record of your communication. Unlike e-mail, you should only send memos to others within your organization. Table 1-4 lists the do's and don'ts for constructing professional memos. case You selected three Olympus cruises that complement Quest tours and want to propose offering the cruises next spring. To prepare for a meeting with Keisha Lane and Ron Dawson, vice president of marketing, you describe the cruises and your recommendations in a memo.

ESSENTIAL ELEMENTS

1. **Use a printed form or include a title**
   If your organization provides printed forms or electronic templates for memos, use them to be consistent with others. Otherwise, you can add a title such as "Memo" or "Memorandum" to the top of the page. Figure 1-5 shows the memo to Keisha and Ron written on a company form.
2. **Include a standard header**
   The memo **header** lists basic information about the document. Most memo headers include at least four lines, similar to an e-mail message: Date, To, From, and Subject (or Re). Some organizations specify additional lines, such as Priority or Routing. Use formatting tools in your word-processing program to align the header labels in one column and the corresponding text in another column.
3. **Spell out the date**
   Date formats vary depending on location. For example, 3/4/14 is March 4, 2014, in the United States, but April 3, 2014, in many other countries. To avoid possible confusion, spell out the month name and include a 4-digit year.
4. **Address your reader by name or title**
   You can address your memo to a single person or to a group of people. If you are sending the memo to only a few people, list their names in the To line. Otherwise, use job titles or a group description, such as "Quest tour developers" or "All employees".
5. **Omit the salutation and signature**
   Instead of starting a traditional memo with a salutation (as in an e-mail message), sign your initials to the right of your name in the From line of the header. This indicates that you've reviewed the memo and take responsibility for its content. You don't need to end a memo with a complimentary closing or signature.

QUICK TIP
In a memo header, "Re" is short for the Latin word *Res*, which means "subject."

QUICK TIP
Use job titles in the To: and From: lines when writing to someone with a higher rank in the hierarchy of your organization.

YOU TRY IT

Practice constructing professional memos by completing a memo. Open the WC1-Y4.docx document and follow the steps in the worksheet. When you are finished, submit the document to your instructor as requested.

Written Communication 8 Communicating with E-Mail and Memos

You Try It activities let students perform tasks to demonstrate their understanding of the lesson objective.

Essential Elements present key points that students need to know to perform the lesson skill successfully.

Every lesson features large illustrations of examples discussed in the lesson.

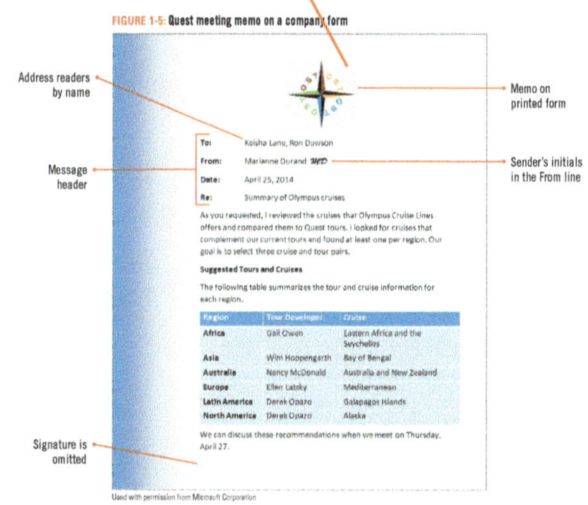

FIGURE 1-5: Quest meeting memo on a company form

Used with permission from Microsoft Corporation

TABLE 1-4: Constructing memos do's and don'ts

memo element	do	don't
Header	• Include standard header lines formatted in two columns	• **Don't** omit the header labels
From line	• Sign your initials after your name in the From line	• **Don't** sign your name at the end of the memo
Opening line	• Start with your main idea or request	• **Don't** start with a salutation
Body format	• Single-space the text • Insert blank lines between paragraphs • Use headings, lists, and bold to highlight information	• **Don't** double-space the text • **Don't** fill the page with one long paragraph

Advancing your career by mastering memos

Mastering the art of writing memos can be vital for advancing your career, especially in the corporate world. Communication skills and a strong work ethic are the top traits that recruiting companies look for in job candidates, according to the *National Association of Colleges & Employers 2008 Job Outlook*. Even technical companies specializing in engineering and computer technology emphasize writing skills. How effectively you communicate your ideas can inform and even inspire others. Bill Gates, cofounder of Microsoft Corporation, wrote a series of memos to colleagues about the potential of computers that set the direction of the computer industry. One laid the groundwork for Microsoft Windows, and another forecast the significance of the Internet. According to Charles Simonyi, a former colleague, Gates "selects the promising ideas that are over the horizon but not too far over, studies them in great detail, and then communicates them very effectively to the company, but also to the industry."

Source: Romano, Benjamin, "Gates' Big-Picture Memos Shaped Microsoft, Changed Tech World," *Seattle Times*, June 27, 2008.

Communicating with E-Mail and Memos | Written Communication 9

Written Communication

Do's & Don'ts tables present key tips for what to do and not do.

News to Use boxes provide real-world stories related to the lesson topic.

Lessons and Exercises

This book is divided into five parts, with each part containing about eight 2-page lessons, or learning objectives. The lessons use Quest Specialty Travel, a fictional adventure travel company, as the case study. The assignments on the peach pages at the end of each part increase in difficulty. Data files and case studies provide a variety of interesting and relevant business applications. Assignments include:

- **Soft Skills Reviews** provide multiple choice questions that test students' understanding of the part material.
- **Critical Thinking Questions** pose topics for discussion that require analysis and evaluation. Many also challenge students to consider and react to realistic critical thinking and application of the part skills.
- **Independent Challenges** are case projects requiring critical thinking and application of the part skills.
- **Real Life Independent Challenges** are practical exercises where students can apply the skills they learned in an activity that will help their own lives. For instance, they might create a resume, write a letter to a potential employer, or role play for a job interview for their dream position.
- **Team Challenges** are practical projects that require working together in a team to solve a problem.
- **Be the Critic Exercises** are activities that require students to evaluate a flawed example and provide ideas for improving it.

Contents

Preface ... iv

Written Communication

Part 1: Communicating with E-Mail and Memos ... Written 1

1: Understanding E-Mail Messages and Memos ... Written 2
2: Composing the Main Elements of Messages ... Written 4
Making sure your message is delivered
3: Creating Professional E-Mail Messages ... Written 6
4: Constructing Professional Memos ... Written 8
Advancing your career by mastering memos
5: Writing Request Messages ... Written 10
Simplifying meeting requests
6: Writing Response Messages ... Written 12
Response e-mail etiquette
7: Writing Bad-News Messages ... Written 14
8: Writing Documentation Messages ... Written 16
Avoiding e-mail overload
Technology @ Work: Wikis ... Written 18
Practice ... Written 20

Part 2: Uncovering the Secrets of Clear Writing ... Written 25

9: Clarifying Written Communication ... Written 26
10: Writing Solid Sentences ... Written 28
11: Developing Effective Paragraphs ... Written 30
12: Mastering Punctuation ... Written 32
E-mail, IM, and posts: writing or texting?
13: Laying Out Your Documents ... Written 34
Selecting the right medium
14: Illustrating Data ... Written 36
15: Adding Tables and Figures to Documents ... Written 38
16: Proofreading and Revising ... Written 40
Plain English is good business
Technology @ Work: Blogs ... Written 42
Blogging is writing
Practice ... Written 44

Part 3: Developing Reports and Proposals ... Written 49

17: Understanding Reports and Proposals ... Written 50
Business reports are not academic papers
18: Planning a Report or Proposal ... Written 52

19: Writing the Beginning .... Written 54
20: Writing the Body .... Written 56
Gathering information
21: Creating the End Matter .... Written 58
Web tools for Web research
22: Writing Short Reports .... Written 60
23: Writing Proposals .... Written 62
24: Citing Sources .... Written 64
Writing in your own words
Technology @ Work: Online Collaboration Tools .... Written 66
Practice .... Written 68

Part 4: Writing for Employment .... Written 73
25: Understanding Job Searches .... Written 74
Searching for jobs on the Internet
26: Writing Effective Cover Letters .... Written 76
27: Planning Résumés .... Written 78
28: Writing Chronological Résumés .... Written 80
Avoiding ethical pitfalls
29: Writing Functional Résumés .... Written 82
Including keywords in your résumé
30: Requesting Letters of Reference .... Written 84
E-portfolios and video résumés
31: Sending Follow-Up Messages .... Written 86
32: Accepting or Rejecting Job Offers .... Written 88
Technology @ Work: Professional Networking Sites .... Written 90
Practice .... Written 92

Part 5: Writing Professional Letters .... Written 97
33: Understanding Professional Letter Writing .... Written 98
The world's most effective business letter?
34: Writing Business Letters .... Written 100
35: Using Salutations .... Written 102
36: Closing Business Letters .... Written 104
37: Writing Routine Letters .... Written 106
38: Answering Request Letters .... Written 108
39: Writing Persuasive Letters .... Written 110
40: Writing for Goodwill .... Written 112
Respond to complaints with goodwill messages
Technology @ Work: Instant Messaging .... Written 114
Practice .... Written 116

Glossary 1

Index 3

Instructor Resources

The Instructor Resources provide instructors with a wide range of tools that enhance teaching and learning. These resources and more can be accessed from the instructor companion site. Log in at www.cengage.com/SSO.

- **Instructor's Manual**—Available as an electronic file, the Instructor's Manual is a valuable teaching tool for your course. It includes detailed lecture topics with teaching tips for each part.
- **Sample Syllabus**—Prepare and customize your course easily using this sample course outline.
- **PowerPoint Presentations**—Each part has a corresponding PowerPoint presentation that you can use in lecture, distribute to your students, or customize to suit your course.
- **Solutions to Exercises**—Solutions to Exercises contains every file students are asked to create or modify in the lessons and end-of-part material. This section also includes a solutions to the Soft Skills Reviews and Independent Challenges.
- **Data Files for Students**—To complete most of the exercises in this book, your students will need Data Files. You can post the Data Files on a file server for students to copy. The Data Files can be downloaded from www.cengage.com.
- **Test Banks**—Cengage Learning Testing powered by Cognero is a flexible, online system that allows instructors to author, edit, and manage test bank content from multiple Cengage Learning solutions and to create multiple versions. It works on any operating system or browser with no special installs or downloads needed, so tests can be created from anywhere with Internet access.

Part 1

Communicating with E-Mail and Memos

Files You Will Need:

WC1-Y2.docx
WC1-Y3.docx
WC1-Y4.docx
WC1-Y5.docx
WC1-Y6.docx
WC1-Y7.docx
WC1-Y8.docx
WC1-TechWork.docx
WC1-IC1.docx
WC1-IC2.docx
WC1-IC3.docx

When you need to communicate with colleagues or anyone else in your organization, send an e-mail message or printed memo. E-mail is the most popular way to exchange information in organizations and is an indispensable productivity tool. You can use an e-mail message to collect information, respond to requests, or confirm decisions, for example. A memo is appropriate when you want to create a permanent or more formal record. In this unit, you learn how to compose professional e-mail messages and memos. case As an assistant at Quest Specialty Travel, you are helping Keisha Lane, the vice president of operations, develop new types of tours. Keisha recently negotiated an agreement with Olympus Cruise Lines so that Quest can add cruise options to its tour packages. She asks you to write a series of e-mail messages and memos to inform the tour developers about the new cruises.

OBJECTIVES

1. Understand e-mail messages and memos
2. Compose the main elements of messages
3. Create professional e-mail messages
4. Construct professional memos
5. Write request messages
6. Write response messages
7. Write bad-news messages
8. Write documentation messages

© Dmitriy Shironosov / Shutterstock Images

Objective 1 Part 1

Understanding E-Mail Messages and Memos

An **e-mail message** is communication composed on and sent with electronic mail technology. A **memo** is a hard, or printed, copy of a document written for people within a single organization. E-mail messages and memos are standard forms of business communication that inform employees, articulate policies, request information, provide responses, and verify decisions. Figure 1-1 shows examples of a professional e-mail message and a memo. However, as described in Table 1-1, each one serves a different purpose. case Before you write the first message for Keisha, you review the guidelines for composing professional e-mail and memos.

DETAILS

Before writing an e-mail message or memo, answer the following questions:

- **What are the purpose and audience of the message?**
  Start by analyzing what you want to accomplish by sending an e-mail or distributing a memo—that purpose should be the main subject of the message. Also clearly identify your audience. A message you write to colleagues can have an informal tone, while a message for your manager should be more professional.

QUICK TIP
In some organizations, the rule of thumb is to send e-mail to colleagues and memos to senior management.

- **Should you create an e-mail message or memo?**
  E-mail messages are generally shorter, more immediate, and less formal than memos. They can also include electronic information stored on your computer, network, or the Internet.

Use e-mail to perform the following tasks:

- **Communicate ideas and information to others in an organization**
  E-mail is popular because it lets you quickly exchange short messages, especially those that request a quick response, confirm a decision, or provide brief information.
- **Notify people of changes in upcoming plans**
  When time is a factor, e-mail is ideal for communicating changes such as rescheduled meetings, project updates, and deadline extensions.
- **Request information or action and reply to requests**
  Instead of making a phone call, send an e-mail message requesting information so that your colleagues can refer to a written record of your question or request to take action. E-mail programs also make it convenient to reply to a message from someone else and include the text of their original message in your response.

QUICK TIP
Phone calls or in-person meetings are appropriate when you need to guarantee privacy or discuss sensitive topics.

- **Make announcements to many people**
  Because you can easily send an e-mail message to many people at the same time, use it to announce changes such as a job vacancy, new product, or promotion.

Use memos to perform the following tasks:

- **Create a permanent record**
  Circulate memos when you need a physical record of the communication, such as to list procedures, provide instructions, or post an announcement in a central location.
- **Communicate a formal message**
  Written memos are more formal than e-mail messages, making them appropriate for official communications such as corporate policies, employment decisions, and other important matters.

FIGURE 1-1: Sample e-mail message and memo

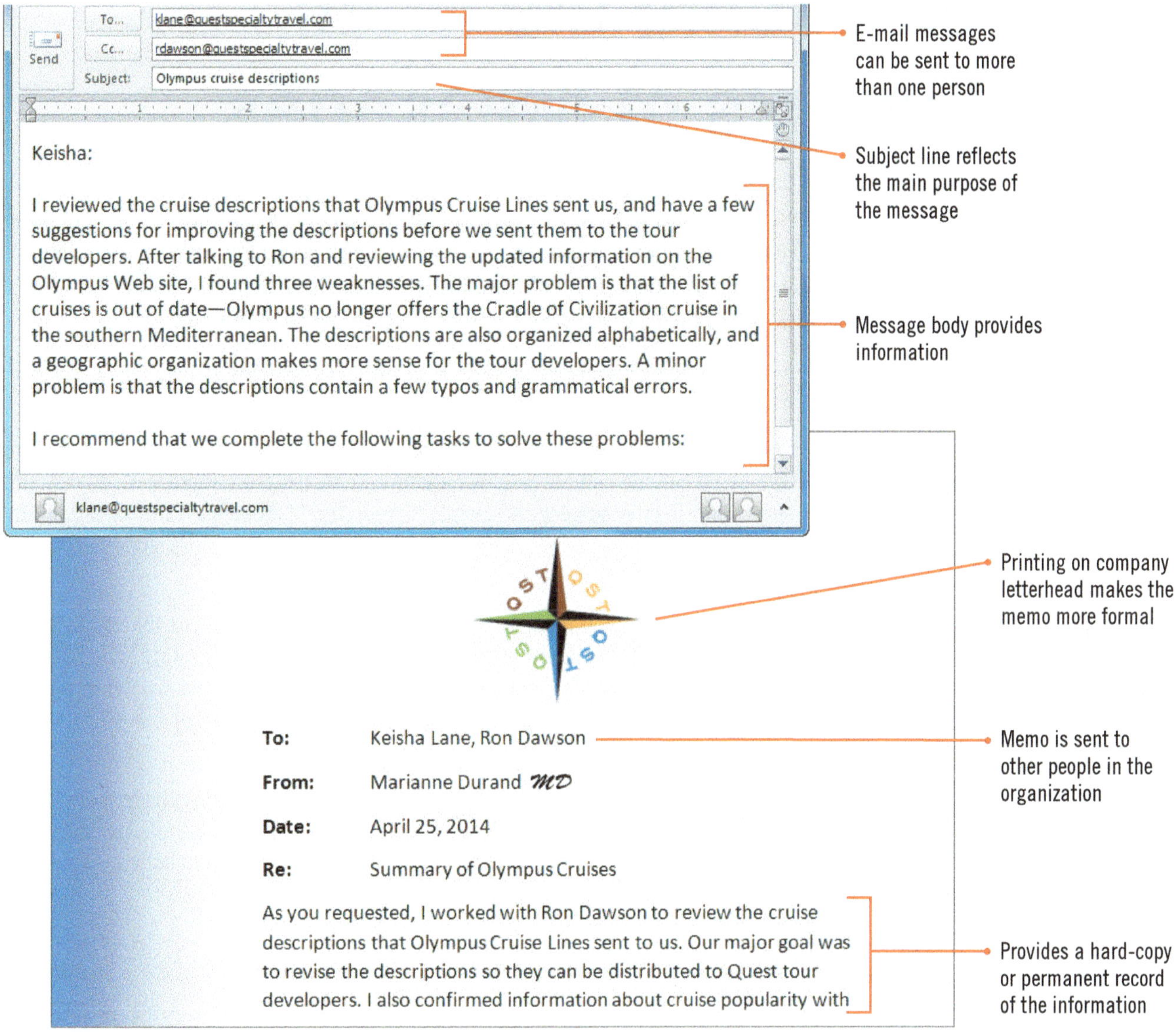
To... klane@questspecialtytravel.com
Cc... rdawson@questspecialtytravel.com
Subject: Olympus cruise descriptions

Keisha:

I reviewed the cruise descriptions that Olympus Cruise Lines sent us, and have a few suggestions for improving the descriptions before we sent them to the tour developers. After talking to Ron and reviewing the updated information on the Olympus Web site, I found three weaknesses. The major problem is that the list of cruises is out of date—Olympus no longer offers the Cradle of Civilization cruise in the southern Mediterranean. The descriptions are also organized alphabetically, and a geographic organization makes more sense for the tour developers. A minor problem is that the descriptions contain a few typos and grammatical errors.

I recommend that we complete the following tasks to solve these problems:

klane@questspecialtytravel.com

To: Keisha Lane, Ron Dawson
From: Marianne Durand *MD*
Date: April 25, 2014
Re: Summary of Olympus Cruises

As you requested, I worked with Ron Dawson to review the cruise descriptions that Olympus Cruise Lines sent to us. Our major goal was to revise the descriptions so they can be distributed to Quest tour developers. I also confirmed information about cruise popularity with

Used with permission from Microsoft Corporation

TABLE 1-1: Appropriate uses for e-mail and memos

scenario	use e-mail	use memo	use other
Many people need to receive the same short message	•		
You want quick answers to one or more questions	•		
You are responding to a colleague's e-mail	•		
Your manager asks you to confirm a decision	•		
You are inviting others to a meeting	•		
You are updating a simple procedure	•	•	
Meeting participants need to review the details of a plan		•	
You are circulating a new set of formal company policies		•	
You want to express enthusiasm to a colleague			Phone call or visit
You need to resolve a conflict			Face-to-face meeting
Your message is confidential			Letter enclosed in an envelope

Objective 2 Part 1

Composing the Main Elements of Messages

ESSENTIAL ELEMENTS

Whether you are writing an e-mail or composing a printed memo, your messages should include four basic elements: (1) a subject line that offers a preview of your message; (2) an opening sentence that communicates your main idea; (3) a message body that explains, supports, or justifies your ideas; and (4) an appropriate closing statement. Figure 1-2 shows an e-mail message with these four elements. case Keisha asks you to send an e-mail message to the tour developers to set up a conference phone call.

QUICK TIP
Subject lines do not need to be complete sentences or end with a period.

1. **Subject line**
   Use a concise phrase that summarizes the main idea of your message. Busy people often decide whether to open an e-mail message based on the subject line. For example, "Meeting on Tuesday at 10:00" and "Report on fall trade show" are effective subject lines, while "Important," "Problems," and "Meeting" are not. Table 1-2 lists the do's and don'ts for including subjects and other basic e-mail elements.
2. **Opening sentence**
   Communicate the main idea of your message in the first sentence. You can do this by restating and expanding the subject line, as in "Let me know if you can attend the project meeting scheduled for Tuesday, April 4, at 10:00 A.M." If you are delivering bad news, however, you should start with a softer approach.
3. **Message body**
   Support your main idea with additional information that explains why you are writing the message. Limit the message to a single topic, and organize the material to make it easy to read. For example, use short sentences, headings, lists, tables, and graphic highlighting techniques such as boldface and bullets. Avoid long paragraphs of text.
4. **Closing statement**
   End the message with a statement that requests specific action from the reader, cites a deadline, summarizes the key points in a complex message, or closes with a positive thought. For example, "Please submit your product descriptions by September 3" is an effective call to action. If you are writing a simple message that does not request action, close with a courteous comment such as "Thanks for all your help on this project."

YOU TRY IT

Practice composing the main elements of messages by revising an e-mail that organizes a meeting. Open the WC1-Y2.docx document and follow the steps in the worksheet. When you are finished, submit the document to your instructor as requested.

Making sure your message is delivered

A recent study by Barracuda Networks found that almost 65 percent of e-mail users receive up to 10 unwanted e-mail messages, or spam, per day. In response, organizations and other users install e-mail filters that block messages containing words typically included in spam. To make sure your e-mail messages are not blocked by filters, avoid the following words in your Subject line: *Free, Deal, Offer, Buy, Special, Call Now, Click Here,* and other terms commonly used to sell products or services, phrases that suggest that the message is urgent or important, and references to money. Also avoid exclamation points, words in all caps, misspelled words, and blank subject lines.

FIGURE 1-2: Four basic elements in an e-mail message

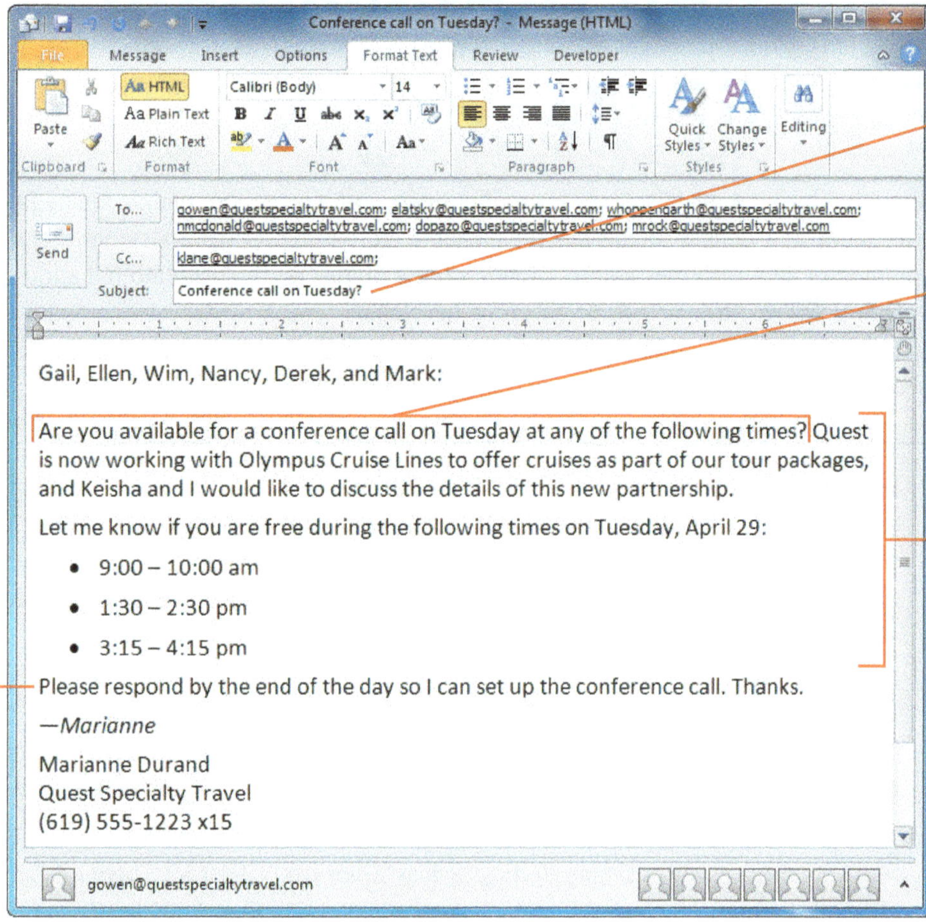

Used with permission from Microsoft Corporation

TABLE 1-2: Basic e-mail elements do's and don'ts

element	do	don't
Subject line	• Summarize the main idea of the message • Use a brief phrase	• **Don't** use vague or wordy language • **Don't** write a complete sentence • **Don't** use terms a spam filter might catch
Opening	• Restate the main idea (unless it is bad news) • Make your request or respond directly to a question	• **Don't** start with a topic other than the main topic • **Don't** explain before making your request • **Don't** restate the request in your reply
Message body	• Focus on a single topic • Organize your supporting ideas logically • Use short sentences, headings, and lists • Include attachments for supplemental material	• **Don't** overwhelm your reader with lengthy narrative • **Don't** include information that doesn't relate to your main topic
Closing	• Include a call to action when you are making a request • Provide a deadline when appropriate • Summarize long messages or end with a closing thought	• **Don't** omit your contact information • **Don't** close abruptly

Objective
3
Part 1

Creating Professional E-Mail Messages

Although e-mail is a relatively new form of business communication, people are beginning to agree on conventions and general guidelines for creating professional e-mail messages. Figure 1-3 shows the beginning of an e-mail message that follows these guidelines by including full addresses and a simple salutation. case After talking to the tour developers, you are ready to compare Quest tours with Olympus cruises, then suggest a few cruises to offer as tour options. Keisha asks you to send her an e-mail message outlining what you need to complete this task.

ESSENTIAL ELEMENTS

1. **Full name and address**

   E-mail addresses such as *bal1966@mymail.com* don't clearly identify the sender. Instead, include full names and e-mail addresses in the To and From fields of an e-mail message. E-mail programs such as Microsoft Office Outlook let you enter a first and last name followed by the e-mail address (Example: Bob Linden <bal1966@mymail.com>).

2. **Carbon copy (Cc)**

   In addition to the main recipient, you can send copies of the message to other people by including their e-mail addresses in the Cc field. Be sure the people listed in the Cc field are directly involved with the message and will benefit from its information—most people only want to receive e-mail that they need to read.

3. **Salutation**

   Start your message with a simple greeting such as "Greetings," "Dear Mr. Dawson," "Hi Katie," or "Ron,". The salutation provides a friendly start to your communication and shows where your message begins, which is especially helpful if someone forwards or replies to your e-mail.

4. **Body format and content**

   Format the opening line and the rest of the message so they are easy to read, as described in Table 1-3. Focus on a single topic and keep the message brief, no more than 25 lines if possible. Ideally, your readers should not have to scroll the message more than once or twice. If you need to discuss more than one topic, send a separate message for each topic. Figure 1-4 shows the opening line and part of the message body for the e-mail message to Keisha.

5. **Closing**

   End with a signature block that includes your name and contact information, such as the name of your organization, address, and your telephone number. Most e-mail programs can insert signature blocks for you.

QUICK TIP
Use the Blind carbon copy (Bcc) field to send copies of your message to others without displaying their e-mail addresses.

QUICK TIP
A salutation is optional when you are sending an e-mail to a colleague at your organization.

YOU TRY IT

Practice creating professional e-mail messages by writing a complete message. Open the WC1-Y3.docx document and follow the steps in the worksheet. When you are finished, submit the document to your instructor as requested.

FIGURE 1-3: **Addressing the e-mail message**

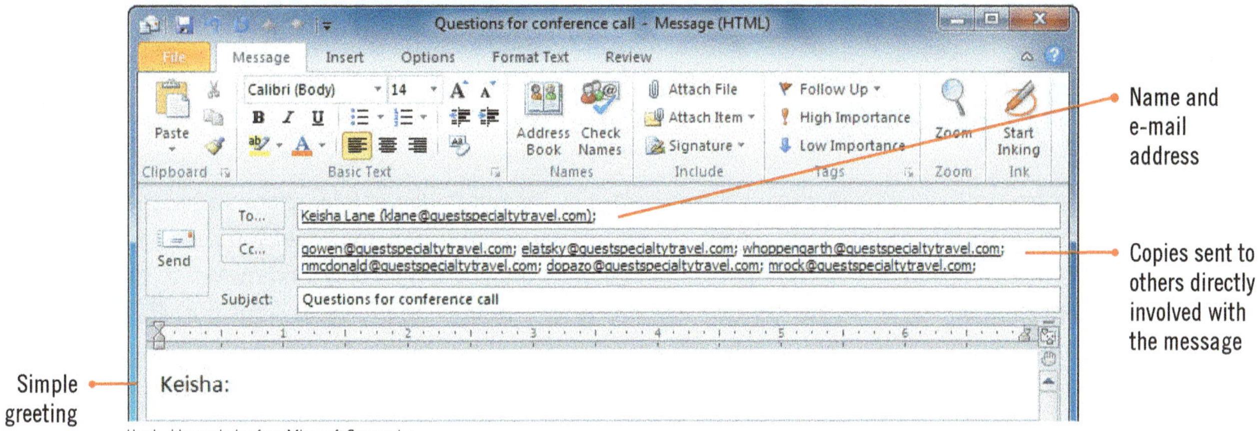

Used with permission from Microsoft Corporation

FIGURE 1-4: **Composing the body of the message to Keisha Lane**

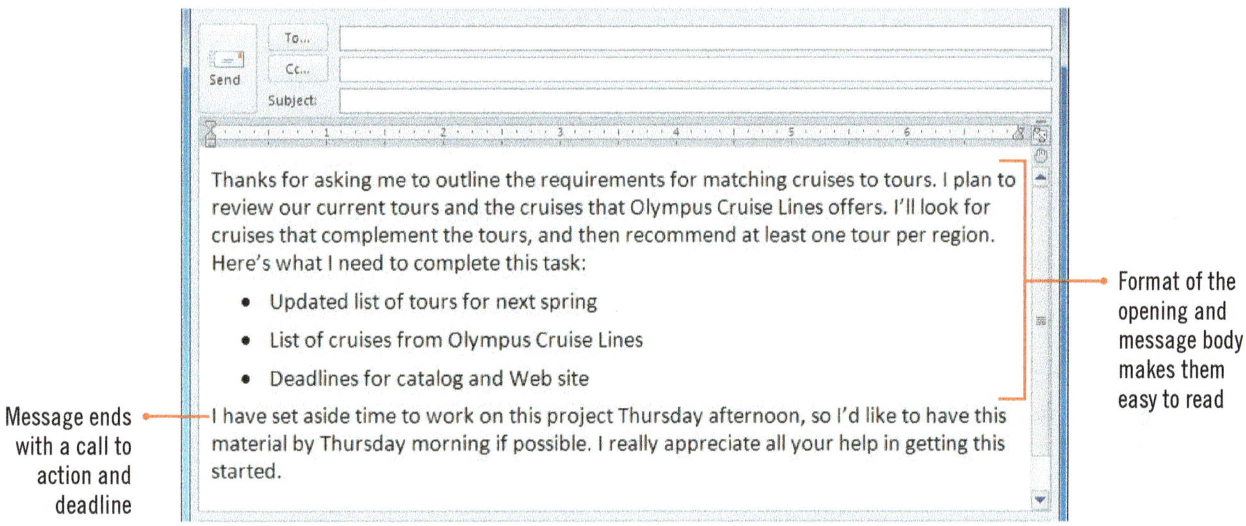

Used with permission form Microsoft Corporation

TABLE 1-3: **Creating e-mail do's and don'ts**

message section	do	don't
To and From lines	• Include both a name and e-mail address in each line	• **Don't** rely on your e-mail address as the only way to identify yourself
Cc line	• Send a copy to people directly involved with the message	• **Don't** send blanket copies to people who are not involved with the message
Salutation	• Start with a short greeting	• **Don't** omit the salutation or use one that's too informal unless you are writing to a friend or close colleague
Body format	• Use standard capitalization and lowercase characters • Insert blank lines and break up text for readability	• **Don't** use all uppercase or all lowercase text • **Don't** include all of the message content in one long paragraph
Closing	• Include a call to action or deadline, if appropriate • End with a signature block	• **Don't** trail off without a conclusion • **Don't** forget to provide your contact information

Objective 4 Part 1

Constructing Professional Memos

Professionals occasionally use traditional hard copy memos to deliver information within their organizations, though memos are not as common as e-mail messages. Write a memo when you need a formal or written, formatted record of your communication. Unlike e-mail, you should only send memos to others within your organization. Table 1-4 lists the do's and don'ts for constructing professional memos. case You selected three Olympus cruises that complement Quest tours and want to propose offering the cruises next spring. To prepare for a meeting with Keisha Lane and Ron Dawson, vice president of marketing, you describe the cruises and your recommendations in a memo.

ESSENTIAL ELEMENTS

1. **Use a printed form or include a title**

   If your organization provides printed forms or electronic templates for memos, use them to be consistent with others. Otherwise, you can add a title such as "Memo" or "Memorandum" to the top of the page. Figure 1-5 shows the memo to Keisha and Ron written on a company form.

2. **Include a standard header**

   The memo **header** lists basic information about the document. Most memo headers include at least four lines, similar to an e-mail message: Date, To, From, and Subject (or Re). Some organizations specify additional lines, such as Priority or Routing. Use formatting tools in your word-processing program to align the header labels in one column and the corresponding text in another column.

3. **Spell out the date**

   Date formats vary depending on location. For example, 3/4/17 is March 4, 2017, in the United States, but April 3, 2017, in many other countries. To avoid possible confusion, spell out the month name and include a 4-digit year.

4. **Address your reader by name or title**

   You can address your memo to a single person or to a group of people. If you are sending the memo to only a few people, list their names in the To line. Otherwise, use job titles or a group description, such as "Quest tour developers" or "All employees".

5. **Omit the salutation and signature**

   Instead of starting a traditional memo with a salutation (as in an e-mail message), sign your initials to the right of your name in the From line of the header. This indicates that you've reviewed the memo and take responsibility for its content. You don't need to end a memo with a complimentary closing or signature.

QUICK TIP

In a memo header, "Re" is short for the Latin word *Res*, which means "subject."

QUICK TIP

Use job titles in the To: and From: lines when writing to someone with a higher rank in the hierarchy of your organization.

YOU TRY IT

Practice constructing professional memos by completing a memo. Open the WC1-Y4.docx document and follow the steps in the worksheet. When you are finished, submit the document to your instructor as requested.

FIGURE 1-5: Quest meeting memo on a company form

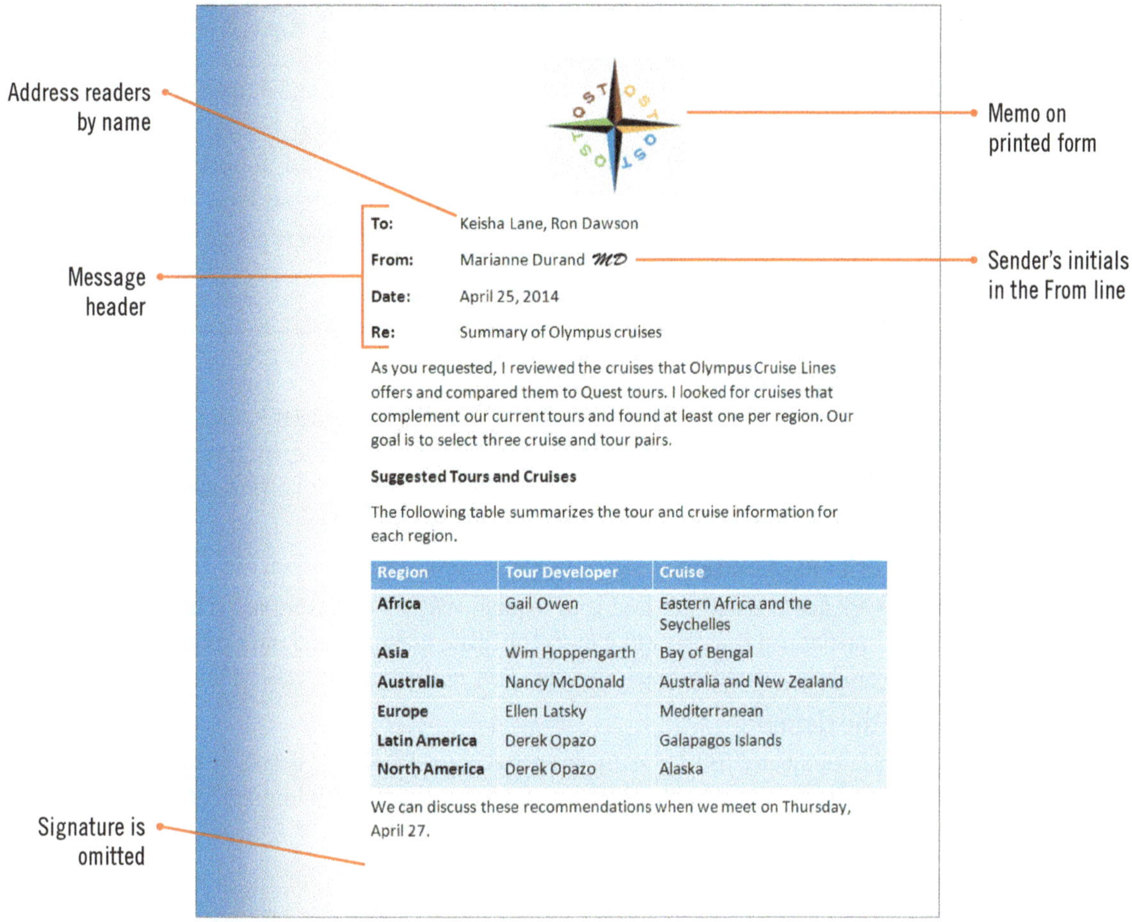

To: Keisha Lane, Ron Dawson

From: Marianne Durand *MD*

Date: April 25, 2014

Re: Summary of Olympus cruises

As you requested, I reviewed the cruises that Olympus Cruise Lines offers and compared them to Quest tours. I looked for cruises that complement our current tours and found at least one per region. Our goal is to select three cruise and tour pairs.

Suggested Tours and Cruises

The following table summarizes the tour and cruise information for each region.

Region	Tour Developer	Cruise
Africa	Gail Owen	Eastern Africa and the Seychelles
Asia	Wim Hoppengarth	Bay of Bengal
Australia	Nancy McDonald	Australia and New Zealand
Europe	Ellen Latsky	Mediterranean
Latin America	Derek Opazo	Galapagos Islands
North America	Derek Opazo	Alaska

We can discuss these recommendations when we meet on Thursday, April 27.

Used with permission from Microsoft Corporation

TABLE 1-4: Constructing memos do's and don'ts

memo element	do	don't
Header	• Include standard header lines formatted in two columns	• **Don't** omit the header labels
From line	• Sign your initials after your name in the From line	• **Don't** sign your name at the end of the memo
Opening line	• Start with your main idea or request	• **Don't** start with a salutation
Body format	• Single-space the text • Insert blank lines between paragraphs • Use headings, lists, and bold to highlight information	• **Don't** double-space the text • **Don't** fill the page with one long paragraph

Advancing your career by mastering memos

Mastering the art of writing memos can be vital for advancing your career, especially in the corporate world. Communication skills and a strong work ethic are the top traits that recruiting companies look for in job candidates, according to the *National Association of Colleges & Employers 2008 Job Outlook.* Even technical companies specializing in engineering and computer technology emphasize writing skills. How effectively you communicate your ideas can inform and even inspire others. Bill Gates, cofounder of Microsoft Corporation, wrote a series of memos to colleagues about the potential of computers that set the direction of the computer industry. One laid the groundwork for Microsoft Windows, and another forecast the significance of the Internet. According to Charles Simonyi, a former colleague, Gates "selects the promising ideas that are over the horizon but not too far over, studies them in great detail, and then communicates them very effectively to the company, but also to the industry."

Source: Romano, Benjamin, "Gates' Big-Picture Memos Shaped Microsoft, Changed Tech World," *Seattle Times*, June 27, 2008.

Written Communication

Objective 5 Part 1

Writing Request Messages

A **request message** asks for information or action from someone else. For example, write a request message when you need to ask colleagues if they are available for a meeting, have information they could send you, or are finished with their tasks on a project. Figure 1-6 shows an original and revised version of a typical request message. case Keisha and Ron approved your plan to add three cruises as extended tour options. They suggest you send e-mail messages to the tour developers asking them to propose specific tours that would work well with the cruises you selected.

ESSENTIAL ELEMENTS

1. **Take a direct approach**

   Start your message by directly making your request. Avoid excessive detail or explanation. For example, "Are you free on Tuesday for a planning meeting?" makes the request in the first line. If you have more than one question, start with a brief statement such as "Please answer the following questions regarding the new project," then list your questions.

2. **Include a brief explanation**

   Your readers ask questions as they read your request. *Why are you asking me? What sales figures do you need? Where is the meeting and how long will it last?* Anticipate questions and offer short explanations. People are more willing to help and respond quickly when they understand the reasons for a request.

3. **Organize the details**

   Use bulleted or numbered lists to clearly present your questions, the details of your request, or the specific actions you want your readers to take. Don't make your reader search through long paragraphs to figure out what you are requesting.

4. **Include a deadline**

   Deadlines help your readers determine the priority of your message and work your request into their schedules. Be sure the deadline is realistic. If you are requesting immediate action or significant effort, make a phone call or a personal visit instead. Figure 1-7 shows a request message that includes a deadline.

5. **Use basic courtesy**

   Because a request message asks your reader to do something for you, use a polite, friendly tone and express appreciation for their efforts. For example, phrases such as "Please consider the following questions," or "I would appreciate your response by..." are courteous sentence openers.

QUICK TIP

Omitting the deadline might result in no response, especially if the reader is busy or tends to procrastinate.

YOU TRY IT

Practice writing request messages by creating one yourself. Open the WC1-Y5.docx document and follow the steps in the worksheet. When you are finished, submit the document to your instructor as requested.

Simplifying meeting requests

Many organizations, especially those that have offices in more than one place, use e-mail to set up online meetings and request attendance. However, employees often have trouble scheduling and preparing for meetings when they use e-mail alone to send messages requesting meetings. Integrating e-mail software with meeting software solves this problem. For example, you can schedule a Web conference using Microsoft Office Outlook, then send a meeting request to participants along with documents they need for the meeting. Instead of composing a separate message, recipients can respond to the request by clicking a button. When it is time for the meeting, participants can click a link in the meeting request message to connect to the online Web conference.

FIGURE 1-6: Original and revised written request

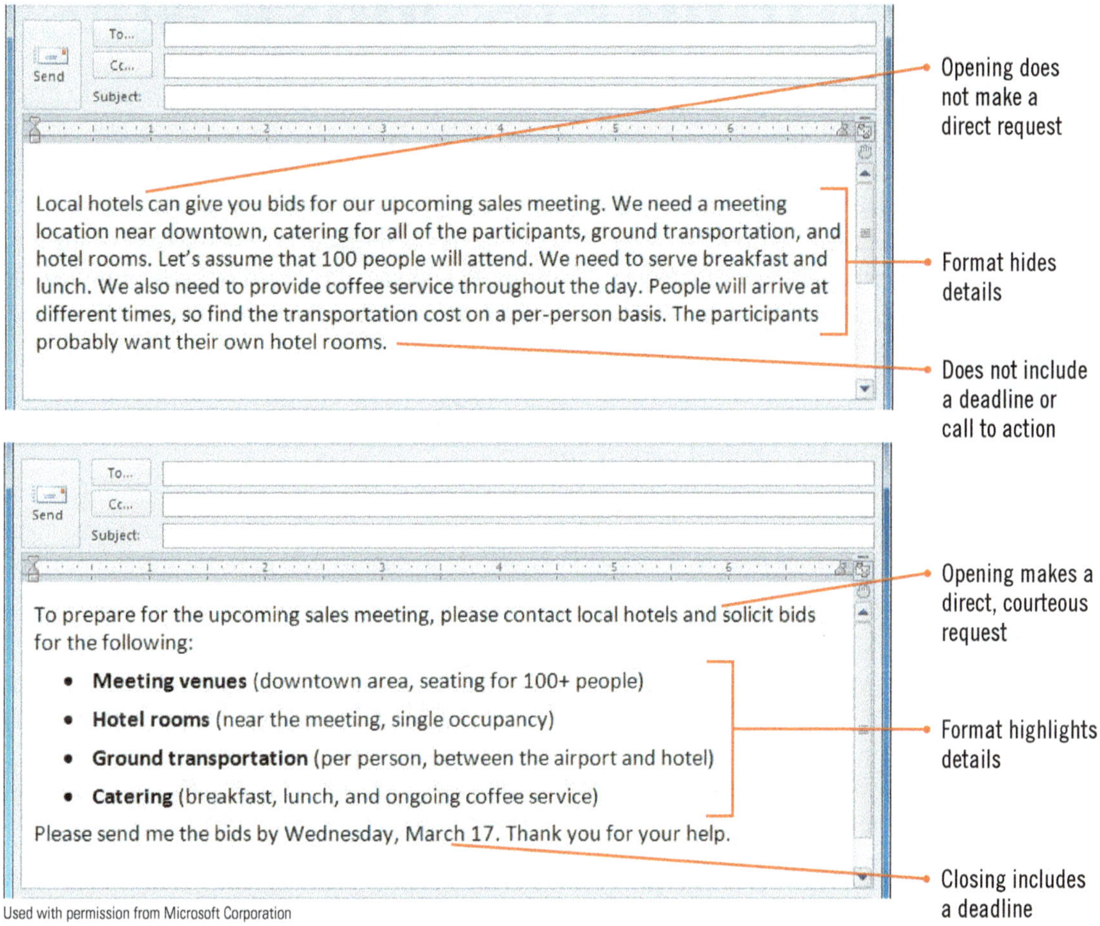

Used with permission from Microsoft Corporation

FIGURE 1-7: Request message to Quest tour developers

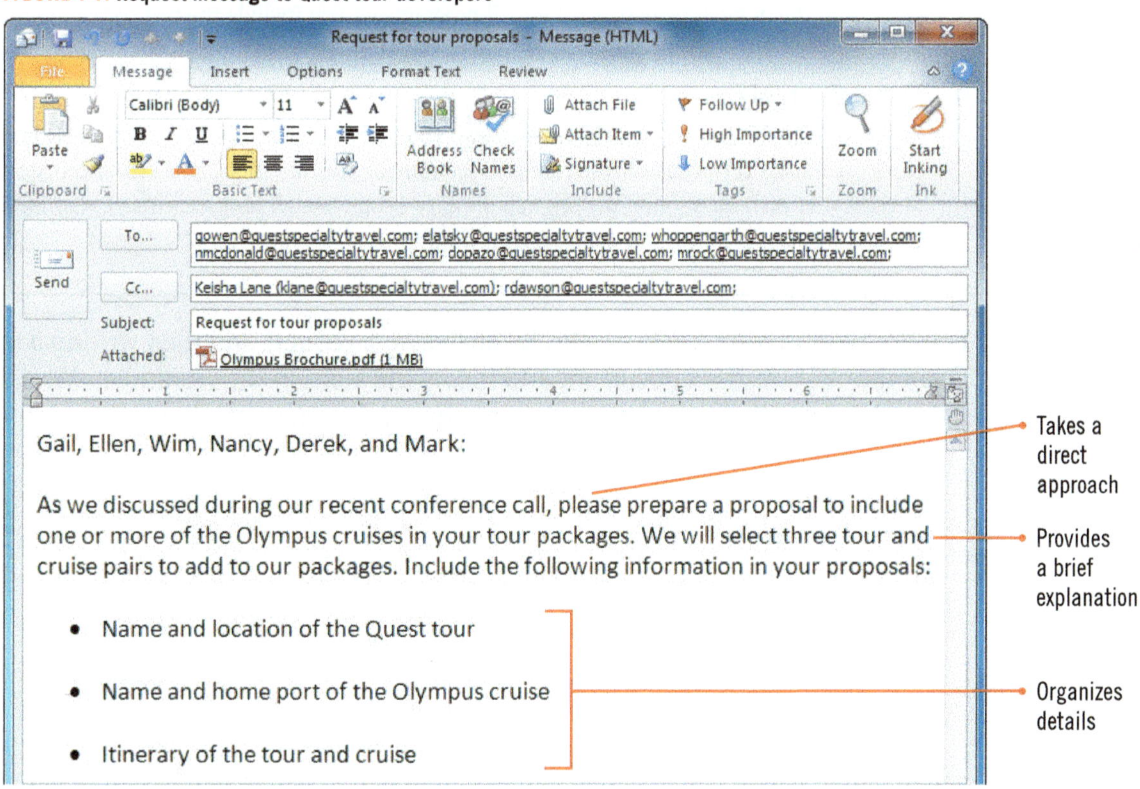

Used with permission from Microsoft Corporation

Objective 6
Part 1

Writing Response Messages

After receiving a request message from someone, you need to send a response to that request and answer any questions. In fact, much of your professional e-mail communication will probably involve creating response messages. As in other types of e-mail messages, you should take a direct approach, format for readability, and use professional, courteous language. Because you are replying to a request, your message should stick to the topic introduced in the original message, and organize your answers or other responses logically and concisely. Figure 1-8 shows an original and revised response message. case Derek Opazo, the tour developer for the Americas, sent you an e-mail message with questions about the cruises that might fit his tours. You need to reply with responses to his questions.

ESSENTIAL ELEMENTS

1. **Use the original subject line**

   When you use the Reply feature in your e-mail program, the program usually inserts "Re:" at the beginning of the Subject line, then inserts the original subject text. The "Re:" indicates your message is a reply, which helps recipients track related messages. If the original subject text is missing or weak, such as "Request", replace it with a more detailed subject, such as "Re: Your request for travel expenses".

2. **Maintain a direct approach**

   When writing a response, you don't need to restate or summarize the original message. Instead, start by directly responding to your reader's initial questions or request. If possible, respond with positive language to generate goodwill and enhance your image as cooperative and helpful. For example, "I am happy to assist you with..." and "As you requested, here are the answers to your questions about..." are effective response-message openers.

   QUICK TIP
   If you cannot answer the questions or comply with the request, write a bad-news message. (See "Writing Bad-News Messages" later in this part.)

3. **Respond completely and in the manner of the original request**

   Make sure you answer all the questions or provide all the requested information. Otherwise, your colleague might need to send you a follow-up message highlighting the missing responses. Your reply should also be consistent with the original request. For example, answer questions or address multiple requests in the same order as in the original request. Most e-mail programs let you include the text of the original message with your response, which helps your readers understand your responses in context. See Figure 1-9.

4. **Prune the reply**

   If you include the text of the original message, you can delete the header, greeting, closing, and signature block so readers can focus on the response sections of your message. You can also insert your responses directly after each question in the original message—some e-mail programs insert your initials before these responses or display them in a contrasting color.

YOU TRY IT

Practice writing response messages by analyzing a request and then writing a response. Open the WC1-Y6.docx document and follow the steps in the worksheet. When you are finished, submit the document to your instructor as requested.

FIGURE 1-8: Original and revised written response

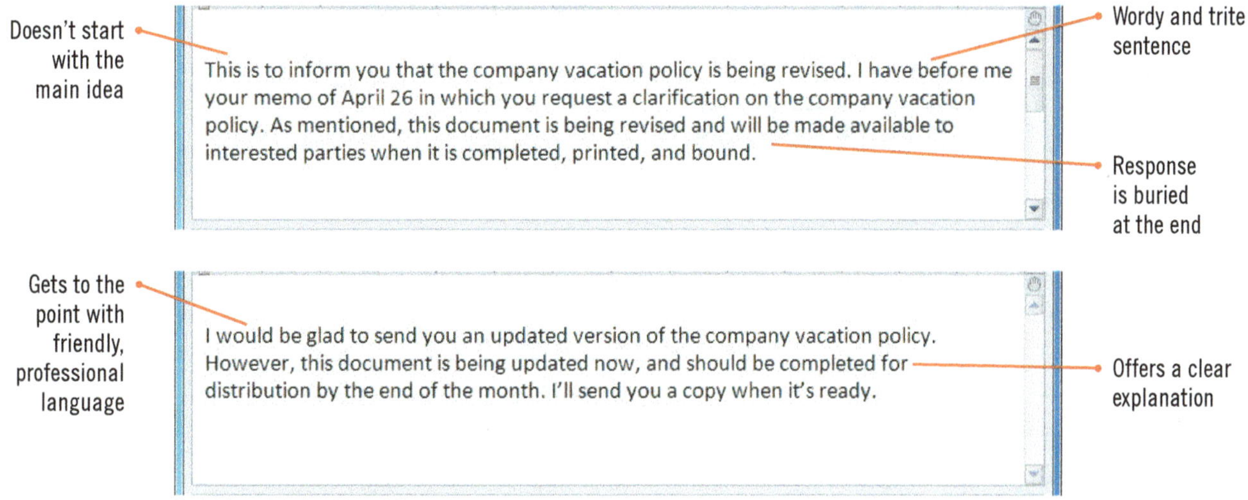

Used with permission from Microsoft Corporation

FIGURE 1-9: Writing a response message to a Quest tour developer

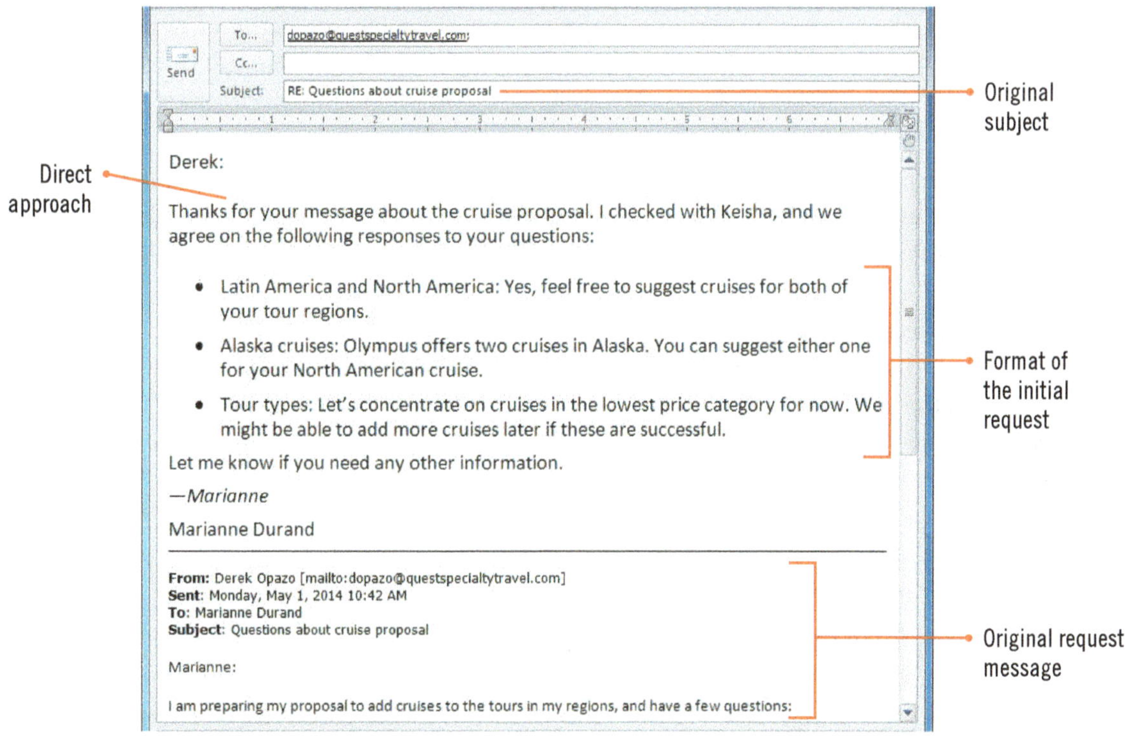

Used with permission from Microsoft Corporation

Response e-mail etiquette

According to the Web site *emailreplies.com,* e-mail responses should be governed by common rules of e-mail etiquette, particularly in the business world. Following e-mail etiquette helps to convey a professional image, ensure efficient and accurate responses, and prevent misunderstandings and even legal problems. Many etiquette guidelines address e-mail responses in particular. For example, when writing and sending e-mail responses, be sure to answer all the questions in the request message, anticipate related questions, respond as quickly as possible (within at least 24 hours), and use the Reply to All feature sparingly. As in any type of e-mail, proofread your complete message before you send it, and look for language your reader might misinterpret. Because e-mail is nearly instantaneous, people expect rapid responses to their requests or by their stated deadline. Responding promptly is professional and courteous. If you don't have an immediate answer to a question, send an e-mail explaining that and identifying when your recipient can expect a response. If you are tardy in your response or fail to respond at all, you can create the impression that you are avoiding the sender's request or have poor time-management skills.

Objective 7
Part 1

Writing Bad-News Messages

Occasionally, you need to write a bad-news message to refuse a request, decline a proposal, highlight disappointing sales, or cancel a project. If your reader does not have a personal stake in the bad news, you can use the direct approach in your message. On the other hand, if your reader is likely to be disappointed, take an **indirect approach** to the bad news, which reveals the message in stages. Figure 1-10 shows the original and revised versions of a bad-news memo. case After the Quest tour developers sent you proposals for including Olympus cruises with their tours, you and Keisha selected three tours that will include a cruise option. You now need to write an e-mail message to the developers of the tours you did not select.

ESSENTIAL ELEMENTS

1. **Start with a statement that establishes goodwill**
   Open with a sincere observation, compliment, or encouraging comment related to your subject. For example, acknowledge your reader's achievement or contribution in a statement such as "Thank you for your detailed, thoughtful request for additional funding." You can also start with facts related to the news, as in "This year, transportation costs have doubled."
2. **Explain the background**
   Presenting the reasons for the negative message is especially important. Briefly describe the circumstances that are relevant to the bad news. Providing some context helps your reader understand the situation and the response. Figure 1-11 shows the beginning of a bad-news message that explains the background of the decision.
3. **Deliver the bad news**
   State the bad news objectively and professionally, using language that softens the message. Provide an alternative or compromise, if possible. For example, you might write, "As a result of increased production, no vacation requests are being honored until after September 1. If you resubmit the request in the fall, I will process it for you immediately."
4. **Close the message appropriately**
   Cushion the bad news by ending with an optimistic statement, or mentioning good wishes. To convey a firm and decisive tone, conclude with the bad news.
5. **Proofread carefully before sending**
   In addition to checking your spelling and grammar, consider how your readers might react to and interpret your message. Refer to Table 1-5 as you edit the message for a list of do's and don'ts when creating bad-news memos.

QUICK TIP
Write one draft of a bad-news message, take a break, then read the message again with a fresh point of view.

YOU TRY IT

Practice writing bad-news messages by writing one that takes an indirect approach. Open the WC1-Y7.docx document and follow the steps in the worksheet. When you are finished, submit the document to your instructor as requested.

FIGURE 1-10: Original and revised version of bad-news message

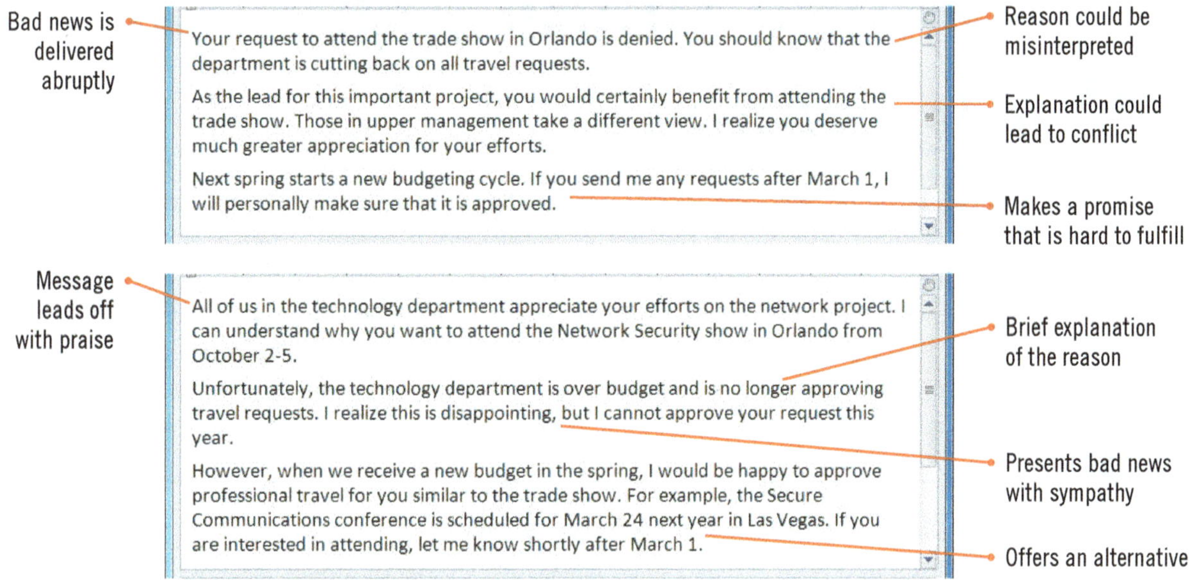

Used with permission from Microsoft Corporation

FIGURE 1-11: Bad-news message to Quest tour developers

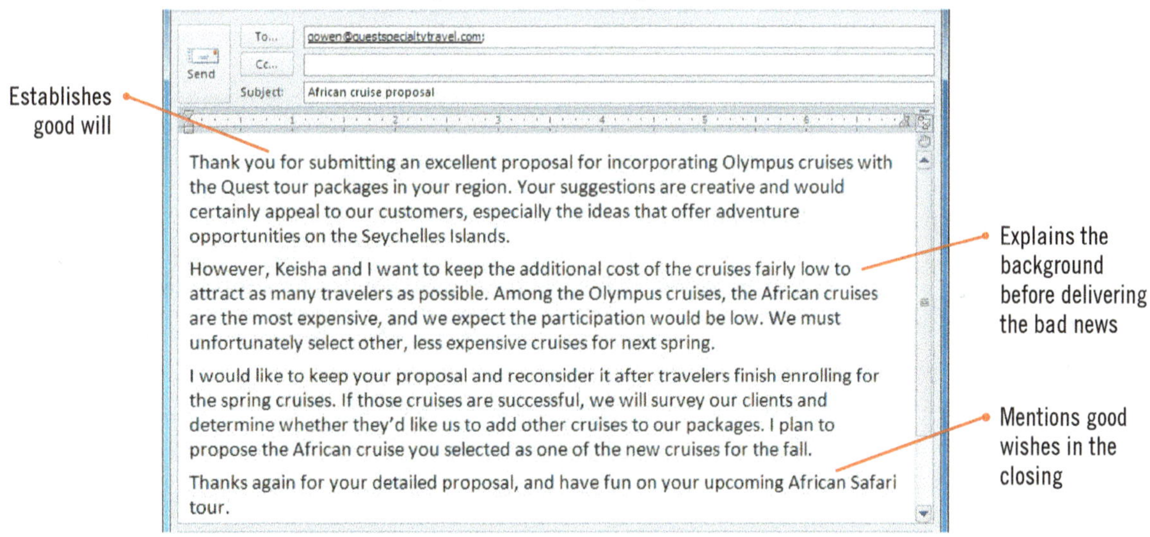

Used with permission from Microsoft Corporation

TABLE 1-5: Delivering bad news do's and don'ts

message element	do	don't
Opening line	• Express appreciation, agreement, or understanding as appropriate	• **Don't** use trite or insincere language
Background explanation	• Explain the reasons for the bad news using neutral language • Demonstrate that you respect the reader	• **Don't** reveal confidential reasons or express opinions • **Don't** blame or accuse the reader of causing a problem
Bad news	• Use clear, neutral language to deliver the bad news • Cite any benefits in the decision • Suggest a compromise or alternative	• **Don't** make unrealistic claims or sound impersonal • **Don't** show benefits if they seem insincere • **Don't** make promises that are difficult to keep
Closing	• End on a positive note • If you need to be firm, end with the bad news	• **Don't** used canned or impersonal language • **Don't** invite further communication

Objective 8 Part 1

Writing Documentation Messages

A **documentation message**, also called a confirmation, to-file, or incident message, confirms events, ideas, discussions, agreements, changes, or instructions. It provides a reminder of an upcoming task or restates an earlier message to avoid misunderstanding. Documentation messages can also provide concise records that might be helpful in the future, especially to settle disagreements. case Now that you've selected three tours that will include a new cruise option, the tour developers need to add the cruise information to the company Web site and tour catalog. You decide to send them a message documenting their next steps.

ESSENTIAL ELEMENTS

QUICK TIP Send documentation messages to the person who is directly involved.

QUICK TIP Avoid including your manager or other superior on the Cc line of a documentation message, which might seem threatening to your recipient.

1. **Use a direct approach and professional tone**

   Because readers often refer back to documentation messages, focus on the most important issues and organize the information logically. For example, use a numbered list to describe a procedure. Use a bulleted list to confirm the main points of a discussion or decision. Figure 1-12 shows the draft of a documentation message that does not take a direct, professional approach. Figure 1-13 shows a revision of the same message that documents a procedure effectively.

2. **Ask for feedback**

   To make sure your readers understand and agree with the message, ask them to send you questions or to note any inaccuracies or disagreements. Your readers often need to clarify or add to the original message so that it accurately and completely reflects the event it documents.

3. **Keep it brief and objective**

   If you are simply acknowledging a change in schedule or verifying that you received a document, create a brief e-mail message with a short confirmation statement. If the message documents sensitive information, such as an agreement to delay a report, use objective, not accusatory language.

4. **Save a copy of the message**

   When sending a documentation message or memo about an important matter, print a hard copy of the message and save it in a file or other appropriate location. Documentation messages sometimes need to be retrieved quickly.

YOU TRY IT

Practice writing documentation messages by revising the rough draft of a message. Open the WC1-Y8.docx document and follow the steps in the worksheet. When you are finished, submit the document to your instructor as requested.

FIGURE 1-12: Original version of the document message

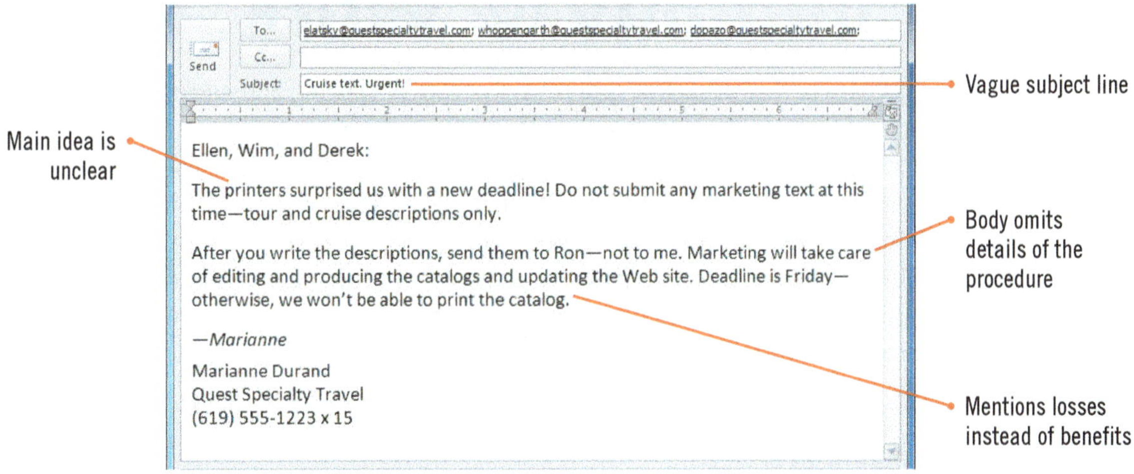

To... elatsky@questspecialtytravel.com; whoppengarth@questspecialtytravel.com; dopazo@questspecialtytravel.com;

Cc...

Subject: Cruise text. Urgent!

Ellen, Wim, and Derek:

The printers surprised us with a new deadline! Do not submit any marketing text at this time—tour and cruise descriptions only.

After you write the descriptions, send them to Ron—not to me. Marketing will take care of editing and producing the catalogs and updating the Web site. Deadline is Friday—otherwise, we won't be able to print the catalog.

—Marianne

Marianne Durand
Quest Specialty Travel
(619) 555-1223 x 15

Used with permission from Microsoft Corporation

FIGURE 1-13: Revised version of the documentation message

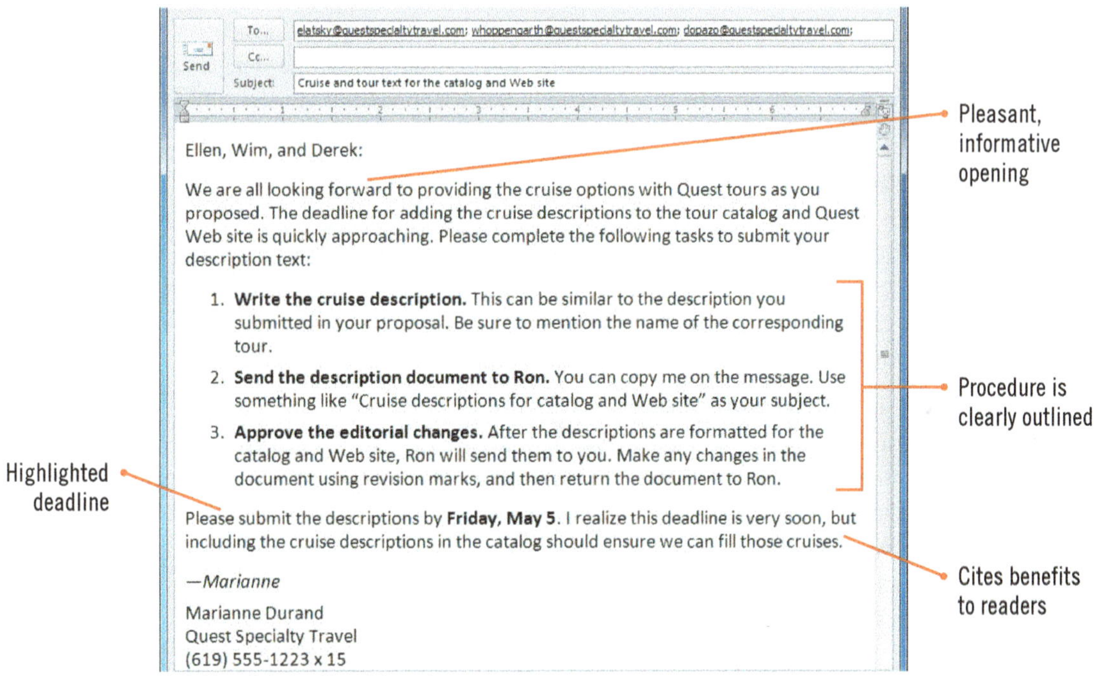

To... elatsky@questspecialtytravel.com; whoppengarth@questspecialtytravel.com; dopazo@questspecialtytravel.com;

Cc...

Subject: Cruise and tour text for the catalog and Web site

Ellen, Wim, and Derek:

We are all looking forward to providing the cruise options with Quest tours as you proposed. The deadline for adding the cruise descriptions to the tour catalog and Quest Web site is quickly approaching. Please complete the following tasks to submit your description text:

1. **Write the cruise description.** This can be similar to the description you submitted in your proposal. Be sure to mention the name of the corresponding tour.
2. **Send the description document to Ron.** You can copy me on the message. Use something like "Cruise descriptions for catalog and Web site" as your subject.
3. **Approve the editorial changes.** After the descriptions are formatted for the catalog and Web site, Ron will send them to you. Make any changes in the document using revision marks, and then return the document to Ron.

Please submit the descriptions by **Friday, May 5**. I realize this deadline is very soon, but including the cruise descriptions in the catalog should ensure we can fill those cruises.

—Marianne

Marianne Durand
Quest Specialty Travel
(619) 555-1223 x 15

Used with permission from Microsoft Corporation

Avoiding e-mail overload

In the corporate world, e-mail overload is a bigger problem than spam. In 2008, the average e-mail user in an organization received about 125 messages a day, which is a 55 percent increase from 2003. Much of this e-mail comes from colleagues, especially those who click the Reply to All button when replying to most messages, send documentation messages to a large group, or send many reminder messages for minor events such as verifying attendance at a regular staff meeting. Some new software products work with e-mail programs to help you reduce the amount of e-mail you send. One product asks you to assign a value to each message sent. For example, you might assign three points to a message asking a colleague to join you for lunch and 30 points to your manager requesting help for an urgent problem. When you meet your point quota for the week, you need to evaluate any other messages you want to send. Another product lets you manage e-mail you receive by color-coding messages from certain users. For example, you might assign green to messages from your manager and blue to messages from a colleague. That way, you know you should open the green messages immediately. Some software even color-codes e-mail automatically by analyzing messages and determining whether the sender is listed in your electronic contacts list.

Technology @ Work: Wikis

A **wiki** is a Web site that many users can contribute to by creating and editing the content. When you are collaborating with colleagues on a project, a wiki can be a more effective communication tool than e-mail. With e-mail, encouraging ideas, making suggestions, and then reaching a consensus can quickly lead to e-mail overload. Because each e-mail message is a separate unit, it is difficult to track conversations and maintain records of decisions, even when using the Reply to All feature. A wiki solves these problems by providing a central location for group editing and quick collaboration. Table 1-6 identifies when to use a wiki. case You've heard that wikis are more effective than e-mail when communicating within a group, and Keisha Lane encourages you to learn more about wikis for Quest Specialty Travel.

ESSENTIAL ELEMENTS

QUICK TIP
The wiki takes its name from the Hawaiian word for "fast."

1. Collaborate on projects

A wiki is a Web site designed for collaboration. If you have access to the wiki, you can visit the Web site, review the latest content, and then update its pages in a Web browser, such as Microsoft Internet Explorer or Mozilla Firefox.

The most well-known wiki is Wikipedia, shown in Figure 1-14, which is an online encyclopedia that anyone with a Web browser can contribute to and maintain. If one Wikipedia user makes an incorrect or inappropriate entry, another user can edit it. Because thousands of users contribute to the wiki, it is a well-researched, high-quality resource.

2. Manage information

You can include all types of business documents on a wiki, such as spreadsheets, text files, presentations, and photos. If you want others to contribute or make changes to the document, you can let anyone in your organization or department access it. Otherwise, you can let only certain users edit the document, while others can view it. If someone does edit a wiki document, the wiki automatically creates a record of who made those changes and when so that you can revert to an earlier version of the document if necessary.

3. Set it up for easy navigation

If you are creating a wiki, start by creating a home page on your computer. In the same folder as the home page, store the documents you want to share with others. For example, one document might be "ToDoToday". Others might be "AllTasks" and "CustomerList". On the home page, list links to these documents.

Use wiki software to create user accounts, which is where you indicate who can access the wiki and what they can do. The rule of thumb for wikis in organizations is to share as much information as possible and secure only what must be private.

4. Access it frequently

If you are using a wiki for a project, access the home page frequently. Check the to-do list or recently modified documents so you can see what needs to be completed on your project. If you edit a document, look for a Summary text box where you can enter a note describing your changes. Then save your changes. The wiki usually updates the list of recent changes.

YOU TRY IT

Practice contributing to a wiki. Open the WC1-TechWork.docx document and follow the steps in the worksheet. When you are finished, submit the document to your instructor as requested.

FIGURE 1-14: Wikipedia, the most well-known wiki

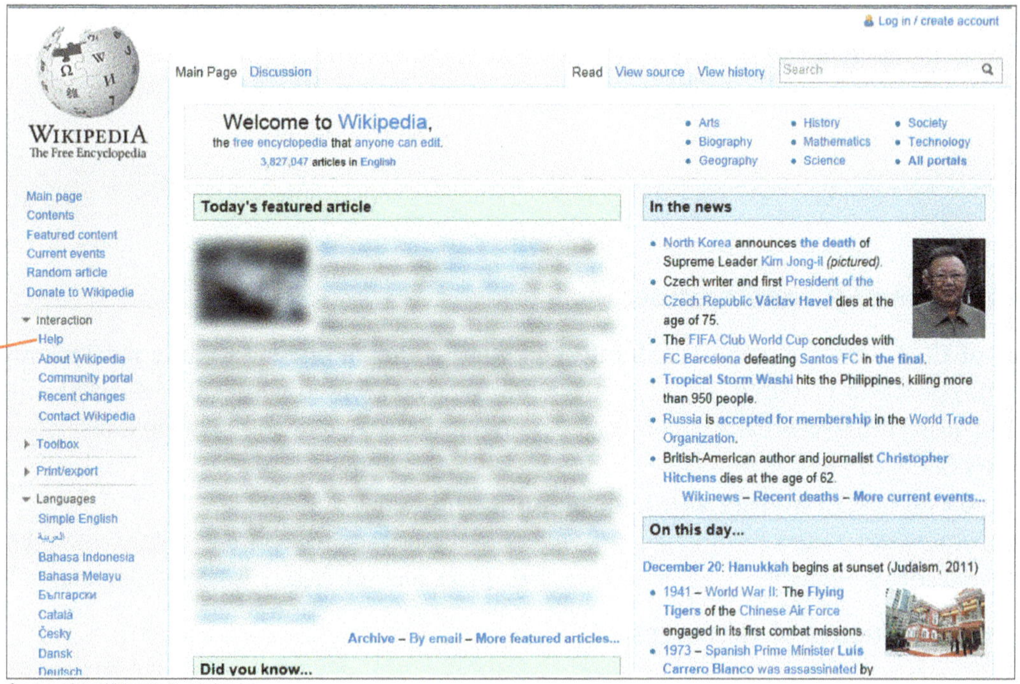

Courtesy of the Wikimedia Foundation, Inc.

TABLE 1-6: Appropriate uses for wikis

scenario	use wiki	use e-mail	use other
Everyone on your project team needs to share a common set of documents	•		
You want to organize meeting notes and team calendars	•		
You are working with colleagues in different locations around the world	•		
You need to make sure you are working with the latest budgets and schedules for your project	•		
Your organization wants everyone to access information about company procedures	•		
No one on your team knows how to set standards for naming wiki pages or maintaining links		•	
You need to exchange confidential documents that are not suitable for peer review		•	Secure Web site
You want to express opinions			Blog

Practice

Soft Skills Review

Understand e-mail messages and memos.

1. **In which one of the following scenarios should you write a memo instead of an e-mail message?**
   - **a.** You are inviting people to a meeting
   - **b.** You are telling many colleagues that a presentation is cancelled
   - **c.** You need a hard copy record of a revised policy
   - **d.** You are responding to a brief question
2. **What should you do before writing an e-mail message or memo?**
   - **a.** Identify the purpose and audience
   - **b.** Send a test message to a colleague
   - **c.** Wait until you have strong feelings about the subject
   - **d.** Make sure your reader is near a computer

Compose the main elements of messages.

1. **Which one of the following is *not* a main element of messages?**
   - **a.** Subject line
   - **b.** Bcc line
   - **c.** Opening sentence
   - **d.** Message body
2. **Which one of the following is an effective subject for a message?**
   - **a.** Questions
   - **b.** Re: Re:
   - **c.** This is a confidential message
   - **d.** Meeting on Friday at 9:00 am

Create professional e-mail messages.

1. **Who should you include in the Cc field of an e-mail message?**
   - **a.** Anyone listed in the original message
   - **b.** Only people directly involved with the message
   - **c.** Your manager in all circumstances
   - **d.** No one
2. **Which of the following is an appropriate way to end an e-mail message?**
   - **a.** Summary of the main idea
   - **b.** Short greeting
   - **c.** Call to action or deadline
   - **d.** Bulleted list of questions

Construct professional memos.

1. **Which of the following is *not* part of a standard memo?**
   - **a.** Header
   - **b.** Salutation
   - **c.** Subject line
   - **d.** Names of recipients
2. **Unlike e-mail, you should send memos only to:**
   - **a.** customers or clients
   - **b.** people who don't like e-mail
   - **c.** managers or supervisors
   - **d.** others in your organization

Write request messages.

1. **What is the purpose of a request message?**
   - **a.** To answer a question
   - **b.** To ask for information or action
   - **c.** To avoid personal contact
   - **d.** To deny a request
2. **What is an effective way to start a request message?**
   - **a.** Make a direct request
   - **b.** Make an apology
   - **c.** Soften the message with a greeting
   - **d.** Include a call to action

Write response messages.

1. **What is a good practice when writing response messages?**
   - **a.** Always use the Reply to All feature
   - **b.** Insert your initials next to your name
   - **c.** Be sure to add your manager's name to the Cc line
   - **d.** Use the Reply feature to include the original subject
2. **What kind of message should you send if you cannot comply with a request?**
   - **a.** Bad-news message
   - **b.** To-file message
   - **c.** Secondary request message
   - **d.** Confirmation message

Write bad-news messages.

1. **Which of the following should you avoid when writing bad-news messages?**
   - **a.** Providing reasons for the bad news
   - **b.** Suggesting an alternative
   - **c.** Expressing an opinion
   - **d.** Using neutral language
2. **Which is the most important part of a bad-news message?**
   - **a.** Using a concise subject
   - **b.** Presenting the reasons for the bad news
   - **c.** Ending with a firm, decisive tone
   - **d.** Listing questions about a request

Write documentation messages.

1. **What is the purpose of a documentation message?**
   - **a.** Persuade your readers
   - **b.** Confirm events, discussions, or agreements
   - **c.** Answer computer questions
   - **d.** Convey cheer and optimism
2. **Which of the following should *not* be part of a documentation message?**
   - **a.** Request for feedback
   - **b.** Direct approach
   - **c.** Confidential information
   - **d.** Short confirmation statement

Technology @ work: wikis.

1. **What is a wiki?**
   - **a.** Audio file you can download
   - **b.** Web site that allows user collaboration
   - **c.** Web log that allows journal entries
   - **d.** Web conference
2. **Which of the following is *not* a scenario for using a wiki?**
   - **a.** You are exchanging confidential documents not appropriate for peer review
   - **b.** Your project team wants to use a central to-do list
   - **c.** You are working with colleagues in different countries
   - **d.** You need to manage a common set of documents

Critical Thinking Questions

1. **"When you click the Send button in your e-mail program, assume that your e-mail message has been published." What implications does this statement have when you compose an e-mail message?**
2. **Suppose you are writing an e-mail message requesting that a colleague attend a meeting. What kind of language and tone do you use? Does the language and tone change if you are writing to a manager in your organization? To a client or customer? To someone in another country? If so, explain how your message changes in each case.**
3. **Because company computers are meant for work-related tasks, employers can legally track your computer usage and monitor your e-mail. Do you consider e-mail monitoring an ethical practice? If you owned your own business, would you monitor your employees' e-mail messages?**

Critical Thinking Questions (continued)

4. **Before e-mail became popular, you corresponded with people outside of your organization using a formal business letter. Although e-mail is now the preferred approach, when would it still be more appropriate to send a formal letter?**
5. **When you send a message to other people, how strictly do you think they judge you on your communication abilities? How does this affect your writing?**

Independent Challenge 1

You work in the Marketing Department of a small Web design company named Overland Designs. The company has grown significantly in the past year. Marshall Aronson, the director of marketing, wants to organize a company celebration to thank employees, honor special accomplishments, and reinforce teamwork. Marshall has made some notes about the celebration, shown in Figure 1-15. He asks you to use the notes to send an e-mail to other department directors requesting their help in organizing the celebration.

FIGURE 1-15

Overland Designs Company Celebration

- Thank employees
- Honor special accomplishments
- Reinforce teamwork
- Send e-mail message to Carl Lansing, Jay Willbourn, Lindsey Rhodes, and Tammy Mitchell. Request their help in organizing the celebration.
- Possible areas of help: sending invitations, designing awards for special accomplishments, developing a (short) process for nominating employees for special accomplishments, enlisting speakers, organizing time, place, and type of celebration–appetizers only? dinner? luncheon?

a. Open the **WC1-IC1.docx** document and follow the steps in the worksheet.
b. Proofread the document carefully to fix any grammar or formatting errors.
c. Submit the document to your instructor as requested.

Independent Challenge 2

You are the manager of the flagship Four Winds Apparel store in Minneapolis, Minnesota. Four Winds Apparel specializes in affordable active wear for men, women, and children and has five other stores in the Minneapolis-St. Paul area. After a year of disappointing sales, Four Winds has decided to close two stores in the twin cities. Allison Crandall, the Four Winds regional manager, sends you a memo explaining this decision and asking you to inform the managers of the stores that will close. You need to revise the memo and send it to the store managers.

a. Open the **WC1-IC2.docx** document and follow the steps in the worksheet.
b. Proofread the document carefully to fix any grammar or formatting errors.
c. Submit the document to your instructor as requested.

Real Life Independent Challenge

This Independent Challenge requires an Internet connection.

You are applying for a summer internship in Washington, D.C., and need to send an e-mail message to a program coordinator to learn the details of the internship.

a. Visit the summer internships page of the National Gallery of Art at www.nga.gov/education/internsumm.shtm, shown in Figure 1-16.

FIGURE 1-16

b. Using your favorite search engine, search for other internship programs in Washington, D.C., such as those in government, media, communications, or the arts. Select an internship that appeals to you. Note the address of the Web site that describes the internship.

c. Select an internship you want to know more about, such as the one at the National Gallery of Art or one you found on your own.

d. Open the **WC1-IC3.docx** document and follow the steps in the worksheet.

e. Proofread the document carefully to fix any grammar or formatting errors.

f. Submit the document to your instructor as requested.

Team Challenge

This Independent Challenge requires an Internet connection.

You work for Farley Worldwide, a company specializing in information services, and have been promoted recently. You now travel overseas with a small group and help your client companies install computers and software. Your next trip is to Beijing, China. Connie Lerner, your project head, will be traveling with you, and mentions she has heard that traveling to China can be quite a culture shock. You and your team need to research how to prepare for the trip to minimize the culture shock.

a. Using your favorite search engine, search for information about westerners in Beijing and tips on doing business there. Note the addresses of the Web sites that provide the most useful information.

b. Meet as a team to discuss your findings.

c. As a team, outline an e-mail to Connie Lerner explaining what to expect in Beijing.

d. Individually, write an e-mail explaining how to prepare for the Beijing trip.

e. Send the message to yourself with a copy to your instructor.

Be the Critic

Review the poorly written message shown in Figure 1-17. Create an e-mail message that lists the weaknesses of the message and makes specific suggestions for improvement. Send the critique to your instructor.

FIGURE 1-17

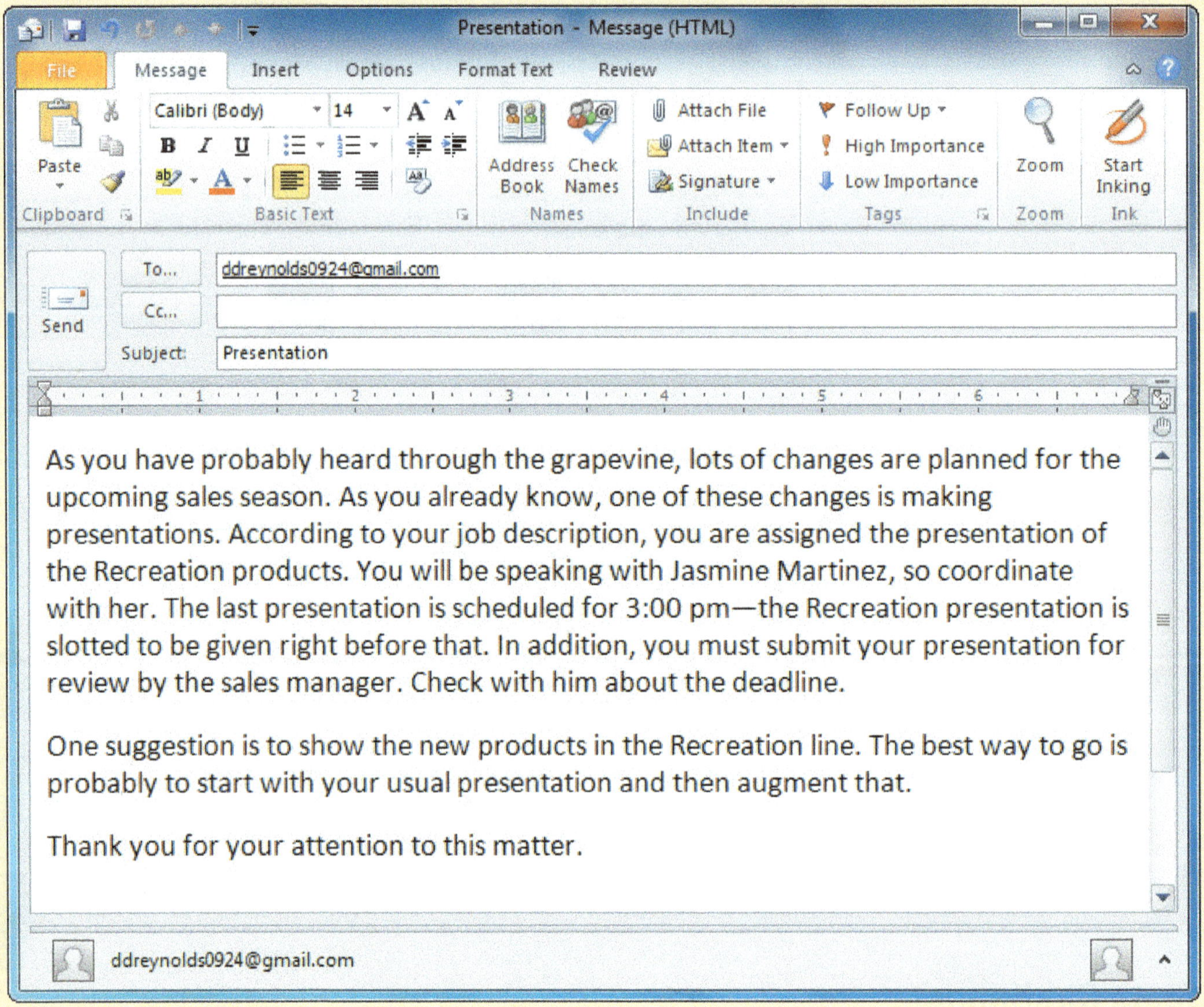

Part 2

Uncovering the Secrets of Clear Writing

Files You Will Need:

WC2-Y10.docx
WC2-Y11.docx
WC2-Y12.docx
WC2-Y13.docx
WC2-Y14.docx
WC2-Y15.docx
WC2-Y16.docx
WC2-TechWork.docx
WC2-IC1.docx
WC2-IC2.docx

Good writers aren't born that way. They develop their skills through practice and careful attention to detail. You can become a good writer the same way—by practicing and paying attention to detail. The skills you develop learning to write clearly will serve you well throughout your career. Some people have the misconception that clear writing means documents that are free from errors (such as spelling and grammar mistakes). Clear writing actually means that you craft your communication to best meet the needs and interests of your readers. A well-written document has a specific purpose, makes its point clearly, organizes supporting and related information logically, and is grammatically correct. case You are a tour assistant at Quest Specialty Travel, currently working with Ellen Latsky, the European tour developer. She is updating a brochure about Quest tours in Eastern Europe and asks for your help in revising the text.

OBJECTIVES

9 Clarify written communication
10 Write solid sentences
11 Develop effective paragraphs
12 Master punctuation
13 Lay out your documents
14 Illustrate data
15 Add tables and figures to documents
16 Proofread and revise

Objective 9 Part 2

Clarifying Written Communication

Professionals in every field must be able to express their ideas clearly, concisely, and completely when writing. If your written communication is unclear or lacks important details, your readers become confused and cannot respond appropriately. To write clearly, be sure you complete the following tasks: prepare, write, and revise. See Figure 2-1. case To prepare for revising the brochure text for Ellen Latsky, you decide to review the guidelines for clarifying written communication.

DETAILS

Before you start to write, review the following guidelines:

- **Know your reader**
  Start your writing projects by identifying your typical reader. Often, you need to help readers understand your topics and ideas, persuade them to your point of view, or motivate them to take action. You'll be successful if you begin by seeing these topics from your audience's point of view rather than your own. If your document is long, complex, or especially important, draft a profile of your reader and refer to it as you write.

- **Relate to your reader's experience and understanding**
  Ideally, your writing is not a surprise to your readers. Instead, you should be adding to their knowledge and exploring alternative ideas with them. A skilled writer identifies topics their readers already understand and builds on those to introduce new concepts. Considering your reader's experience helps make your writing clearer, more accessible, and relevant.

- **Define your objective**
  Before you start to write, determine the exact purpose of your document. Why are you writing and what do you expect to achieve? The purpose of most professional writing is to inform, such as to announce meetings, summarize decisions, or list procedures. The objective of many other business documents is to persuade, such as to convince managers or colleagues; motivate employees; or stimulate customers to action. As you write, double-check to make certain every sentence and paragraph contributes to your objective.

- **Keep it simple**
  Professional writing should be efficient, which means it is easy to read and understand. Keep your words, sentences, and paragraphs short and to the point. Trim the fat from your writing by eliminating vague and unnecessary words. Watch out for long sentences and carefully review any that are longer than two printed lines. Table 2-1 lists the do's and don'ts for clarifying your writing.

- **Make your documents attractive**
  Your reader actively decides whether to read the message you've prepared. One important influence on this decision is how your writing looks. Documents that are clearly written and use an attractive layout are much more inviting and likely to be read. In contrast, long blocks of text intimidate your readers and reduce the chances that they will carefully consider your work.

  Overall, your writing can follow these guidelines by taking the reader's point of view, focusing on information that meets your objective, and selecting language carefully.

QUICK TIP
Some messages have a primary audience and a secondary audience. The tone, language, and content should be appropriate for both audiences.

QUICK TIP
Another typical objective in business writing is to promote goodwill, especially when you write to customers.

QUICK TIP
The purpose and audience of your message determine its format, approach, and vocabulary.

FIGURE 2-1: Clear writing process

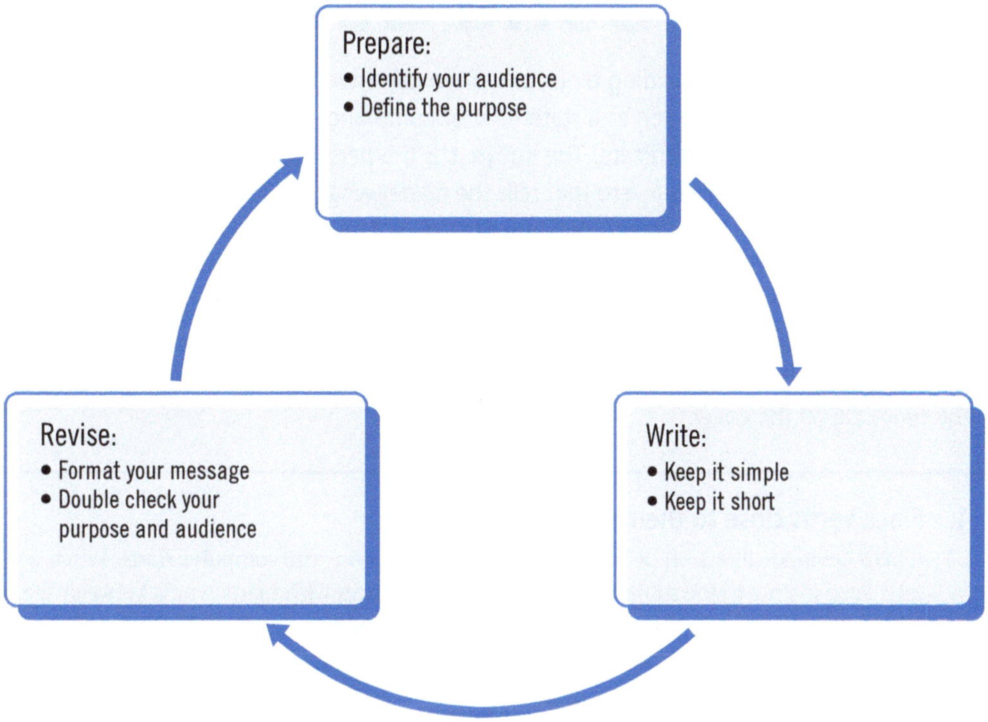

Written Communication

TABLE 2-1: Clarifying your writing do's and don'ts

guideline	do	don't
Know your reader	• Determine whether you are writing to colleagues, decision makers, or customers • Consider how much the reader already knows about your subject • Identify the benefits of the message to your readers	• **Don't** overlook the secondary audience • **Don't** skip this step for short messages
Relate to your reader	• Picture your typical reader • Anticipate your reader's reaction • Shape the message to the reader • Adapt the vocabulary and tone to the reader • Address the reader directly as "you"	• **Don't** use language that is not appropriate for the reader, such as jargon or abbreviations • **Don't** choose words that can be interpreted as being biased • **Don't** forget about tone • **Don't** focus on your needs and goals
Define your objective	• Determine the purpose of your message • Identify what you want to achieve with the message	• **Don't** include a sentence that doesn't meet your objective
Keep it simple	• Choose short, familiar words • Write short sentences and paragraphs	• **Don't** use vague or unnecessary words • **Don't** include sentences longer than two lines
Make your documents attractive	• Organize and format your message so it is appealing to your reader	• **Don't** format your message in one long block of text

Objective 10 Part 2

Writing Solid Sentences

The sentence is the basic building block of written communication. Sentences are groups of words that form a complete thought, such as a statement or command. A sentence makes sense because it is composed of a subject and a predicate. The **subject** is the person, place, or thing that the sentence is talking about. The **predicate** is a verb that tells the reader what the subject is, what the subject is doing, or what is happening to the subject. Beyond writing sentences that are grammatically correct, also consider **style**, which refers to the tone, formality, and voice of your sentences. To write with style, you should organize and simplify your message so it is easy for your reader to understand. Table 2-2 lists the do's and don'ts of writing sentences. case Ellen Latsky explains that the purpose of the brochure is to encourage customers to take a Quest tour in Eastern Europe. You start updating the brochure by revising the sentence on the cover.

ESSENTIAL ELEMENTS

1. **Place verbs close to their subjects**

   A verb describes an action or state of being: I *am*, you *write*, the computer *starts*. When a verb is the predicate, keep it close to the subject of the sentence. Sentences with many words between the subject and verb are complicated because your readers must identify both the subject and verb before they can understand the sentence. Figure 2-2 shows how keeping the verb close to the subject makes sentences easier to read.

2. **Keep sentences short and concise**

   The longer the sentence, the harder it is to read and understand. Keep your sentence length between 10 and 25 words to make sure readers do not need to reread the sentence to understand it. Shorten your sentences by removing unnecessary words and using vigorous, direct language.

QUICK TIP
The beginning of a long sentence often contains unnecessary words, such as "This is to inform you that...."

3. **Use simple, direct language**

   The hallmark of clear sentences is simple, uncluttered language that readers can immediately understand. To achieve this clarity, you must know what you want to say. As William Zinsser, author of *On Writing Well*, says, "Clear thinking becomes clear writing." Cluttered writing often comes from fuzzy thinking.

4. **Write affirmatively**

   Your writing is easier to understand when you avoid using negative language. Positive language is usually more concise and creates goodwill. Be sure you use positive language when requesting action because it is easier to understand what to do instead of what not to do.

QUICK TIP
Negative language includes verbs that use "not," such as "do not," "cannot," and "should not."

5. **Add variety to your sentences**

   If all of your sentences are simple statements that follow the same pattern, your document will seem monotone and dull. Add variety to your writing with an occasional question, exclamation, or command. Using sentences of varying lengths also provides interest.

YOU TRY IT

Practice writing solid sentences by revising the text for a brochure. Open the WC2-Y10.docx document and follow the steps in the worksheet. When you are finished, submit the document to your instructor as requested.

FIGURE 2-2: Original and revised brochure cover

Used with permission from Microsoft Corporation

TABLE 2-2: Writing sentences do's and don'ts

sentence element	do	don't
Verbs	• Keep verbs close to the nouns they describe • Use active verbs	• **Don't** insert too many words between the subject and the verb • **Don't** rely on forms of "to be" such as "is" and "are"
Length	• Strive for sentences that contain an average of 20 words • Make your main point quickly • Delete redundant words	• **Don't** regularly lengthen sentences by adding new ideas after "and" or "but" • **Don't** pad the beginning of a sentence with a wordy opener such as "It is important to note that"
Word choice	• Choose simple, direct language • Use familiar, concrete words • Identify what you want to say before you write	• **Don't** write to impress with long, abstract words • **Don't** use empty buzzwords or jargon
Tone	• Emphasize the positive • Strive for language that sounds warm and friendly	• **Don't** rely on negative words and phrases • **Don't** use language that sounds stuffy or demeaning
Variety	• Use different types of sentences, such as statements, questions, and commands • Vary sentence length	• **Don't** write a series of sentences of the same length and pattern • **Don't** be afraid of conversational language, which is typically varied

Objective 11 Part 2

Developing Effective Paragraphs

ESSENTIAL ELEMENTS

A **paragraph** is a group of sentences that collectively presents or describes a single topic or idea. Each sentence in a paragraph should relate to the main idea. Paragraphs in business documents usually begin by directly expressing the central message, continue by presenting supporting details, and end with a concluding sentence. When you are ready to shift your focus from one topic to another, start a new paragraph. case After clarifying the sentence on the front of the Quest brochure, you read the paragraphs on the first page and plan how to revise them.

QUICK TIP
Choose one of these paragraph formatting techniques and use it throughout your document.

QUICK TIP
The number of sentences does not determine whether a section of text is a paragraph—the unity and coherence of ideas among those sentences does.

1. **Signal your reader**
   Each time you begin a new paragraph, provide a visual cue by indenting the beginning of the first sentence or inserting a blank line between paragraphs. These visual cues improve the readability of your documents.
2. **Start with a topic sentence**
   In most cases, begin each paragraph with a sentence that summarizes the main idea. This helps prepare your readers for what follows and clarifies the topic of the paragraph. Table 2-3 explains when to insert the topic sentence in other locations in a paragraph.
3. **Follow with detail sentences**
   Follow the topic sentence with one or more detail sentences that provide additional information about the subject. Include as many sentences as you need to explain the main topic, but strive for readability by keeping the sentences and paragraph short.
4. **Repeat your main idea**
   A paragraph makes more sense if you mention the main idea or key word more than once. Occasionally referring to the topic helps make your paragraph cohesive and builds continuity.
5. **Use pronouns to connect ideas**
   After introducing your subject at the beginning of a paragraph, use pronouns such as "these," "that," "they," and "it" to refer to the subject in subsequent sentences. Figure 2-3 shows a paragraph that uses pronouns to connect an idea from one sentence to another.
6. **Finish with a concluding sentence**
   Conclude each paragraph with a summary, final thought, or transition to the next paragraph. Arrange your paragraphs so that one flows logically to the next. Figure 2-3 also shows a paragraph that begins and ends logically.
7. **Break up blocks of text**
   Paragraphs become difficult to read after 8–10 printed lines. Long paragraphs usually signal that you need to break your topic into shorter subtopics.

YOU TRY IT

Practice developing effective paragraphs by revising paragraphs of brochure text. Open the WC2-Y11.docx document and follow the steps in the worksheet. When you are finished, submit the document to your instructor as requested.

FIGURE 2-3: Paragraph in a Quest brochure

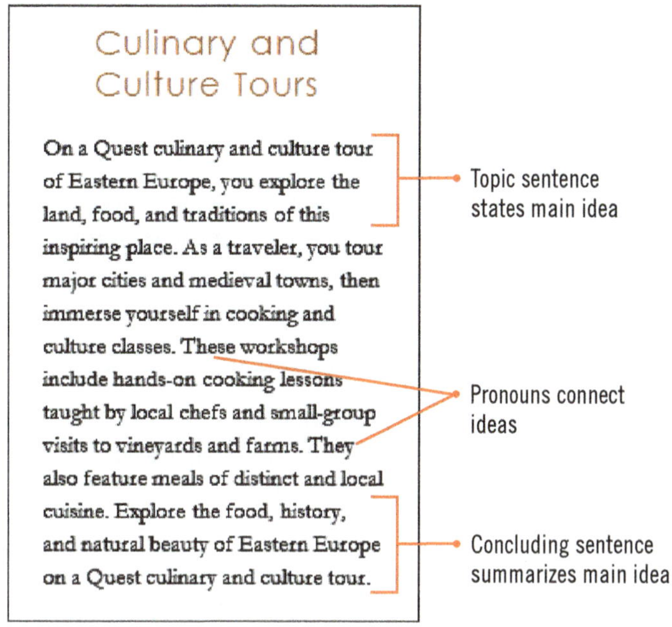
Culinary and Culture Tours

On a Quest culinary and culture tour of Eastern Europe, you explore the land, food, and traditions of this inspiring place. As a traveler, you tour major cities and medieval towns, then immerse yourself in cooking and culture classes. These workshops include hands-on cooking lessons taught by local chefs and small-group visits to vineyards and farms. They also feature meals of distinct and local cuisine. Explore the food, history, and natural beauty of Eastern Europe on a Quest culinary and culture tour.

Used with permission from Microsoft Corporation

TABLE 2-3: Developing paragraphs do's and don'ts

paragraph element	do	don't
Format	• Provide a visual cue when you start a new paragraph • Indent the beginning of the first sentence or insert a blank line between paragraphs • Break a long paragraph into shorter blocks, each concentrating on a subtopic	• **Don't** use a pronoun without clearly introducing your subject first • **Don't** mix formats—stick to indenting the first line or inserting a blank line • **Don't** divide text into short blocks more than necessary
Topic sentence	• Include a sentence that summarizes the main idea • Start with the topic sentence to introduce the main idea directly • Insert the topic sentence in the middle to compare and contrast • End with the topic sentence to draw a conclusion or persuade	• **Don't** include more than one main topic in a paragraph • **Don't** bury the topic sentence; insert it at the beginning or compose the paragraph so that the topic is clear
Detail sentences	• Illustrate, explain, or strengthen the main topic • Cite evidence to support your main idea • Include as many sentences as you need	• **Don't** introduce details that are not related to the main topic • **Don't** follow the outdated recommendation that paragraphs should have five sentences
Main idea	• Repeat a key word or phrase to remind readers about the main idea • Organize sentences so that one idea logically leads to the next • Use transitions to connect subtopics	• **Don't** repeat the main idea too often • **Don't** write disjointed sentences that are independent of one another
Pronouns	• Connect detail sentences to the main idea by using pronouns • Use pronouns to signal you are continuing to discuss a previous subject	• **Don't** use a pronoun without clearly introducing your subject first • **Don't** use a pronoun if it is not clear what the pronoun refers to
Conclusion	• Conclude with a summary, final thought, or transition to the next paragraph	• **Don't** end abruptly or fade without concluding

Objective 12 Part 2

Mastering Punctuation

When you talk with someone, the way you speak conveys much of your meaning. Your pauses, voice inflections, and rate of speaking help you express thoughts and clarify meaning. Written communication uses a set of symbols called **punctuation marks** to perform these tasks and help readers interpret text. The most common punctuation symbols are the period, comma, and question mark. Table 2-4 summarizes punctuation do's and don'ts. Figure 2-4 shows examples of some types of punctuation. case Ellen Latsky mentions that the brochure text on the inside panel uses confusing punctuation. You review and then revise the punctuation in that text.

ESSENTIAL ELEMENTS

QUICK TIP
Avoid combining a question mark with other punctuation, as in "Are you finished!?" unless the writing is very informal.

1. **Period (.) and question mark (?)**
   Use a period to end a complete sentence, even in a bulleted or numbered list. Use a question mark at the end of a sentence that asks a direct question.
2. **Comma (,)**
   Insert commas to show readers which words belong together in a sentence. Typical uses of commas include setting off introductory text, listing items in a series of three or more, and separating independent clauses linked by "for," "and," "nor," "but," "or," "yet," and "so" (these are connectors, or **conjunctions**, sometimes abbreviated as FANBOYS).

QUICK TIP
When formatted as a sentence (not as a numbered list), use a semicolon between items in a list if any item contains a comma.

3. **Semicolon (;)**
   Use a semicolon when you want to join two independent clauses and show they are related in their meaning without using a conjunction such as "and" or "so." An **independent clause** has a subject and a verb and can stand alone as a sentence.
4. **Colon (:)**
   Use a colon to alert your reader that the following information explains or enhances the current idea. For example, a colon often introduces a list, example, or quotation.
5. **Ellipsis (...)**
   An ellipsis indicates that you've omitted one or more words from a quotation. If the ellipsis falls at the end of a quoted sentence, be sure to include a final period after the ellipsis.

QUICK TIP
The dash is sometimes called an em dash because its width is the same as the letter "m."

6. **Dash (—)**
   Insert a dash to set off or highlight part of a sentence. A single dash emphasizes the information that immediately follows it; a pair of dashes highlights the information in between them.
7. **Parentheses ( ) and brackets [ ]**
   Use parentheses to insert a thought that is not essential to the meaning of the sentence. You can also enclose supplemental explanations or references in parentheses. Use brackets when you want to insert your own remarks or observations into the middle of a paragraph. These remarks are generally used to explain or illustrate the point that is being made in the main text.

YOU TRY IT

Practice mastering punctuation by revising brochure text that does not have correct punctuation. Open the WC2-Y12.docx document and follow the steps in the worksheet. When you are finished, submit the document to your instructor as requested.

FIGURE 2-4: Examples of some types of punctuation

Semicolon

Call me on Friday; I will have the sales data then.

New group tours originated in Toledo, Ohio; Fort Wayne, Indiana; and Rockford, Illinois.

Ellipsis

Original quotation – "The results of the survey show that customers rank most of our services highly, but after further analysis, customers are most satisfied with the variety of destinations."

Abbreviated quotation – "The results of the survey show that ...customers are most satisfied with the variety of destinations."

Dash

Customer service, tour quality, and tour value–these are areas customers also rate highly.

Many customers–but not all–completed the survey.

Parentheses

The tour-by-tour sales figures are available for your review (see Appendix A).

Bracket

The CEO thanked the tour developers for their *enthusiasm* [emphasis added].

TABLE 2-4: Comma and colon do's and don'ts

punctuation	do	don't
Comma	• Set off introductory text *Example*: Generally, employees arrive on time • List items in a series *Example*: She writes, copies, and prints the articles • Separate independent clauses *Example*: The Web page is colorful, but it isn't accurate	• **Don't** omit the final comma if doing so causes confusion • **Don't** use a comma to separate independent clauses without a FANBOYS
Colon	• Introduce a list, example, or quotation *Example*: You'll receive the following items at the conference: handouts, samples, and exhibition passes • Indicate the end of a greeting in a business letter *Example*: Dear Mr. Wolff: • Separate a label or short heading from information *Example*: Subject: Budget decisions	• **Don't** insert a colon unless text on one side forms a complete sentence

E-mail, IM, and posts: writing or texting?

How much time do you spend creating and responding to e-mail, instant messages, cell phone text messages, and posts on social networking sites? If you're under 30, you are probably engaged in these activities throughout the day. But are you writing or texting when you communicate using these channels? According to "Writing, Technology, and Teens," a 2008 study by the National Commission on Writing (NCW), "Teens write a lot, but they do not think of their e-mails or instant and text messages as writing." This finding echoes what corporations reported in 2004 in another NCW survey. That survey found a third of employees in top U.S. companies wrote poorly and required up to $3.1 billion annually on remedial training. A *New York Times* article on the study said, "Millions of inscrutable e-mail messages are clogging corporate computers by setting off requests for clarification, and many of the requests, in turn, are also chaotically written, resulting in whole cycles of confusion." The flip side of this news is that people entering the workforce who can write clearly and in complete sentences are in high demand. "It's not that companies want to hire Tolstoy," said Susan Traiman, a director at the Business Roundtable, an association of leading chief executives whose corporations were surveyed in the NCW study. "But they need people who can write clearly."

Source: National Commission on Writing, "Writing, Technology, and Teens," 2008, and Dillon, Sam, "What Corporate America Can't Build: A Sentence," *New York Times*, December 7, 2004.

Objective 13 Part 2

Laying Out Your Documents

Effective writing involves more than just choosing the words that you use. Your document's appearance, layout, and design details all influence its readability. Word-processing software and printer technology make it easy to develop professional-looking documents from your desktop. As you plan your writing, be sure to consider issues related to layout and white space. White space is the area on your page where there is neither text nor graphics. White space helps to break up the elements on the page and makes it easier for your reader to navigate. case Ellen also notes that the brochure has an appealing layout except on an inner panel. See Figure 2-5. She asks you to recommend ways to change the layout of the inner panel to make the text easier to read.

ESSENTIAL ELEMENTS

1. **Use left, not full, justification**

   Set your word processor to use **ragged-right alignment**, also called left justification. Aligning the text along the left margin adds white space at the end of each line of text and helps your reader locate the beginnings of new lines. Text with a ragged-right edge is usually more legible in paragraphs that span four or more inches.

QUICK TIP

The page gutter is blank space between adjacent pages.

2. **Use white space effectively**

   If your document contains both text and illustrations, add white space around the edges of the page by increasing the size of the margins and page gutter. Wrap text around a graphic, photo, or illustration leaving plenty of white space between the text and figure. Do not let text run into the edge of a photo or graphic.

3. **Separate headings and subheadings from body text**

   Include white space before and after headings and subheadings to make them easier to read. This white space makes it easier for your reader to browse your document and locate sections. If your space is limited, reduce the amount of text to preserve headings.

4. **Choose heading and paragraph fonts**

   Word processors offer a tempting array of fonts, but most are not appropriate for business writing. Choose a traditional font (such as Times Roman, Helvetica, or Courier) for headings and another for paragraphs, and use those throughout your document. Avoid using more than two fonts on a page. For most business documents, body text size should be 11 to 12 points. Headings can be larger and darker, but avoid using all caps, which are generally hard to read.

5. **Use moderation with page layout**

   Your document effects should be subtle and balanced. Limit your use of graphics, clip art, different typefaces, and other elements. Use them when they support the content and add to the appeal and goals of your document. Use effects such as lines, bold, italic, and color sparingly.

   Figure 2-6 shows the revised inner panel of the Quest brochure.

YOU TRY IT

Practice laying out your documents by revising text so it is appropriate for a brochure. Open the WC2-Y13.docx document and follow the steps in the worksheet. When you are finished, submit the document to your instructor as requested.

FIGURE 2-5: Original layout of inner panel

AUSTRIAN EXPERIENCE

Explore the best of Austria, place of cultural and historical beauty. You'll tour Vienna and Salzburg and see for yourself places such as the Schönbrunn Palace, once home to the Habsburg family. The grounds include Europe's largest greenhouse, Wagenburg, and the world's oldest zoo, Tiergarten. In Salzburg, enjoy a city tour that includes Mirabell Palace, Mozart's birthplace, the Festival Halls, the Cathedral of Salzburg, and the Hellbrunn and Leopolkskron palaces. The tour ends at Mozart's residence before a seasonal cultural performance. Priced from $1,750 per person (does not include airfare). You can also opt for a bicycling tour through the Austrian Lake District, which allows relatively easy cycling through stunning, mountainous terrain. Starting and finishing in the wonderful city of Salzburg, the cycling ranges from flat lakeside tracks to quiet country lanes across scenic rolling hills. Priced from an additional $650. Another option is a train ride to the Tyrol and the historical town of Innsbruck. You can then take one of three walking tours: through the old town, including the Cathedral of St. Jacob; through modern Innsbruck, including the Northern Chain railway; or through sporty Innsbruck, including Olympic Hall. Innsbruck tours also allow plenty of time for exploring on your own.

Used with permission from Microsoft Corporation

FIGURE 2-6: Revised layout of inner panel

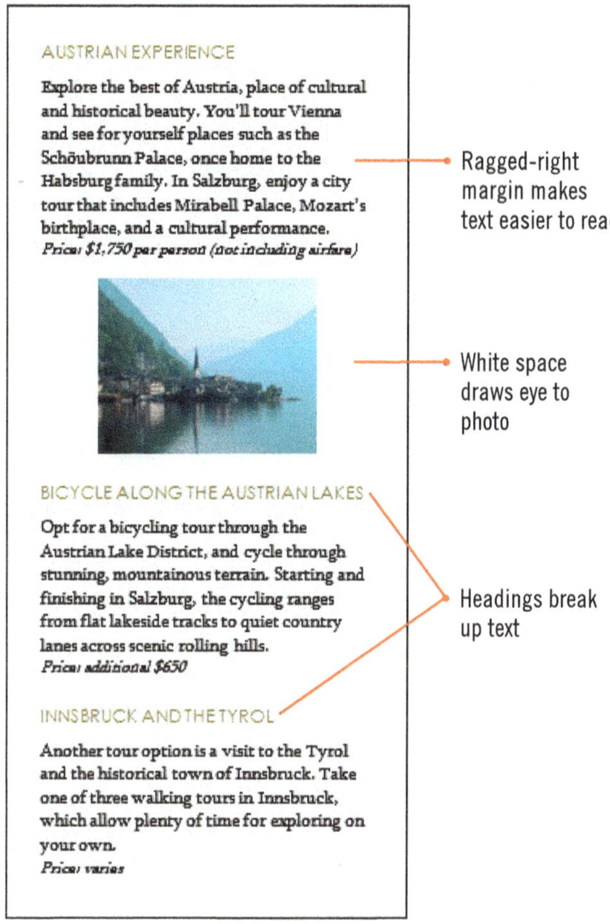

AUSTRIAN EXPERIENCE

Explore the best of Austria, place of cultural and historical beauty. You'll tour Vienna and see for yourself places such as the Schöubrunn Palace, once home to the Habsburg family. In Salzburg, enjoy a city tour that includes Mirabell Palace, Mozart's birthplace, and a cultural performance.
Price: $1,750 per person (not including airfare)

BICYCLE ALONG THE AUSTRIAN LAKES

Opt for a bicycling tour through the Austrian Lake District, and cycle through stunning, mountainous terrain. Starting and finishing in Salzburg, the cycling ranges from flat lakeside tracks to quiet country lanes across scenic rolling hills.
Price: additional $650

INNSBRUCK AND THE TYROL

Another tour option is a visit to the Tyrol and the historical town of Innsbruck. Take one of three walking tours in Innsbruck, which allow plenty of time for exploring on your own.
Price: varies

Used with permission from Microsoft Corporation; Fuse/Jupiterimages

Selecting the right medium

E-mail, fax, voice mail, videoconference—these are a few of the methods you can use to communicate with colleagues, customers, decision makers, and others in your professional life. Each medium provides advantages and drawbacks, so you should choose the one that suits your purpose, audience, and message. The medium, in turn, determines the layout of your message.

- *E-mail*: Use e-mail for a fast delivery of information. Format messages using short sentences and bullets for easy scanning.
- *Instant messages*: If you are online and need a quick response, send an instant message, especially to find out if someone is available for a phone call.
- *Voice mail*: Leave a voice mail message when you want to convey important or routine information and let the receiver respond when it is convenient.
- *Phone call*: Call someone when you want to exchange information and allow a give and take without needing nonverbal cues.
- *Face-to-face meeting*: Meet with one person to deliver a persuasive or personal message or to convey bad news. Meet with a group to arrive at a group consensus.
- *Web, video, or voice conference*: Meet online or on the phone when you need group interaction but members of the group are not working in the same place.
- *Fax*: Send a fax when you need a written record or signature, especially from someone in another location.
- *Blog*: Use a blog (a Web site where one person generally posts comments that others can respond to) when you want to keep other people, such as customers and employees, informed and up to date.
- *Letter or memo*: When you need a written record, write a letter to someone outside your organization or a memo to someone in your organization.

Objective
14
Part 2

Illustrating Data

When you need to compare data, illustrate it with a **chart** or graph. Representing data graphically makes the information easier to understand and remember. Graphics can make numerical information meaningful, reveal trends or patterns, simplify complex relationships, and add visual interest to your documents. Become familiar with the most popular chart types, their strengths and weaknesses, and when each is appropriate. Table 2-5 lists the do's and don'ts for using charts in business documents. case You want to add an illustration to the Quest brochure to increase its visual appeal, and Ellen suggests adding a chart to one of the panels.

ESSENTIAL ELEMENTS

QUICK TIP

You can create charts using a tool such as Microsoft Excel.

1. **Column and bar charts**

   Column and bar charts present categorical and numeric data that are grouped in intervals, such as sales per month or expenses for each product. A column chart includes a horizontal bar for each category, and the height or length of each bar represents the value of that category. A bar chart is similar, but uses vertical bars. Figure 2-7 shows an example of a column chart.

2. **Line charts**

   Line charts reveal trends or patterns in your data. A line chart shows how two values are related to each other. The vertical (y) axis usually indicates a quantity, such as dollars, or a percentage. The horizontal (x) axis typically represents units of time. Because of this, line charts are ideal for showing changes in quantity over time. Figure 2-7 also shows a line chart.

3. **Pie charts**

   A pie chart is drawn as a circle divided into segments, where each segment represents a category. Sometimes, a segment is separated from the rest of the pie to give it special emphasis. Pie charts compare the whole to its parts. Figure 2-7 also shows a pie chart with an emphasized segment.

4. **Process charts**

   Process charts show the steps in a procedure, and are sometimes called flow charts. Different shapes represent various types of activities. For example, circles or ovals represent the beginning and end of the procedure, diamonds represent a decision or choice that must be made, and rectangles represent a major activity or step in the process.

5. **Organization (or hierarchy) charts**

   When people or objects are organized into a hierarchy, you can represent them with an organizational chart. Organizational charts are typically drawn as a horizontal or vertical tree using geometric shapes to represent its various elements. Lines connect the shapes to indicate relationships between the elements. Organizational charts show the formal structure of a business. Hierarchy charts show the relationship among objects. Figure 2-7 also shows an example of an organizational chart.

YOU TRY IT

Practice illustrating data by creating an organizational chart. Open the WC2-Y14.docx document and follow the steps in the worksheet. When you are finished, submit the document to your instructor as requested.

FIGURE 2-7: Examples of charts

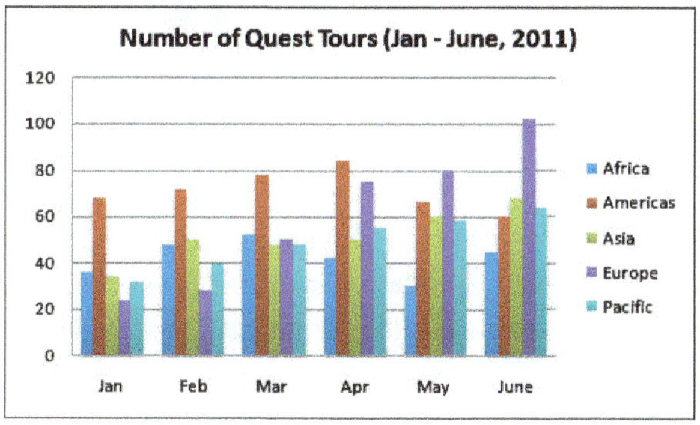

Column chart

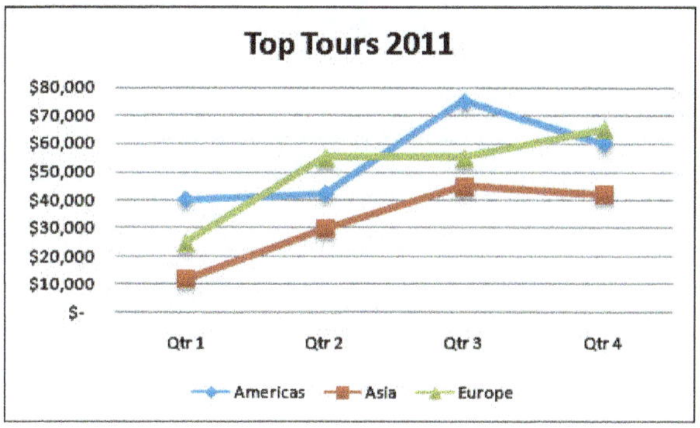

Line chart

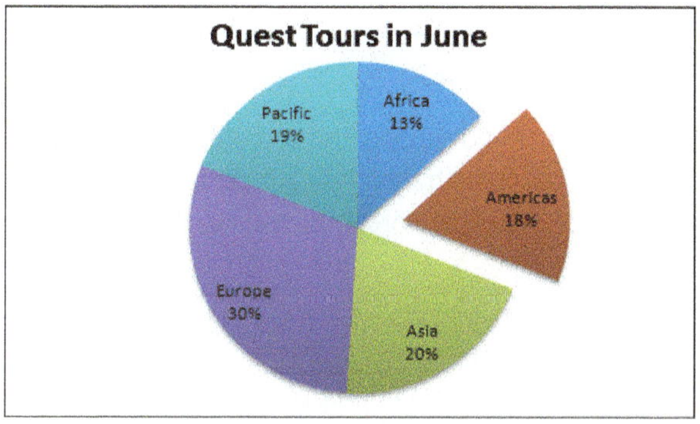

Pie chart

Used with permission from Microsoft Corporation

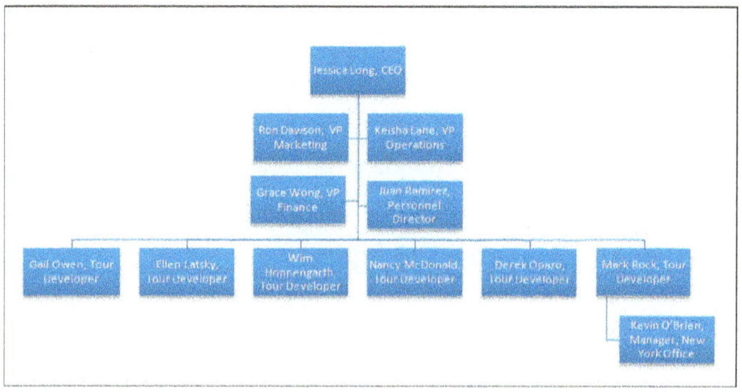

Hierarchy chart

TABLE 2-5: Illustrating data do's and don'ts

chart type	do	don't
Column and bar chart	• Show data changes over a period of time • Compare items • Choose bar charts when comparing durations	• **Don't** compare too many items—five or six is a typical maximum • **Don't** use column charts when the categories have long names; use bar charts instead
Line chart	• Show trends or patterns in data	• **Don't** use if the values are spaced evenly, such as by months or years
Pie chart	• Show the size of one category of data in proportion to other categories and to the whole	• **Don't** chart more than one category of data in a pie chart
Process chart	• Show the steps in a procedure • Use common shapes to represent parts of the process	• **Don't** change the meaning of the common shapes
Hierarchy chart	• Show the reporting relationships in an organization	• **Don't** include too many details in each box of the chart

Objective 15 Part 2

Adding Tables and Figures to Documents

One way to make documents more appealing and easy to read is to include graphics, photographs, and illustrations. These visual elements are appealing to the eye and help draw your reader's attention to the text. Tables also provide visual interest, and are designed to compare lists of information. Table 2-6 lists the do's and don'ts for adding tables and figures to documents. case After adding a chart to the brochure, you and Ellen decide to include a figure illustrating the tours, which would be informative and appealing on the back panel. You also want to add another photo to an inner panel.

ESSENTIAL ELEMENTS

QUICK TIP
A particular table or figure should only appear once in a document.

1. **Use illustrations when appropriate**
   Include graphics only when they add value to your document and support the content. For example, use company logos for corporate documents. Don't include visuals only to decorate a page, break up blocks of text, or to increase the length of a document. Figure 2-8 shows the Quest brochure with an additional figure.
2. **Label the figures**
   Every figure and table usually includes a label and caption to identify the item. Use "Figure #" to label figures such as charts, diagrams, photos, maps, and drawings. Use "Table #" to label tables. Number figures and tables independently of one another in sequence. Table labels generally appear above the table, and figure labels appear below the illustration. Follow the label with a short caption that describes what is being displayed, such as "Figure 2: Tyrol region."
3. **Refer to each figure or table**
   In nearby text, refer to each figure and table that you include. The figure reference ideally falls before the figure appears, as in "Figure 2 shows a photo of the Tyrol region." See Figure 2-9.
4. **Resize the illustration**
   When you insert photos, charts, and graphics in a document, they are displayed at their original, or native, size and resolution. If necessary, resize the image so that it fits the page and balances the content. Be sure to maintain the **aspect ratio** when you resize.
5. **Position the illustration**
   Position the graphic so that it balances the page. For example, two graphics on the left side of the page and all of the text on the right probably looks unbalanced.

QUICK TIP
Aspect ratio is the relationship between the width and height of an illustration.

YOU TRY IT

Practice adding tables and figures to documents by organizing brochure text to use tables and figures. Open the WC2-Y15.docx document and follow the steps in the worksheet. When you are finished, submit the document to your instructor as requested.

FIGURE 2-8: Graphics added to Quest brochure

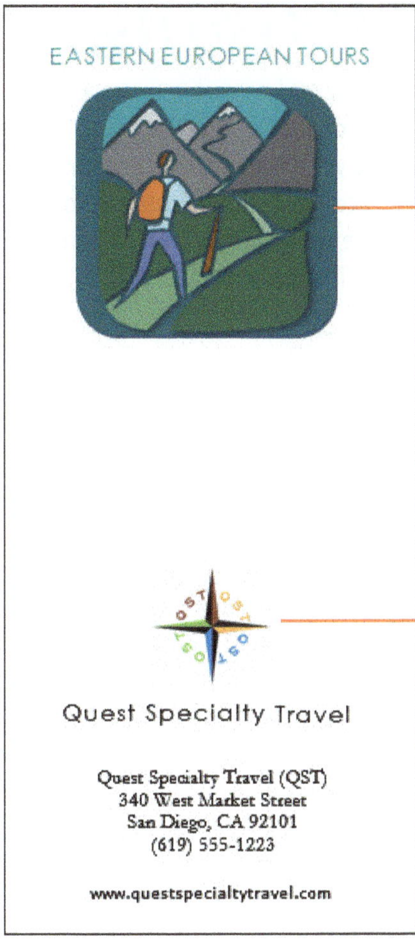

Used with permission from Microsoft Corporation

FIGURE 2-9: Photo and caption added to brochure

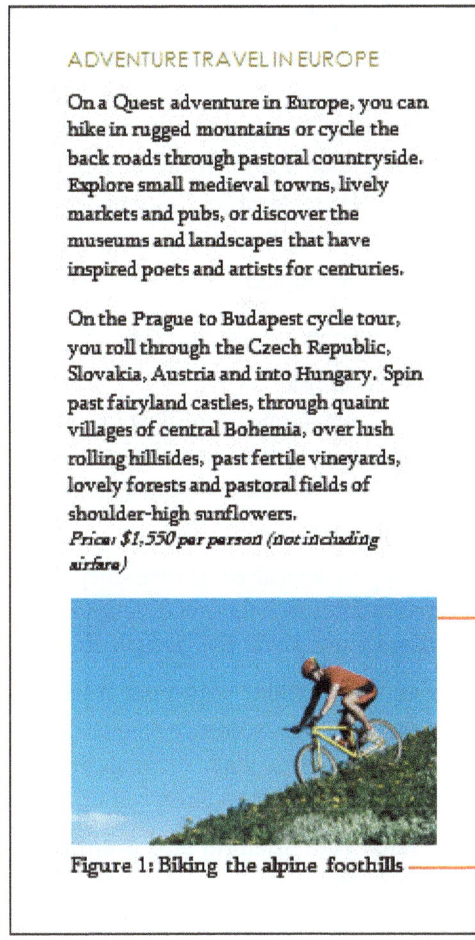

Used with permission from Microsoft Corporation; Fuse/Jupiterimages

TABLE 2-6: Adding tables and figures do's and don'ts

guideline	do	don't
Illustrations	• Include an illustration only when it adds value to the document • Add an illustration if it supports the content	• **Don't** add a figure merely to decorate the document • **Don't** include a figure only to break up blocks of text or lengthen a document
References	• Label each figure and table so you can refer to it in the text • Number each figure or table in order • Refer to each figure and table in nearby text	• **Don't** include a figure or table without referring to it in the content
Formatting	• Resize graphics to fit the page • Position the graphic so that it balances the page	• **Don't** resize so that you change the aspect ratio of the graphic

Objective 16 Part 2

Proofreading and Revising

To make a positive impression in your writing, you should carefully review and correct your work. When you proofread, you search your writing for errors, such as grammatical and typographical mistakes, before submitting your document to your reader. Revising involves changing your content and improving its structure and presentation. Like writing itself, proofreading is a skill you acquire. Table 2-7 lists the do's and don'ts of proofreading and revising. case After all the changes you've made to the Eastern European brochure, Ellen suggests you proofread it carefully before producing the final copy.

ESSENTIAL ELEMENTS

1. **Take a break**

   Give yourself time between writing and proofreading. Complete your writing project and start editing the next day, if possible. Even a short break will be helpful if your schedule is tight. The goal is to distance yourself from what you've written and return with a fresh perspective.

2. **Slow down**

   Most people make errors when they speed through the writing process. You risk overlooking these errors if you rush through the proofreading. Read through your writing slowly and deliberately. If you composed the message using electronic tools, it often helps to print a copy of your writing and read it on paper.

3. **Become familiar with your mistakes**

   As you develop experience proofreading your own work, you will recognize common errors that you make repeatedly. These might be words that are routinely misspelled, grammatical errors, or punctuation faults. Pay attention to these errors and look for other examples of them.

4. **Check your spelling and grammar manually**

   The automatic spelling and grammar checkers in word processing software are helpful, but they can't identify every mistake. They often flag as errors words or phrases that are in fact correct. Don't rely on these electronic tools exclusively. Use the automated features as a first pass in your proofreading, and follow them with a manual review of your documents. Use a dictionary to check the spelling of any word that looks suspect or that you are unsure of.

5. **Ask a colleague to look it over**

   It is easier to detect mistakes in the work of others than it is in your own. Usually, you become involved with your message, and you tend to skip over misspelled words and grammatical errors. A trusted colleague or friend can provide an objective look at your work. Ask them to proofread it as well as comment on the content and ways that you can improve it.

Figures 2-10 and 2-11 show part of the Quest brochure before and after proofreading and revision.

QUICK TIP

It often helps to read documents aloud to catch errors that your eye often misses, such as words repeated often in a paragraph.

YOU TRY IT

Practice proofreading by revising text that contains errors. Open the WC2-Y16.docx document and follow the steps in the worksheet. When you are finished, submit the document to your instructor as requested.

FIGURE 2-10: First draft of brochure text

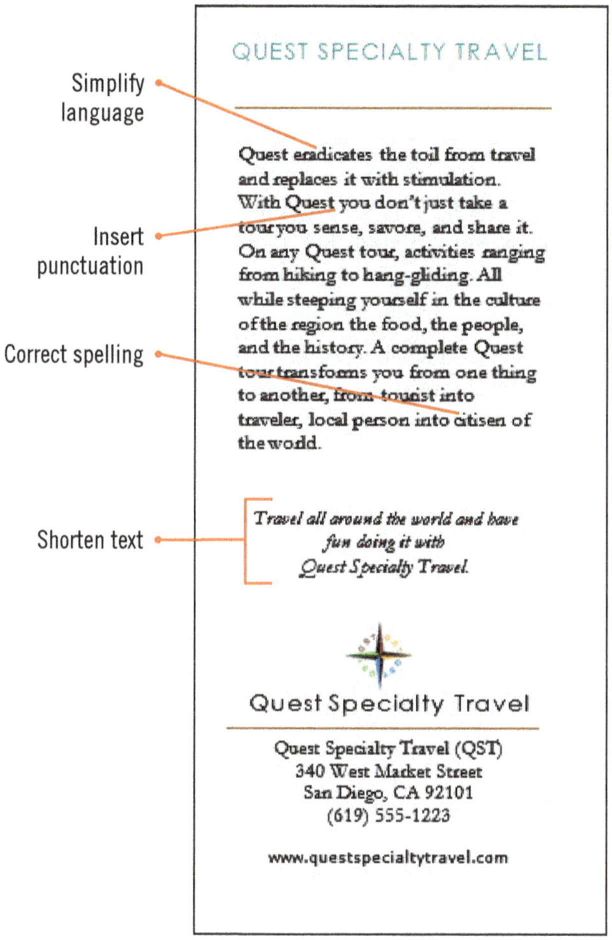

Used with permission from Microsoft Corporation

FIGURE 2-11: Revised brochure text

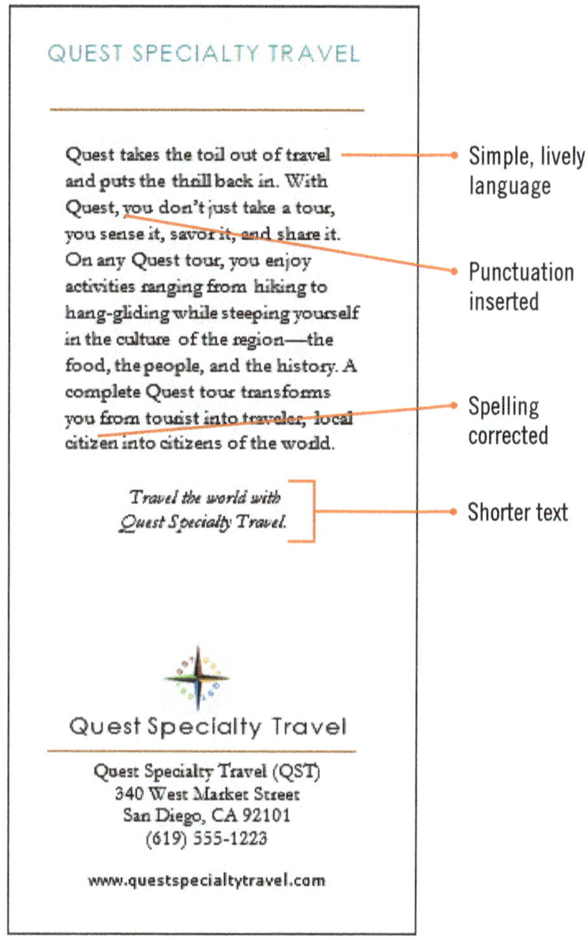

Used with permission from Microsoft Corporation

TABLE 2-7: Proofreading and revising do's and don'ts

guideline	do	don't
Timing	• Finish writing, take a break, then proofread • Read through your writing slowly and deliberately	• **Don't** write and proofread a document hastily
Checking for errors	• Learn to recognize your typical mistakes • Check for errors using automated tools, then check manually • Ask a colleague to proofread and comment on your documents	• **Don't** exclusively rely on electronic tools such as spell checkers

Plain English is good business

Some business people write to impress readers rather than express their ideas. They ask you to "execute a signature" instead of "sign the form." They start a letter with "Pursuant to our recent communication," when "As I mentioned in our phone call" is clearer and friendlier. As Deborah Dumaine, founder of Better Communications, says, "Grammar isn't the biggest problem in business writing; it's getting the message across." Dumaine's clients report a 73 percent increase in productivity after they are trained to write in plain English. The biggest difference, however, might be in communications with customers. According to the Federal Trade Commission, some major insurance companies, retailers, and banks have voluntarily redrafted their consumer communications into plain English over the last 10 years. Many other companies have simplified their forms in response to changes in state law. These companies report fewer customer inquiries, less litigation, and improved customer relations.

Sources: Penttila, Chris, "Well-written Business Documents, Leadership Qualities, and More," *Entrepreneur Magazine*, March 2005, and the Better Business Bureau Web site, *www.bbb.org*, accessed January 5, 2009.

Technology @ Work: Blogs

ESSENTIAL ELEMENTS

A **blog** (short for Weblog) is an interactive online journal. In general, one person writes blog entries on a Web site, and others read and comment on the content. In business, blogs can be internal or external. Internal blogs are designed for employees and others within an organization, and are often used instead of meetings and e-mail discussions, especially for routine company or project matters, such as policies, procedures, and announcements. External blogs are available to the public and let company employees or spokespersons air their views. For example, the Small Business Administration uses its external blog (*http://community.sba.gov*) to announce programs and services, clarify policies, and for other public relations purposes. See Figure 2-12. Because both types of blogs project an image of an organization and blog posts are usually archived for later searching, they require clear writing more than most forms of corporate communication. case Ellen Latsky is considering whether to create a blog for customers interested in Quest's European tours. She asks you to research the basics of writing an external company blog.

1. **Determine whether blogs are appropriate for your audience**

   As with any type of writing, start by analyzing the purpose and audience of the blog. Profile your target readers and determine whether a blog is an effective way to reach them. Does your audience spend much time online? Are they comfortable using technology tools to read and respond to information? Be sure to clarify your goals in publishing a blog. The strength of blogs is that they can stimulate discussion if the writing is lively and has personality. If you want to post corporate announcements, newsletters and Web sites are better options.

2. **Write with a personal voice**

   Most personal and internal blogs are written by a single person. External blogs often have more than one author, especially in companies with many products or services. In that case, the person who knows the product or service well should be the blogger. Each blogger should write in a professional, but identifiable style. Personalities and points of view make a blog interesting, though they must always be appropriate for the audience.

QUICK TIP

Experts recommend that you update your blog regularly, at least once a week.

3. **Develop and follow writing guidelines**

   Although a blog should have a personal voice, it projects an image of your organization and must be written to meet professional standards. Create a list of best practices and writing tips for the blog in your organization. Decision makers should review and approve of this list, and bloggers should take care to follow it.

QUICK TIP

Respond to all comments—positive and negative—in a professional and businesslike way.

4. **Establish a policy for comments**

   Remember that blogs are not electronic press releases for your organization—they should allow a two-way conversation between the company and the customer (or between one member of the organization and other members). Encourage readers to participate, but publish and distribute a strict policy about allowable comments. For example, the USA.gov blog provides clear comment-posting guidelines (*http://blog.usa.gov*). See Figure 2-13. Constructive criticism should be allowed, but rumors and inappropriate language should not.

YOU TRY IT

Practice working with blogs by reviewing a corporate blog. Open the WC2-TechWork.docx document and follow the steps in the worksheet. When you are finished, submit the document to your instructor as requested.

FIGURE 2-12: Small Business Association blog

Courtesy of the U.S. Small Business Administration

FIGURE 2-13: Comment posting guidelines on the USA.gov blog

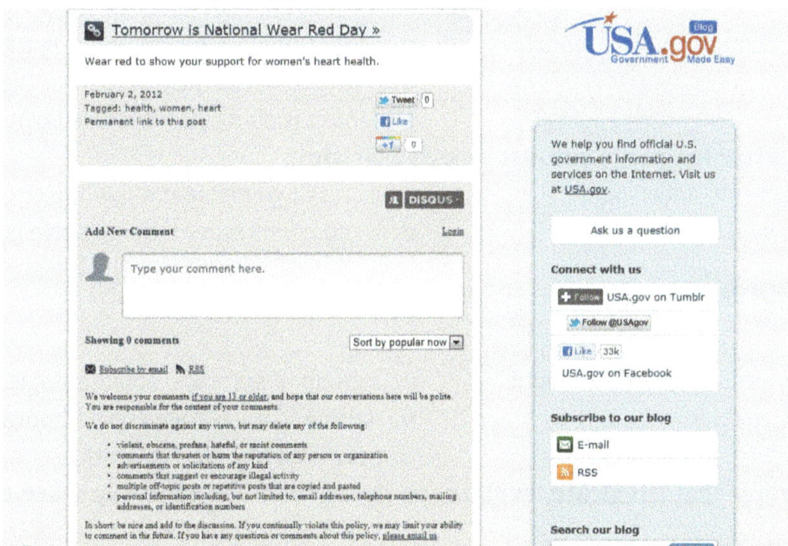

Courtesy of USA.gov

Blogging is writing

More than other forms of electronic communication such as e-mail, blogs are crafted pieces of writing that people can access long after they are first published on a Web site. If you are writing a blog, at a minimum, make sure you are using clear sentences and a logical organization for your ideas. Build on these fundamentals with the following techniques to devise an appealing and useful blog:

- *Include descriptive titles and headings*: Your titles and headings tell potential visitors what you are writing about. Make sure these elements use concrete details and active verbs.
- *Get to the point*: People read content on the Web more quickly than they do printed material. Make your point quickly—in the first sentence, if possible. Write economically throughout the post so people keep reading.
- *Stick to one topic*: A blog post can be long or short, but it should cover a single topic. An effective strategy is to present a single problem, discuss a solution, and then describe the results. Support your ideas with facts and references. Come to conclusions based on evidence rather than unsupported opinions.
- *Make it worth your reader's time*: Share knowledge and experiences to teach your readers or stimulate them to think. Write with energy and conviction, and show readers something in a new way to make your post worthwhile.
- *Edit and revise before publishing*: You can write quickly to put your words on the page, but those ideas are likely to remain fuzzy unless you edit them. Professional writers spend more time editing and revising than writing first drafts. Make sure the words you post on a blog today will be valuable and clear in the future.

Practice

Soft Skills Review

Clarify written communication.

1. **Start your writing projects by:**
   - **a.** illustrating data
   - **b.** proofreading your work
   - **c.** identifying your typical reader
   - **d.** laying out the document
2. **Which of the following is *not* a typical purpose of professional writing?**
   - **a.** To summarize decisions
   - **b.** To persuade customers
   - **c.** To list procedures
   - **d.** To chat informally

Write solid sentences.

1. **A sentence is:**
   - **a.** a group of words that form a complete thought
   - **b.** a type of noun
   - **c.** a set of symbols for interpreting text
   - **d.** a verb that tells the reader what the subject is, what the subject is doing, or what is happening to the subject
2. **You should avoid negative language because positive writing:**
   - **a.** is more concise and easier to understand
   - **b.** usually contains your own words
   - **c.** is free of grammar and spelling errors
   - **d.** is more impressive than negative language

Develop effective paragraphs.

1. **A paragraph is:**
   - **a.** a group of words that form a complete thought
   - **b.** the process of finding errors in writing
   - **c.** a group of sentences about a single topic
   - **d.** writing that has been copied from someone else and presented as your own work
2. **Sentences in a paragraph that illustrate, explain, or strengthen the main topic are called:**
   - **a.** topic sentences
   - **b.** detail sentences
   - **c.** concluding sentences
   - **d.** formatted sentences

Master punctuation.

1. **Why should you include correct punctuation in your documents?**
   - **a.** To avoid charges of plagiarism
   - **b.** To add variety to sentences
   - **c.** To increase white space on the page
   - **d.** To help readers interpret text
2. **Which of the following is *not* a situation where you should use a colon?**
   - **a.** Introduce a list, example, or quotation
   - **b.** Set off introductory text
   - **c.** Indicate the end of a greeting in a business letter
   - **d.** Separate a label or short heading from information

Lay out your document.

1. **What is the advantage of including white space on a page?**
   - **a.** It helps you stick to one topic
   - **b.** It adds value and supports the content
   - **c.** It concisely conveys numeric information
   - **d.** It makes it easier for your reader to navigate a document
2. **When designing a document, you should limit your use of:**
   - **a.** graphics, clip art, and different typefaces
   - **b.** white space and page gutters
   - **c.** complete sentences
   - **d.** colons and dashes

Illustrate data.

1. **Which of the following is *not* a goal of graphics in a business document?**
   - **a.** To make numbers meaningful
   - **b.** To separate a heading from information
   - **c.** To simplify complex relationships
   - **d.** To add visual interest to documents
2. **What kind of information can column and bar charts illustrate?**
   - **a.** Data changes over a period of time
   - **b.** Steps in a procedure
   - **c.** Reporting relationships in an organization
   - **d.** The size of one category of data in proportion to other categories

Add tables and figures to documents.

1. **When should you add a figure to a document?**
   - **a.** To decorate a page
   - **b.** To break up blocks of text
   - **c.** To illustrate content
   - **d.** To increase the length of a document
2. **When you include a photo as figure in a document, what else should you include in the text?**
   - **a.** Footnote
   - **b.** Name of the photographer
   - **c.** Figure reference
   - **d.** Aspect ratio

Proofread and revise.

1. **What do you do when you proofread?**
   - **a.** Search for and correct writing errors
   - **b.** Search for correct citations
   - **c.** Increase the length of the document
   - **d.** Search for proof of your claims
2. **When is the most effective time to use digital spelling and grammar checkers?**
   - **a.** After publication
   - **b.** Before you lay out the page
   - **c.** After converting a document to digital form
   - **d.** During the first pass of your proofreading

Technology @ work: Blogs.

1. **A blog is:**
   - **a.** an interactive online journal
   - **b.** a new form of instant messaging
   - **c.** a chart representing inexact data
   - **d.** a type of style checker
2. **Internal blogs are often used to:**
   - **a.** communicate with the public
   - **b.** take the place of company meetings
   - **c.** announce products to customers
   - **d.** conduct research

Critical Thinking Questions

1. **You are researching a new technology and copied some quotations from a relevant Web site. When you verify the Web site address to use in a citation, you find the Web site is no longer online. Can you use the text as your own?**
2. **Suppose you are working for a company that designs high-tech gadgets. You are part of a team developing guidelines for company publications. Should you allow people to use high-tech buzzwords and jargon?**
3. **You have recently been promoted and are now in charge of the company online newsletter. You want your colleagues to contribute to the newsletter, so you decide to write guidelines for contributors. What guidelines do you include?**
4. **You are reading your manager's blog and discover that it includes text taken from another source without reference. What should you do?**
5. **Besides copying text, the Web and other digital technologies have made it easy to copy images. Do you think plagiarism applies to photos and drawings as well as text?**

Independent Challenge 1

You are working in the Marketing Department of a small Web design company named Overland Designs. You are writing a description of your general services that will eventually be published on the company Web site. So far, you've made the notes shown in Figure 2-14. You need to assemble these notes into a coherent paragraph before sending it to the Web designer.

a. Open the **WC2-IC1.docx** document and follow the steps in the worksheet.
b. Proofread the document carefully to fix any grammar or formatting errors.
c. Submit the document to your instructor as requested.

FIGURE 2-14

Web site, Web pages, online brochures–name it, and it can be created by Overland Designs.
Great idea for a Web site now need someone to build it?
Just contact us for a free quote.
Ideas and concepts can be given to use along with sample Web pages, they are especially helpful.
After our first meeting in person or online, Overland Designs will get to work on your site.
Overland Designs is excellent at creating corporate identities online and advertising products.

Independent Challenge 2

You are working at the flagship Four Winds Apparel store in Minneapolis, Minnesota. Four Winds Apparel specializes in affordable active wear for men, women, and children and has five other stores in the Minneapolis-St. Paul area. Your boss asks you to update a flyer for an annual sale, shown in Figure 2-15. You need to revise the flyer so it is clearly written.

a. Open the **WC2-IC2.docx** document and follow the steps in the worksheet.
b. Proofread the document carefully to fix any grammar or formatting errors.
c. Submit the document to your instructor as requested.

FIGURE 2-15

Real Life Independent Challenge

This Independent Challenge requires an Internet connection.

To prepare for writing in your career area, learn about the kind of writing professionals do in various fields. Then try your hand at a typical document, which you can use in your portfolio when you hunt for jobs.

a. Identify a field in which you'd like to work.

b. Using your favorite search engine, research the field that interests you. The online *Occupational Outlook Handbook* (*www.bls.gov/oco*) is also a good resource for information about occupations.

c. Use the Web or personal resources to learn what kinds of writing people do in that field. For example, you could interview someone who works in a law office or ad agency.

d. Create a document that reflects the type of writing professionals do in your chosen field. Be sure to perform the following tasks:

- Identify the audience of the document.
- Define the purpose of the document.
- Use the writing and organizing techniques described in this unit.

e. Format the document effectively.

f. Proofread the document carefully to fix any grammar or formatting errors.

g. Save and close the document, then submit it to your instructor as requested.

Team Challenge

You are working for Farley Worldwide, a company specializing in information services, and you are part of a group preparing to travel to Europe and Thailand. To prepare for the trip, you and your team decide to research typical expressions that are often misinterpreted in other cultures.

a. Use the Web and other resources to research at least three examples of expressions, sayings, cultural references, and proverbs that are ambiguous or often misinterpreted when translated from English to other languages and vice versa.

b. Meet as a team and compile two lists of expressions: those that cause problems when translated from English, and those that cause problems when translated to English.

c. Brainstorm other examples of practices such as tips, business meetings, greetings, and negotiations that might differ from one culture to another.

d. Select one of these practices, and then research it on the Web.

e. As a team, meet again to discuss your findings.

Be the Critic

Review the poorly written document shown in Figure 2-16. Create an e-mail message that lists the weaknesses of the document and makes specific suggestions for improvement. Send the critique in an e-mail message to your instructor.

FIGURE 2-16

Attendance and Reporting to Work Policy

It should be noted that each employee is considered important to the overall success of the operation. The paramount thing to keep in mind is that when you are not here, someone else must fill in for the uncompleted job. Consequently, all employes are expected to report to work on time at the scheduled start of the workday. Do not arrive at work unless you are prepared to at your scheduled starting time. Every employee is expected to wear his badge at all times.

The company depends on its employees to be at work at the times and locations scheduled so excessive absenteeism and/or tardiness will immediately lead to disciplinary action, up to and including termination. The determination of excessive absenteeism will be made at the discretion of the company. It is impossible for the company to exist without complete cooperation from its employees. To expedite your agreement to these policies, your signature is required.

Part 3

Developing Reports and Proposals

Files You Will Need:

WC3-Y18.docx
WC3-Y19.docx
WC3-Y20.docx
WC3-Y21.docx
WC3-Y22.docx
WC3-Y23.docx
WC3-Y24.docx
WC3-TechWork.docx
WC3-IC1.docx
WC3-IC2.docx

Reports and proposals are the most common types of long documents you write in business. Both answer questions about a topic or project or offer solutions to a problem. Your readers will study your report and use the conclusions and analysis to help them make decisions. Besides commercial businesses, nonprofit and government agencies write and request reports to summarize or analyze research. Organizations sometimes hire professional writers to develop proposals that earn contracts or otherwise result in sales. Knowing how to compose these important documents is a valuable professional skill. case Keisha Lane, vice president of operations for Quest Specialty Travel, wants to expand the tours Quest offers and supplement the types of activities tour developers organize, especially those involving adventure and educational travel. Keisha asks you to research the tours and activities that Quest's competitors provide, and then write a report describing your findings.

OBJECTIVES

17 Understand reports and proposals
18 Plan a report or proposal
19 Write the beginning
20 Write the body
21 Create the end matter
22 Write short reports
23 Write proposals
24 Cite sources

Objective 17 Part 3

Understanding Reports and Proposals

A **report** is a written document designed to communicate information about a particular subject. Reports are written objectively, though some can include analysis or recommendations. A **proposal** is similar to a report but is intended to persuade and inform. A proposal provides information about a product, service, or idea and tries to convince the reader to adopt the recommended solution. A key difference between reports and proposals is when they are written. A proposal is normally developed early in the decision-making process when it can influence decisions. A report is usually written after some action has been taken. Some reports document the status of an activity or project as it occurs. Other reports are written at the conclusion of the activity or project. See Figure 3-1. case Before you begin your report on the tours and activities that Quest's competitors offer, you prepare to write by analyzing your purpose and audience.

DETAILS

QUICK TIP
The general goals of reports and proposals are to answer questions and solve problems.

QUICK TIP
The primary audience is often a decision maker.

Before you start to write a report or proposal, review the following questions:

- **What is your purpose for writing?**
  The first step in writing a report is clearly defining your purpose. Start by analyzing what you want to accomplish. Is your goal to inform, update, analyze, or persuade? Your objective will help you to decide on the format that you should use.
- **Who are your readers?**
  As with other types of documents, write a report or proposal with your readers in mind. To best meet your readers' needs, identify how well they understand your subject. What do they want to learn from reading your report or proposal? How are they likely to react? How should you write to make the information clear and understandable to your readers? Be sure to consider your primary (main) audience and the secondary audience, which includes anyone else who might read the document.
- **Should you write a report or a proposal?**
  You write a report to share information with someone else. You write proposals to persuade your readers to adopt your idea, product, or solution. They are similar to analytical reports except that you are presenting only one recommendation. Table 3-1 lists suggestions for when you should write a report or a proposal.
- **Will your report present information or analyze a topic?**
  Reports can be one of two types. **Informational reports** present information in a clear, objective format. An informational report is appropriate when you want to provide a written summary of a subject for your reader. Opinions and recommendations are not included in an informational report. **Analytical reports** typically present data, analysis, and a conclusion. Analytical reports often provide different options, identify pros and cons for alternatives, and include specific recommendations.
- **Is your proposal for an internal or external audience?**
  Proposals are also one of two types. **Internal proposals** recommend how to solve problems within an organization, such as by changing a procedure or using different products or services from vendors. **External proposals** are designed to sell products or services to customers and are usually written in response to a request.

  The answers to these questions help you decide how long your report should be, what information to include, and the degree of formality that is appropriate.

FIGURE 3-1: Types of reports and proposals

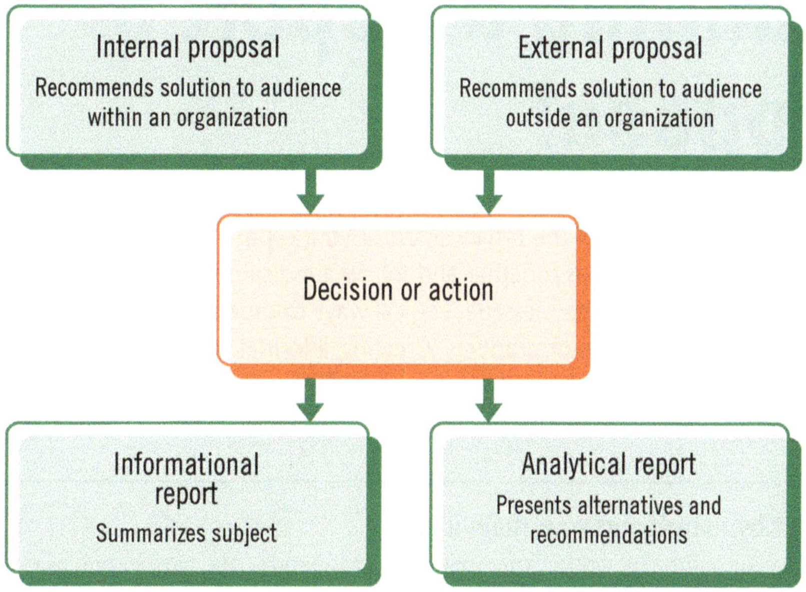

TABLE 3-1: When to write a report or proposal

scenario	report	proposal	other
You attended a trade show and want to inform others about your competitors' products.	•		
You need to document company procedures.	•		
You are analyzing whether to purchase new computer equipment or upgrade the current equipment.	•		
You are proposing to purchase new computer equipment.		•	
You are recommending a new way to schedule staff resources.		•	
You are offering your company's services to a person or organization.		•	
You are summarizing notes you took at a conference for your own future reference.			Informal notes or outline
You are promoting your company's services for a general audience.			Advertisement
You are describing your company's products and providing examples to potential customers.			Presentation

Business reports are not academic papers

A recent study by the College Board confirmed that writing is a "threshold" skill for hiring and promoting salaried employees. Most companies expect that anyone with a post-secondary school degree has some writing skills. However, few recent graduates have direct experience in workplace writing, which is very different from academic writing. Alan Pike, who teaches management writing and oral communication at Cornell University, describes a survey of 2,000 college professors asked to grade short answers to exam questions." . . .they were given a plain English set of responses to those exam questions . . . And then they were sent a second set of responses that were indirect . . . just full of words, verbal, and almost without exception, these 2,000 college professors graded the second set of responses higher than they did the first." Managers, customers, and others in business would prefer the plain English responses. In addition to style, a significant difference between academic and workplace writing is the audience. "Business writing?" says Alan Pike. "Are they interested in your thought processes, how you got to you conclusions? They couldn't care less . . . Will they reward you for self-expression? No. What are they interested in? What is this gonna do to the company, to our market share . . . It has to be action oriented, and user oriented, and it has to be written for your reader's perspective."

Sources: College Board staff, "Writing: A Ticket to Work or a Ticket Out," Report of the National Commission on Writing, September, 2004; and Pike, Allen, "Business Writing: Understand the Difference Between an Academic and Business Audience," www.allbusiness.com/lecture/11702094-1.html.

Objective 18
Part 3

Planning a Report or Proposal

Organize your business reports and proposals so that the information is easy to read and follow. You should have a good idea of the organization of your report or proposal before you write the first sentence. Group common ideas together and follow a logical sequence that suits your purpose and helps the reader to understand the message. Logical ways to order information are by time, importance, and categories, such as location or products. Creating a formal or informal outline helps you plan an effective report. Table 3-2 summarizes the do's and don'ts for creating an outline. case After identifying the purpose and audience for your report on Quest competitors, you are ready to outline the report.

ESSENTIAL ELEMENTS

1. **Start by identifying your main idea**
   Start your outline by writing your main idea at the top of the page in one or two sentences. If your main idea is longer, refine your message. Stating the main idea at the top of the page helps you focus on your objective as you develop the rest of the outline. The main idea of many reports and proposals is to describe a solution to a problem.

QUICK TIP
A report should have at least three to five major headings.

2. **Use headings for your important ideas**
   Review the ideas and topics for your report and select the most important ones. These are the major headings in your outline. List these in a logical order, such as from most to least important or chronologically if your report emphasizes time. The headings will become the major sections of your report. Figure 3-2 shows the headings in an informal and formal outline, including the standard use of Roman numerals, uppercase letters, numbers, and lowercase letters.

3. **Create subheadings for subtopics**
   Divide each of your main topics into several ideas so you can discuss them in detail. List these ideas in your outline as subheadings. Provide two or more subheadings for each major heading, as shown in Figure 3-2. You can break subtopics into smaller divisions if you are writing a long or complex report.

4. **Include appropriate sections**
   Most reports and proposals include standard sections such as the introduction, background, current situation, facts, proposed solution, summary, conclusions, recommendations, pros and cons, reference list, and appendices. Choose the sections that serve the purpose of your report or proposal.

QUICK TIP
Many reports and proposals are written by a group of people; circulate the outline to everyone in the group for their approval.

5. **Review your outline**
   Review a complete draft of your outline to answer the following questions: Are your ideas arranged in a logical order? If you read the outline aloud to yourself, does it make sense? Are your headings and subheadings logical and balanced? Are they similar in terms of their significance? Rearrange the order if necessary. Do your topics have enough detail or evidence to support your main idea? If not, you should either add to your outline or restructure it.

YOU TRY IT

Practice planning a report or proposal by reorganizing material so it matches its purpose. Open the WC3-Y18.docx document and follow the steps in the worksheet. When you are finished, submit the document to your instructor as requested.

FIGURE 3-2: Formal and informal outlines

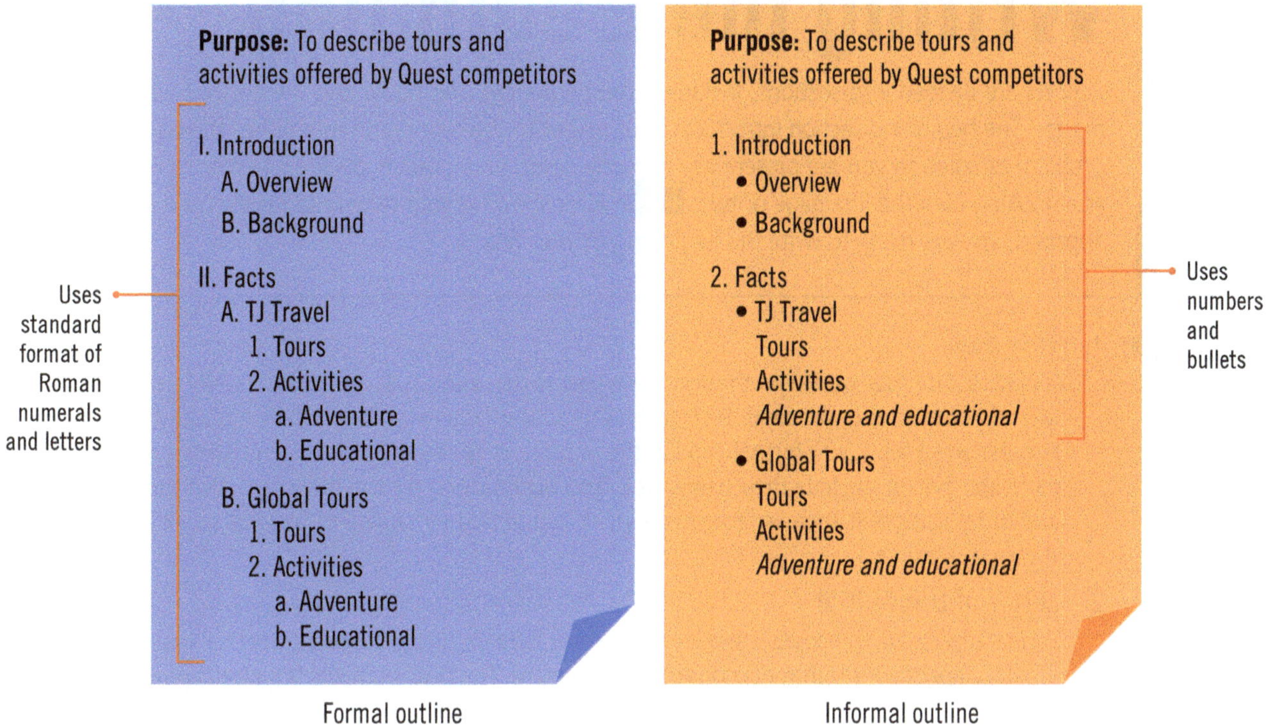

TABLE 3-2: Outline do's and don'ts

element	do	don't
Main idea	• Start by brainstorming and listing all the ideas you want to include • Select one as the main idea • List at the top of the outline	• **Don't** keep all of the ideas—only those that serve the purpose and audience of the report or proposal • **Don't** use more than two sentences to state the main idea
Major headings and sections	• Select the topics and write corresponding headings • Use standard headings such as Introduction and Conclusion • List in logical order • In a formal outline, use Roman numerals for major headings	• **Don't** deviate from a standard pattern of (1) introduction, (2) facts or findings, and (3) conclusion unless a different organization is clearer • **Don't** include topics that do not have enough details or evidence
Subheadings	• Divide major topics into subtopics with subheadings • List the subtopics in logical order, such as by time, importance, or category • In a formal outline, use uppercase letters for the first level of subheadings, numbers for the next level, and lowercase letters for the last level	• **Don't** list subtopics in random order • **Don't** use subheadings that are hard to interpret

Objective 19

Part 3

Writing the Beginning

Reports are divided into sections, including the beginning, the body, and the conclusion and other end matter. The beginning section introduces your reader to the report and establishes the background of the problem or solution you are presenting. In many cases, your readers decide whether to read your report after looking over the first page or two. case After showing your outline to Keisha Lane and gaining her approval, you are ready to write the beginning of your report.

ESSENTIAL ELEMENTS

QUICK TIP

Most word-processing programs include report templates with place-holders for standard report elements such as title pages.

1. **Title page**

   Include a title page on a report unless the report is very short. Use a title that briefly describes the main idea of your report or proposal. Format the title so it is larger and darker than surrounding text. You can also include a subtitle to further explain the purpose of the report. If you are preparing your report for a particular person, include their name, title, and organization on the title page. Also indicate the report author by using text such as "Prepared by" or "Submitted by" followed by your name and the date, as shown in Figure 3-3.

2. **Letter of transmittal**

   Formal reports and proposals often include a cover letter or memo called a **letter of transmittal**, which provides a personalized introduction to your document. The letter or memo is typically printed on organization stationery and summarizes your important findings, conclusions, or recommendations. Address the letter of transmittal to a particular person. Use separate letters, each personally addressed, if you are distributing multiple copies of the report.

QUICK TIP

A rule of thumb is that the executive summary should not be longer than 10 percent of the complete report.

3. **Executive summary**

   An **executive summary** is designed for busy managers and other decision makers who might not have time to read the complete report. The executive summary is a short synopsis of the important ideas, observations, problems, and conclusions contained in your report. Use clear, nontechnical language to highlight the main points in the same sequence they appear in the report.

4. **Table of contents**

   A table of contents (TOC) lists the headings of your report and their page numbers. See Figure 3-3. Although the TOC appears at the beginning of your report, it should be one of the last elements you create because page numbers often change when you edit the document.

5. **Introduction**

   Formal reports and proposals start with an introduction that announces your topic and guides readers into the body of your document. The introduction should clearly explain the purpose of the report. It can also describe the background or current situation, introduce the main issue or problem that your report addresses, and preview your main idea or objective. End your introduction by outlining the contents and the format of your report. See Figure 3-4.

YOU TRY IT

Practice writing beginnings by revising material so that it's clear, appealing, and appropriate for a report introduction. Open the WC3-Y19.docx document and follow the steps in the worksheet. When you are finished, submit the document to your instructor as requested.

FIGURE 3-3: Title page and table of contents for a report

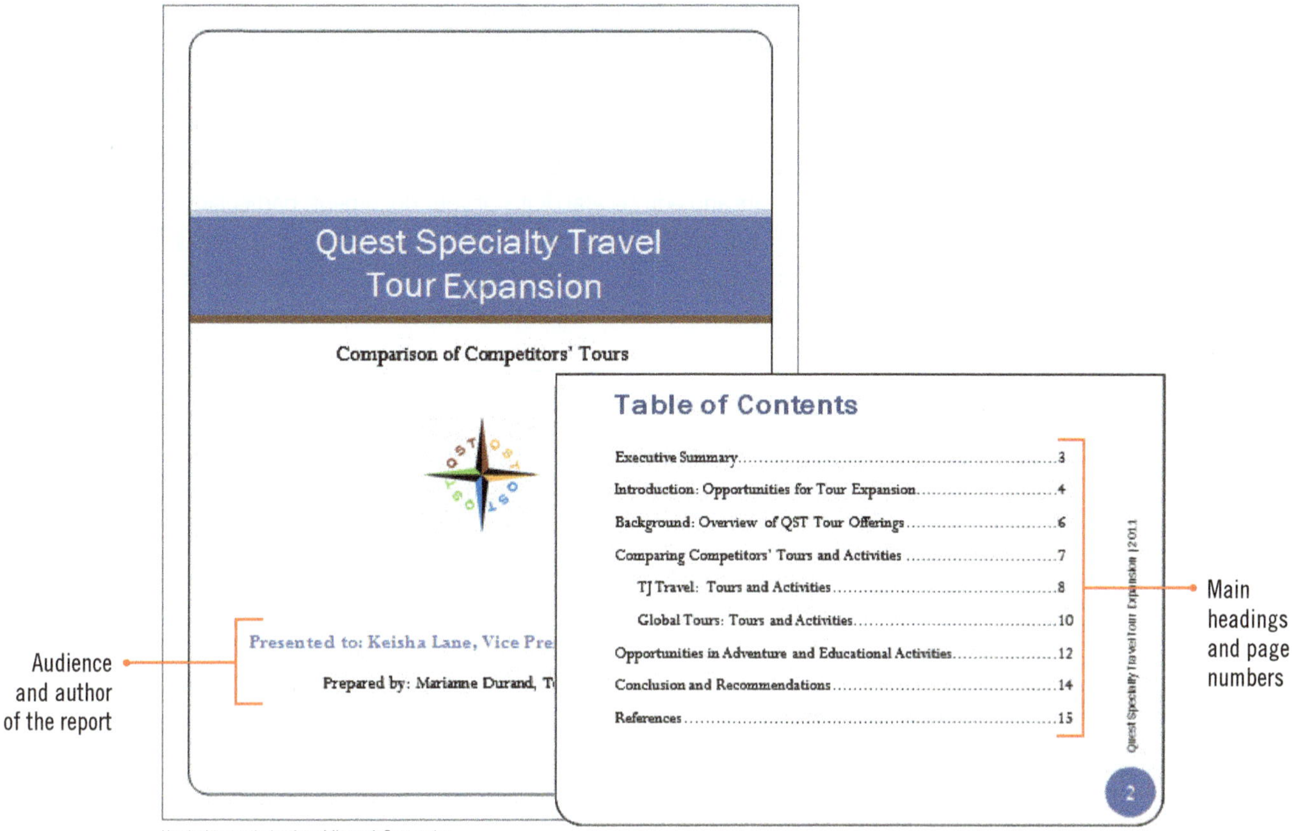
Quest Specialty Travel
Tour Expansion

Comparison of Competitors' Tours

Presented to: Keisha Lane, Vice Pre

Prepared by: Marianne Durand, T

Table of Contents

Executive Summary..3
Introduction: Opportunities for Tour Expansion........................4
Background: Overview of QST Tour Offerings........................6
Comparing Competitors' Tours and Activities........................7
TJ Travel: Tours and Activities........................8
Global Tours: Tours and Activities........................10
Opportunities in Adventure and Educational Activities........................12
Conclusion and Recommendations........................14
References........................15

Quest Specialty Travel Tour Expansion | 2011

2

Used with permission from Microsoft Corporation

FIGURE 3-4: Report introduction

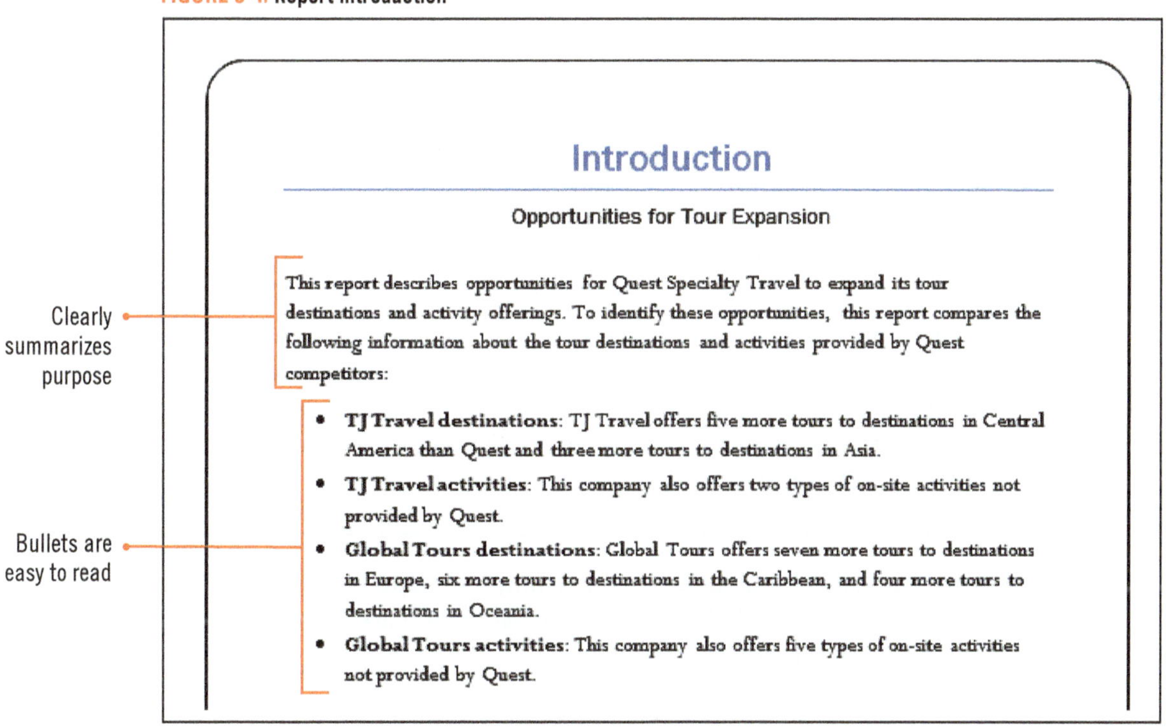
Introduction

Opportunities for Tour Expansion

This report describes opportunities for Quest Specialty Travel to expand its tour destinations and activity offerings. To identify these opportunities, this report compares the following information about the tour destinations and activities provided by Quest competitors:

- **TJ Travel destinations**: TJ Travel offers five more tours to destinations in Central America than Quest and three more tours to destinations in Asia.
- **TJ Travel activities**: This company also offers two types of on-site activities not provided by Quest.
- **Global Tours destinations**: Global Tours offers seven more tours to destinations in Europe, six more tours to destinations in the Caribbean, and four more tours to destinations in Oceania.
- **Global Tours activities**: This company also offers five types of on-site activities not provided by Quest.

Used with permission from Microsoft Corporation

Objective
20
Part 3

Writing the Body

The body of your report is the main part of the document and contains all of the material that supports your central idea. The body typically makes up 85% of the overall content, and includes a detailed discussion of research, supporting evidence, and solutions. Organize the body using the headings listed in your outline. Budget enough time to create and edit several drafts of your document, particularly for long or complex reports. Carefully proofread your work and have a colleague read it over as well. case You have refined the outline of your report and written the first draft of the beginning sections. Now you are ready to write the body of the report on the tours and activities that Quest competitors offer.

ESSENTIAL ELEMENTS

1. **Review headings and sections**
   Review the headings listed in your outline to make sure they clearly identify each section in the body. Keep in mind that some people are likely to scan rather than read the report, so the headings should be meaningful. You can use combination headings such as "Findings: Competitors' Tours and Activities" when you need to cover multiple items.

2. **Explain your methods**
   If your report includes data such as charts, figures, or tables of facts, identify in a brief paragraph where you found the material, as shown in Figure 3-5. Explaining your approach and disclosing the sources of your information helps your readers interpret the data.

3. **Present the evidence**
   Present facts and findings that are useful, important, or necessary to your reader and that support your conclusion or solution. Use tables, graphs, lists, photos, and drawings to clarify data, create visual interest, and illustrate concepts. Identify each figure with a label such as "Figure 1" and a descriptive caption such as "Quest tours and activities in Asia." Refer to each figure in a nearby paragraph, as shown in Figure 3-5.

QUICK TIP
For every figure you include, you need to mention the figure by number in the text.

4. **Prepare recommendations and identify alternatives**
   If the purpose of the report is to solve a problem, include specific, practical recommendations. If your audience is not familiar with the topic or might not agree to a suggestion, identify alternative options or actions. Present alternatives objectively and give each a similar amount of coverage.

5. **Discuss or evaluate the recommendations**
   Besides providing recommendations and alternatives, explain their implications for your organization. For example, if you report that sales have increased for three consecutive quarters and you recommend continuing the current sales campaign, explain how the increased sales affect production schedules and inventory levels. If you present several alternatives, discuss the pros and cons of each.

QUICK TIP
Be objective in your analysis. Biased writing discredits your report.

6. **Conclude the report**
   Bring your report to a clear conclusion by summarizing the important parts of your presentation. Some readers look only at the last page of a report, so be sure to highlight your main message as you close. If you are writing a proposal, you should finish with a call to action. Recommend your solution and explain why it is in your reader's best interest to adopt it.

YOU TRY IT

Practice writing the body of a document by revising text. Open the WC3-Y20.docx document and follow the steps in the worksheet. When you are finished, submit the document to your instructor as requested.

FIGURE 3-5: Body of the report

Identifies source of the material

Refers to figure

Figure label and caption

Quest meets this need through its ACE activities. To maintain a competitive edge, Quest should make sure its ACE offerings are more appealing, fresh, and authentic than its competitors' offerings. This report surveys the tours and activities that two of Quest's closest competitors—TJ Travel and Global Tours—include as part of their travel packages.

A study of current TJ Travel and Global Tours brochures and Web sites provided the data for this report. (See www.tjtravel.course.net and www.globaltours.course.net.)

The chart in Figure 1 compares the number of tours in the five major regions for destination travel.

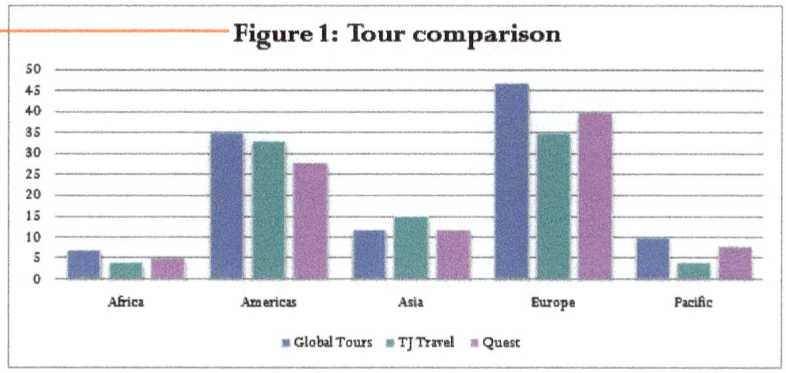

Used with permission from Microsoft Corporation

TABLE 3-3: Writing the body do's and don'ts

element	do	don't
Headings	• Make sure the headings clearly identify each section in the body • Writing headings that are meaningful	• **Don't** use generic, undescriptive headings • **Don't** write long headings that are difficult to decipher
Content	• Present facts and findings that are useful, important, or necessary to your reader • Use tables, graphs, lists, and graphics to support the content • Present solutions to problems, if appropriate	• **Don't** use graphics merely to decorate the material • **Don't** provide an opinion—support your material with facts

Gathering information

You can gather information for a report or proposal from primary and secondary sources. **Primary sources** are forms of firsthand experience, such as interviews and observations. **Secondary sources** are written documents describing a topic or experience, such as articles, books, and Web pages. The Web is a popular resource for gathering information because it provides access to billions of secondary sources. However, to find the best sources for your report, you need to become adept at using search engines and providing keywords as search terms. For general topics, popular search engines such as Google and Yahoo are a good place to start. If you want to restrict your search to a subject area, you can use a specialty search engine, such as FindLaw (*www.findlaw.com*), which is limited to legal topics. Specialty search engines are also helpful if your keyword or phrase has more than one meaning, such as *stock management*, which yields pages of links to stock market sites, though you might be looking for articles about managing merchandise in a store. Popular search engines actually search databases of Web sites, which index what is called the visible Web, not the entire Web. To search other databases, you can use the **invisible Web**, Web sites that popular search engines cannot access, such as university libraries and online almanacs.

Objective 21 Part 3

Creating the End Matter

A complete report or proposal often includes **end matter**, one or more sections that follow the conclusion. End matter typically includes reference material that supports the main document, such as a list of books and other works you cited in the report. Supporting information helps explain the key ideas in your report, adds to your credibility, and is intended for some readers, but not all. Table 3-4 summarizes the do's and don'ts for creating end matter. case Keisha Lane reviews a draft of your report, and reminds you to add a reference list to the end matter. You also want to include an appendix showing the tours and activities Quest Specialty Travel currently offers.

ESSENTIAL ELEMENTS

QUICK TIP
Check to see if your organization prefers a particular citation format.

1. **Reference list**

   If you are using various sources of information in your report, identify them in a reference list. (See Figure 3-6.) Select one of the standard ways to cite references; many word processors provide a tool that guides you to include the author, title, publication, date of publication, and other citation information in the correct format.

2. **Table of figures or illustrations**

   If you use illustrations in your report, you can list them in a table in your end matter, especially if readers might want to refer to the illustrations later. A table of figures lists the figure label, figure caption, and page number of each illustration. Many word processors can search your report and create a table of figures for you.

QUICK TIP
If your reader wants to adopt your proposal, an approval page or attached contract is a convenient way for them to do so.

3. **Approval page**

   Proposals often include an authorization or approval page, which contains a short paragraph that authorizes the action that you have recommended in the proposal. Include a place for your reader to sign and date their approval.

4. **Appendices**

   Supplemental material of secondary interest to some readers belongs in an appendix. Include information as an appendix if it is relevant to your subject but is too detailed or distracting to include in the body of your report, such as lists of raw survey results or copies of a survey form. Refer to the appendix in the report itself, as in "See Appendix B."

YOU TRY IT

Practice writing the end matter by editing a report. Open the WC3-Y21.docx document and follow the steps in the worksheet. When you are finished, submit the document to your instructor as requested.

FIGURE 3-6: Reference list

References

Bergman, L. (14 January 2011). Selling High-End Tours in Hard Times. *Travel Business*, 35-40

Chapman, A. (2011). Appealing to Discerning Travelers. Retrieved May 12, 2011, from Travel Professionals: http://www.tpg.course.com/pub/030811/article05.htm

Global Travel home page (2011). Retrieved May 20, 2011 from http://www.globaltravel.course.net

Global Travel. (2011). *The Adventurer's Guide to Global Travel* [Brochure]. San Diego: Global Travel

TJ Tours home page (2011). Retrieved May 20, 2011 from http://www.tjtours.course.net

TJ Tours. (2011). *TJ Tours featured tours and activities* [Brochure]. San Diego: TJ Tours

Used with permission from Microsoft Corporation

TABLE 3-4: End matter do's and don'ts

element	do	don't
Reference list	• List the articles, books, Web pages, and other works used as sources • Include the author, title, publication, and date of publication at a minimum • Select an accepted reference format and use it consistently	• **Don't** include a reference list if you used footnotes for only a few references
Appendices	• Include a cover page for each appendix • Label the first appendix Appendix A, followed by Appendix B, and so on • Include a title that identifies the contents of the appendix	• **Don't** use appendices as a catch-all to add material that isn't relevant to your main document

Web tools for Web research

The Web is full of excellent sources of information for business reports and proposals—far too full. Most people use a time-consuming method of using search engines to find Web pages related to their topic, and then cutting and pasting text into a separate program such as Microsoft Word or an e-mail message. Now you can use Web tools that work like electronic research assistants. For example, Zotero (*www.zotero.org*) works with browsers such as Firefox. As you visit Web sites, it automatically senses content and lets you add information including sources, files, and snapshots of Web pages to a personal library. Zotero also indexes your library so you can find information quickly. Google has a custom search tool that lets you collect and search related Web pages, such as all Web pages related to green building technology. With a search tool named Kartoo (*www.kartoo.com*), you enter a keyword and then Kartoo draws a visual map, with links to other topics that help you refine your search. It shows you relationships among Web sites along with the links. Search engines such as Hakia (*www.hakia.com*) also track your search words and display links to pages that might interest you. Hakia combines Web searching with human expertise—librarians recommend Web sites that are free of commercial bias.

Source: Buckman, Rebecca, "Yahoo!'s Intelligent Search," *Forbes.com*, February 4, 2009.

Objective 22 Part 3

Writing Short Reports

Short reports focus on a single idea or topic and do not require the formality or detail of a longer document. The short format is commonly used for periodic (or activity) reports, progress updates, trip reports, and other situations where brevity is appropriate. If you need to discuss several of these topics, address each in a separate short report. Short reports should not be used for important matters, when formality is required, or when writing a proposal. case After completing your report on expanding Quest's tours and activities, Keisha Lane sent you to the annual Adventure Travel convention in San Francisco. She now asks you to write a short conference report summarizing the event.

ESSENTIAL ELEMENTS

QUICK TIP
Ideally, a five-paragraph report fits on one to two printed pages.

QUICK TIP
In a short report, use only two levels of headings.

1. Use the five-paragraph format

As shown in Figures 3-7 and 3-8, the simplest report format uses five paragraphs to present information on a specific topic: an introduction that provides a brief overview and states your main idea in the first paragraph; three paragraphs that support your topic; and a concluding paragraph that summarizes your message and restates your main idea. Short reports don't need to include as much detail or cover as many topics as a full formal report. Stick to what your reader wants or needs to know.

2. Start each section with a heading

Readability is important when writing short reports. Include headings at the beginning of each section so your readers can quickly navigate the report. Use heading levels to signal the importance of the information. For example, level 1 headings are the largest and darkest headings, so use them for the main headings. Level 2 headings are smaller and lighter, so use them for the subheadings.

3. Use a letter format for external audiences

If a reader of your short report is someone outside of your organization, use a business letter format. Print the first page on company letterhead. Follow the basic guidelines for a traditional business letter and include an inside address, date, salutation, and complimentary close. The report is the body of your letter.

4. Use a memo format for internal audiences

If you are preparing the short report for someone within your organization, use a memo format. Prepare your report as you would a business memo. Start the report with a traditional memo header and include the To, From, Date, and Subject fields.

5. Consider a title page

Short reports typically omit many of the elements that are part of more formal documents, such as a table of contents and executive summary. However, you can include a title page, which provides a descriptive cover for your report and communicates the subject to your reader. Readers can learn the title, date, and your name at a glance. A title page also helps distinguish your report from other documents and correspondence on your reader's desk.

YOU TRY IT

Practice writing short reports by reorganizing a report. Open the WC3-Y22.docx document and follow the steps in the worksheet. When you are finished, submit the document to your instructor as requested.

FIGURE 3-7: Beginning of convention report

Memo format for internal audience

Date: May 25, 2011

To: Keisha Lane

From: Marianne Durand *MD*

Subject: Report on the Adventure Travel Convention

Paragraph 1 is an overview of the conference

I attended the Adventure Travel convention sponsored by the Travel Professionals Association. This one-day meeting, held in San Francisco on May 23, highlighted trends in current adventure travel and offered advice and techniques for appealing to our customers. Although the presentations covered a wide range of topics, this report focuses on adventure tourism trends, typical adventure travelers, and destination rankings.

Paragraphs 2–5 summarize details

Adventure Tourism Trends

Despite the struggles in the economy, adventure travel is proving to maintain its popularity, especially among travelers ages 35-50. More than one speaker noted the following trends in adventure tourism:

- Activities with growing demand include biking, diving, sailing, and surfing.
- Special services are popular, such as unexpected luxury in remote locations.
- Messages that emphasize the personal growth benefits of adventure tourism are the most successful.

Each section starts with the same level of heading

Adventure Travelers

Adventure travelers are maturing and continue to look for flexibility and quality. A recent National Geographic study describes the typical adventure traveler as follows:

- Married without children living at home
- Household income between $75,000 and $149,000

Used with permission from Microsoft Corporation

FIGURE 3-8: Ending of convention report

Destination Trends

Three organizations track destination rankings. Mr. Alan Bittman, president of Travel Professionals Association, provided the following composite statistics:

- The five most popular adventure destinations in 2011 in developed countries are Switzerland, Sweden, New Zealand, United Kingdom, and Spain (in order of popularity).
- The five most popular adventure destinations in 2011 in developing countries are Estonia, Chile, Slovak Republic, Czech Republic, and Hungary (in order of popularity).
- Air travel is 20% more expensive this year than two years ago, so countries and regions that are investing in improved high-speed rail systems will be in demand.

Conclusion offers a follow-up presentation

Summary Presentation

This report covers the most striking findings at the conference. Many more topics were discussed that would be valuable to most people at Quest Specialty Travel. I would be happy to develop a presentation summarizing the conference and give the presentation at a staff meeting or luncheon. If this is acceptable to you, let me know when I can schedule the meeting.

Used with permission from Microsoft Corporation

Objective
23
Part 3

Writing Proposals

Although proposals are similar to business reports and contain many of the same elements, they have a different purpose. In addition to informing your readers and answering their questions, the goal of a proposal is to persuade readers to adopt your product, service, or idea. Most proposals are written for people outside of the organization to offer goods and services for sale. Nonprofit agencies use proposals to solicit funding and support for their organizations. However, you can also write a proposal to people within your organization. If you have a new idea that you want to present to management, a proposal is often the appropriate format. Table 3-5 lists the do's and don'ts for writing proposals. case Stimulated by the travel conference you attended, you want to establish a monthly meeting and invite speakers from the travel and tourism industries to make presentations. Keisha suggests you create a proposal that describes the monthly meeting and includes a budget for the speakers.

ESSENTIAL ELEMENTS

1. **Write solicited proposals**

   You write a solicited proposal when someone asks you for one, often using a **request for proposal (RFP)**, which specifies the proposal's requirements. Customers use RFPs when they want to purchase a product or service that is too complex or unique to order through traditional channels. The RFP describes what they want in detail.

2. **Write unsolicited proposals**

   You write an unsolicited proposal when you are offering products or services to someone who has not requested them. In this case, you need to be particularly convincing because your readers are not anticipating your offer. Quickly explain what you are proposing and why it is of value to them so they continue reading beyond the first page.

3. **Write product proposals**

   Proposals that suggest your readers buy a product or service are called **product proposals** or commodity proposals. They present information about goods and quote a price for their purchase. Product proposals focus on what you will deliver, offer supporting information about the goods, discuss how the reader would benefit from the items, and estimate the cost.

4. **Write solution proposals**

   Solution proposals (sometimes called service proposals) suggest ideas, services, or complex solutions. They begin by describing a problem and defining how you propose to solve it. Follow this with a detailed plan for accomplishing the solution and the schedule you will follow.

5. **Focus on key elements**

   The goal of a proposal is to persuade your reader. Without the element of persuasion, you are writing an informational report. To be persuasive, proposals should include solutions, benefits, and credibility. See Figure 3-9.

6. **Ask for the sale**

   Your reader might be motivated by your presentation, but not know how to pursue your offer. Conclude your proposal with a call to action that tells the reader what they need to do to accept your proposal and move ahead with the process.

QUICK TIP
Product proposals often include an acceptance page or a contract for the reader to sign.

YOU TRY IT

Practice writing proposals by editing a proposal. Open the WC3-Y23.docx document and follow the steps in the worksheet. When you are finished, submit the document to your instructor as requested.

FIGURE 3-9: Key elements of proposals

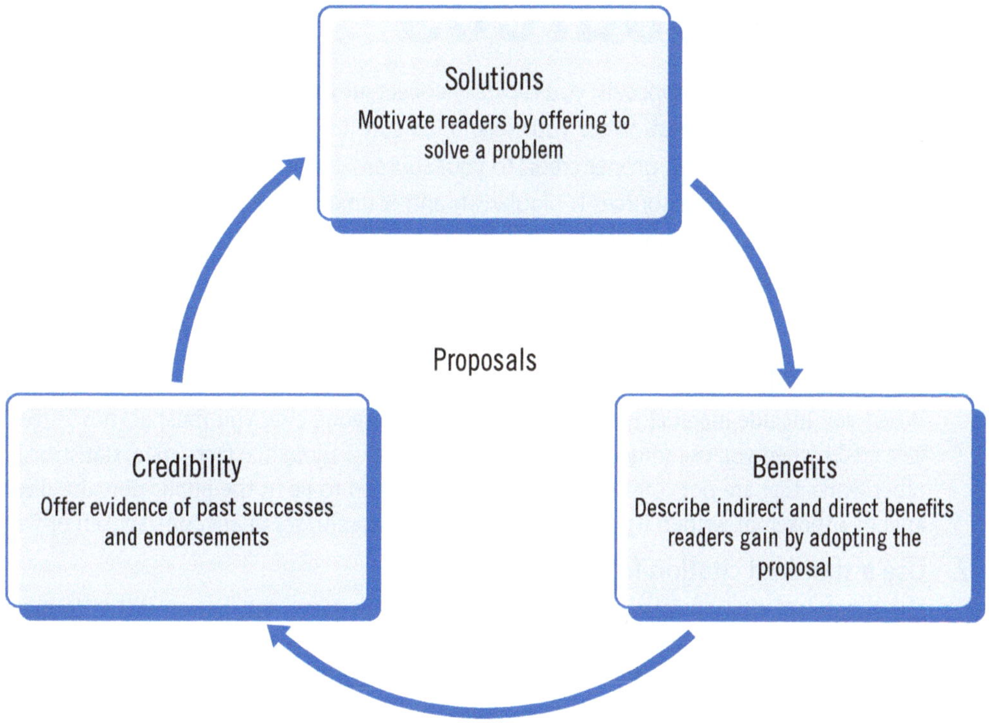

TABLE 3-5: Proposal do's and don'ts

element	do	don't
Solicited proposal	• Write when someone asks you for a proposal, often with an RFP • Use a formal format similar to formal reports, including a title page, executive summary, and table of contents	• **Don't** propose solutions you can't deliver • **Don't** overlook the requirements in the RFP
Unsolicited proposal	• Write when you can offer a product or service your audience might not know about • Use an informal format similar to short business reports • Include an introduction, background information, proposed product or solution, staff requirements, budget, and schedule	• **Don't** create a proposal as a way to make a sales contact—make sure you have a valuable solution • **Don't** rush the budget or estimate—this often becomes the basis for a contract
Product proposal	• Suggest your readers buy a product or service • Include what you will deliver, offer supporting details about the goods, discuss how the reader benefits, and estimate the cost	• **Don't** provide so much detail that the service or idea is no longer needed • **Don't** estimate a budget without including a deadline for acceptance
Solution proposal	• Suggest ideas, services, or complex solutions to a problem • Describe the benefits of adopting your proposal • Provide evidence of your credibility	• **Don't** offer vague solutions; use concrete examples • **Don't** forget to mention indirect and direct benefits

Objective
24
Part 3

Citing Sources

When writing reports and proposals, you typically collect information from various sources, and then organize and evaluate the information for your reader. Be sure to indicate when you have used materials that someone else created. Giving proper credit to your sources of information is both professional and ethical. Failing to properly cite your sources is plagiarism and is unacceptable in academic and professional environments. case You are finishing your proposal to Keisha Lane about hosting monthly speakers at Quest Specialty Travel. Your last step is to cite all your sources.

ESSENTIAL ELEMENTS

QUICK TIP
Ideas that are common knowledge do not need to be cited.

1. Recognize what to cite

When you include material that was developed by someone else, you must acknowledge it. In particular, give credit when you use someone else's ideas, theories, or thoughts; facts, data, statistics, illustrations, and other works that are not common knowledge or assumed to be in the public domain; direct quotations of anyone's spoken or written words; and summaries or paraphrases of anyone's spoken or written words.

QUICK TIP
You can find guides for these and other popular citation formats on the Internet.

2. Use a standard citation format

Use a standard citation format, such as the Modern Language Association (MLA) format, which is commonly used in the liberal arts and humanities fields, but is also popular in business. The American Psychological Association (APA) format is the most popular format in the social sciences. The Chicago style is based on the *Chicago Manual of Style* published by the University of Chicago Press.

QUICK TIP
The titles "Bibliography," "Works Cited," and "Reference List" are used by different citation formats.

3. Use in-text citations

Immediately follow any quotation or paraphrasing of a source's ideas with a parenthetical citation. At the end of the sentence, insert an open parenthesis, the last name of the author, either the page number (MLA) or the year of publication (APA), and a closed parenthesis, as in "We have nothing to fear, but fear itself (Roosevelt, 1933)." Word processors can help you manage citations and source material.

4. Paraphrase or use quotations

Paraphrasing means to use your own words to state or explain someone else's ideas. Plagiarism is writing or using someone else's ideas or words without acknowledging the source. If you copy text from a Web page, for example, and then replace a few words with synonyms, that is still considered plagiarism. Paraphrasing uses a different grammatical structure than the original text and often presents ideas from a different point of view. Figure 3-10 compares the plagiarized version of text with an acceptable paraphrase.

YOU TRY IT

Practice working with source material by paraphrasing text. Open the WC3-Y24.docx document and follow the steps in the worksheet. When you are finished, submit the document to your instructor as requested.

FIGURE 3-10: Text that needs citation

Belize is a popular destination for North American travelers.

→ Common knowledge; does not need citation

Belize attracts more than 850,000 annual visitors. Tourism is the country's top source of employment and investment. The irony is that it is also the country's biggest environmental threat.

→ Not a common fact; needs citation

With one foot planted in the Central American jungles and the other dipped in the Caribbean Sea, Belize blends the best of both worlds. Offshore, kayakers glide from one sandy, palm-dotted islet to another, while snorkelers swim through translucent seas, gazing at a kaleidoscope of coral, fish, dolphins and turtles. Inland, explorers investigate ruins of ancient civilizations, and birders aim their binoculars at some 570 species.
(http://www.lonelyplanet.com/belize)

→ Original text

With the Central American jungles on one side and the Caribbean Sea on the other, Belize is a mix of both worlds. On the water, people in kayaks paddle smoothly among small, sandy islands. Swimmers and snorkelers in the translucent seas gaze at a carousel of coral, fish, and other sea life. On the land, travelers explore the grounds of ancient civilizations or look to the skies to catch some of the 570 species of birds.

→ Though slightly different, still plagiarized

Belize is a paradise for the adventure traveler. For those who want to revel in the natural world, Belize offers pristine Caribbean beaches for water sports such as swimming, snorkeling, and kayaking. For others who want to explore on shore, Belize is renowned for its hundreds of species of resident and migratory birds and for its Mayan temples.

→ Paraphrase

Writing in your own words

Plagiarism, writing that has been copied from someone else and presented as your own work, is considered a serious violation in the academic world. Due to well-publicized incidents of plagiarism at the *New York Times* and the *Washington Post*, and because digital writing makes it easy to copy text, businesses are also looking for plagiarism and punishing those who plagiarize, usually by firing the violator. The most effective way to avoid plagiarism is to write mostly in your own words. When you need to refer to other sources, be sure to cite the source and make it clear what you are quoting from that source. To cite a source, you can use footnotes or insert the name of the source between parentheses. Quotations should contain the exact words of the original text or use ellipses for text you don't include. Paraphrasing causes the most confusion because you are summarizing text while maintaining the original ideas or facts, even if you change some of the words or the word order. Start paraphrased text with lead-ins such as "According to" so it is clear the idea originated with someone else. A common rule of thumb is that if you are paraphrasing more than three lines of text, change it to a quotation and cite it properly.

Technology @ Work: Online Collaboration Tools

Online collaboration tools are Web-based software designed to help groups work together to achieve their goals, such as completing a project, designing a new product, or writing a long report or proposal. Google Docs is a free Web-based collaboration tool that includes word processing, spreadsheet, presentation, and form applications. The main page is shown in Figure 3-11. With Google Docs, one central version of a document is stored online, which means you can access the document from any Internet-connected computer and know you are working with the latest version of that document. case Keisha Lane asks you to prepare for creating a report with the Quest tour developers. She suggests you investigate Google Docs as a tool to use for online collaboration.

ESSENTIAL ELEMENTS

1. **Create and edit documents**
   Google Docs includes typical business applications, including word processing, spreadsheet, and presentation software. You can create new documents from scratch or from a template, post existing files, and edit them using familiar tools.

2. **Share and collaborate online**
   You designate who can access your documents by entering their e-mail addresses at the Google Docs Web site, and then sending them an invitation. People you've invited can either edit or view your files. More than one person can view and make changes at the same time. Document revisions show who changed what so you can track changes. In addition, Google Docs saves all versions of documents, so you can revert to an earlier version if necessary.

> **QUICK TIP**
> If you publish a Google document, it becomes public and anyone can access it.

3. **Manage your work**
   Compared to desktop tools, the main advantage of online collaboration tools is that you can access your documents from any device with an Internet connection—including laptop computer and cell phone. You can organize them using folders the same way you do on your desktop computer. Because the documents are stored on servers with excellent security and data protection, you don't have to back up frequently or worry about virus infections.

> **QUICK TIP**
> You can store up to 5,000 Google documents of up to 500 KB each and 1,000 spreadsheets of up to 1 MB each.

4. **Use basic office application features**
   Although the Google Docs applications do not have as many features as their more robust counterparts, such as Microsoft Office and Open Office, they meet basic business needs—the 20 percent of the tools you use 80 percent of the time.

5. **Access Google Docs through a Google account**
   To access Google Docs, you create a Google account. Start your browser and go to *http:/docs.google.com*. Create an account to use Google Docs. See Figure 3-12. If you signed up for Gmail, you already have a Google account. You become the owner of any files you create or import to your Google account. You invite others to be collaborators or viewers.

YOU TRY IT

Practice using online collaboration tools by creating and sharing a document on Google Docs. Open the WC3-TechWork.docx document and follow the steps in the worksheet. When you are finished, submit the document to your instructor as requested.

FIGURE 3-11: **Google Docs main page**

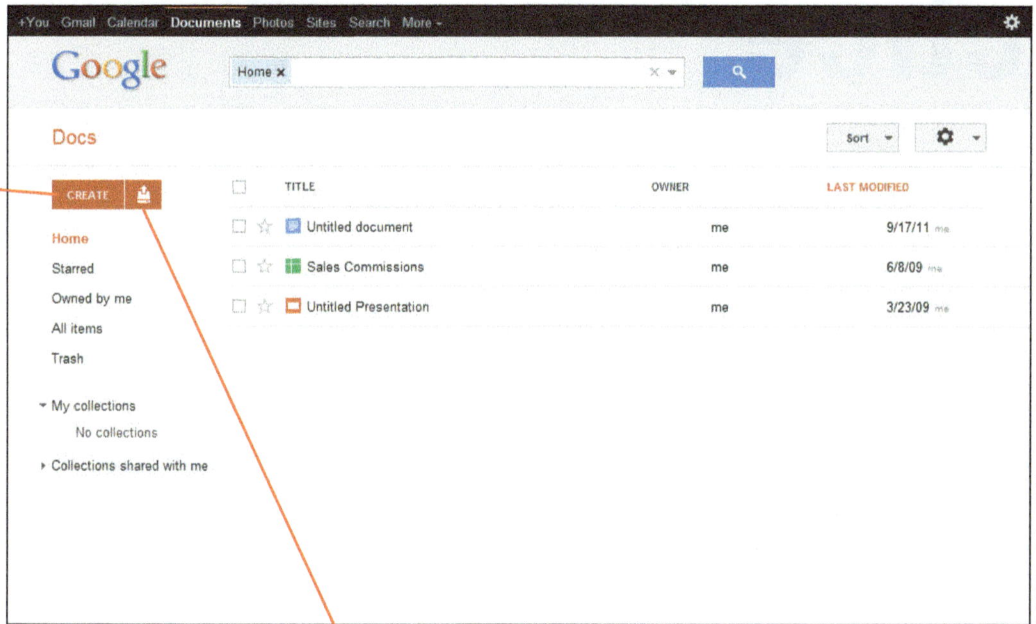

FIGURE 3-12: **Creating a Google account**

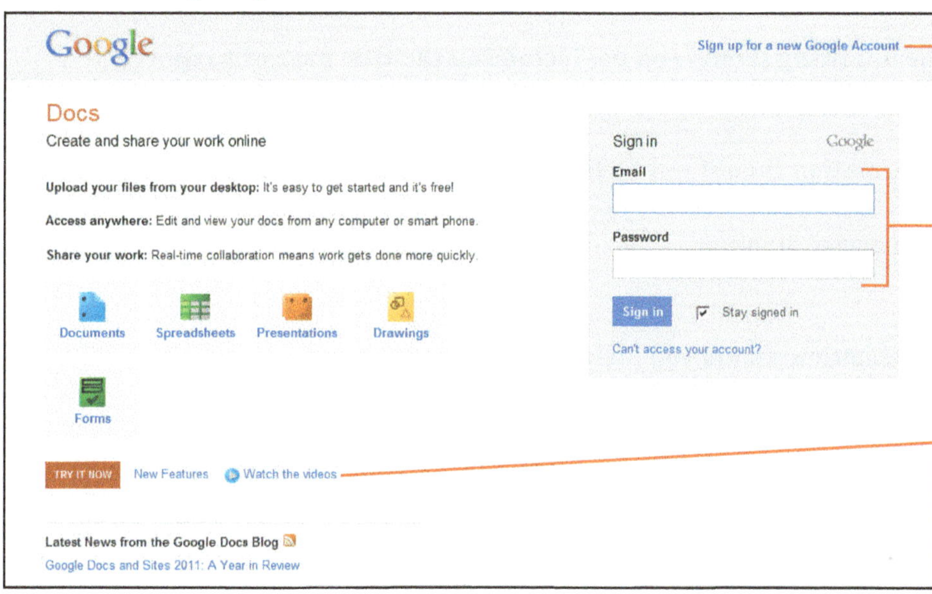

Practice

Soft Skills Review

Understand reports and proposals.

1. **What kind of long document presents information in a clear, objective format?**
   - **a.** Electronic notes
   - **b.** Analytical report
   - **c.** Informational report
   - **d.** Interview
2. **What type of long document often provides different options, identifies pros and cons for alternatives, and includes specific recommendations?**
   - **a.** Analytical report
   - **b.** Informational report
   - **c.** Informational proposal
   - **d.** Citation

Plan a report or proposal.

1. **Which one of the following is *not* a logical way to order information?**
   - **a.** Time
   - **b.** Random
   - **c.** Importance
   - **d.** Category
2. **Which one of the following is a heading for a standard section in a report or proposal?**
   - **a.** Recommendations
   - **b.** Anticipations
   - **c.** Work Plan
   - **d.** Graphics

Write the beginning.

1. **Which one of the following should you *not* include on the title page of a report?**
   - **a.** Report title
   - **b.** Subtitle
   - **c.** Reader's name and title
   - **d.** Table of contents
2. **What kind of information should you include in a report introduction?**
   - **a.** Figure references
   - **b.** Complete paraphrasing of the report
   - **c.** Purpose of the report
   - **d.** Identification of author

Write the body.

1. **What kind of information should you include in the report body?**
   - **a.** Facts and findings
   - **b.** Letter of transmittal
   - **c.** Reference list
   - **d.** Appendix
2. **If the purpose of the report is to solve a problem, the body should offer:**
   - **a.** contact information about the author
   - **b.** name, date, and other source information
   - **c.** specific, practical recommendations
   - **d.** secondary sources

Create the end matter.

1. **What is end matter?**
   - **a.** Table of contents
   - **b.** The last blank page in the report
   - **c.** Reference material that supports the main document
   - **d.** A chart type
2. **Supplemental material of secondary interest to some readers belongs in a(n):**
   - **a.** table of figures
   - **b.** appendix
   - **c.** reference list
   - **d.** approval page

Write short reports.

1. **Which one of the following is a type of short report?**
   a. Trip report
   b. Reference report
   c. Proposal report
   d. Flowchart report
2. **The five-paragraph format for a short report includes an introduction, three paragraphs that support the topic, and:**
   a. at least one figure
   b. a paragraph of responses
   c. a concluding paragraph
   d. partial findings paragraph

Write proposals.

1. **The purpose of a proposal is to:**
   a. specify in detail what a company wants
   b. avoid plagiarism
   c. make a sales contact
   d. persuade readers to adopt your product, service, or idea
2. **When would you write a solution proposal?**
   a. To report on a conference
   b. To provide suggestions for solving a problem
   c. To avoid persuading the reader
   d. To describe an ongoing project

Cite sources.

1. **For which of the following types of material do you *not* need to cite sources?**
   a. Common knowledge
   b. Someone else's theories
   c. Little known statistics
   d. Quotations of someone's spoken words
2. **Which of the following types of citations are *not* allowed in business reports?**
   a. In-text citations
   b. Footnotes
   c. List of references
   d. Uncredited quotations

Technology @ work: Online collaboration tools.

1. **Businesses can use online collaboration tools to:**
   a. find primary sources
   b. help a group work together to write a report
   c. separate plagiarism from paraphrasing
   d. accept an RFP
2. **What is one advantage of using online collaboration tools instead of standard desktop software?**
   a. They provide tools for organizing citations.
   b. They can print long reports.
   c. You can access your documents from any device with an Internet connection.
   d. They have sophisticated formatting features.

Critical Thinking Questions

1. **Proposals are different from reports because they persuade readers to take action. Do you think that makes proposals basically unethical?**
2. **Suppose you are using online collaboration tools to develop an analytical report for your company and you are gathering research that documents negative impressions about your best-selling product. Should your employer have the right to monitor your group's work? What if the research catalogs positive impressions of the product?**
3. **You are part of a group brainstorming to solve a problem for your company. During the brainstorming sessions, the group leader lists ideas on a white board for discussion. Later, one of the group members approaches your employer with a report listing these solutions, letting the employer think they are all her ideas. What should you do?**

Critical Thinking Questions (continued)

4. **Your team has written a proposal for a client that will generate millions of dollars in revenue for your company. After the client accepts the proposal, you discover that a colleague plagiarized some of the material in the proposal. Should you keep quiet or speak out?**
5. **Your employer asks you to respond to a request for proposal by including a very high budget because your company does not actually want to perform the specified work. Is it ethical to write and send the proposal?**

Independent Challenge 1

You work in the Marketing Department of a small Web design company named Overland Designs. Recently, a few of Overland Designs clients have asked whether you provide video services so they can include product and service videos on their Web sites. Marshall Aronson, the director of marketing, asks you and three other employees to create a report on Web video. You meet with the others to generate ideas and assign tasks. Your task is to create an outline for the report based on the notes shown in Figure 3-13.

FIGURE 3-13

Purpose:

Background
- Client requests
- Current capability

Reference List

Services

Video Development: Potential
- Production planning
- Photo and graphic development

Video Production: Potential
- Professional digital video production
- State-of-the-art formats

Video Post-Production (Editing): Potential
- Digital editing
- Video to state-of-the-art formats Web formats

Video Development: Current
- Creative services
- Script development

Video Production: Current
- Videotaping production
- Studio production
- Stock photos and stock video production

Video Post-Production (Editing): Current
- Video to CD and the Web
- Computer/digital video conversions
- Audio production

Introduction
- Current video services
- Other Web video services

Summary

Used with permission from Microsoft Corporation

a. Open the **WC3-IC1.docx** document and follow the steps in the worksheet.
b. Proofread the document carefully to fix any grammar or formatting errors.
c. Submit the document to your instructor as requested.

Independent Challenge 2

You work in the flagship Four Winds Apparel store in Minneapolis, Minnesota. After a year of disappointing sales, Four Winds has decided to close two stores in the area, and morale is low at your store. However, you have an idea for improving morale by boosting group exercise among employees. You decide to prepare a proposal to Allison Crandall, your manager. See Figure 3-14.

a. Open the **WC3-IC2.docx** document and follow the steps in the worksheet.
b. Proofread the document carefully to fix any grammar or formatting errors.
c. Submit the document to your instructor as requested.

FIGURE 3-14

Healthy staff means a healthy business.

Common knowledge: healthy body = a healthy mind.

But a fit staff can also improve the bottom line.

Studies (see International Fitness Club Network) conclude that the results of employee health and wellness programs show a 100% to 300% return on investment after five years. The return comes primarily in fewer lost days, reduced health insurance premiums, and reduced employee turnover.

The goals of an employee fitness program are to keeping morale high, maintain employee health, lower costs of medical insurance and personal medical expenditures, lower levels of stress, and improve employee health and fitness.

The program can begin with an initial health assessment completed by a medical professional or a fitness professional. Progress can be tracked on a form similar to the one shown in ???

Fitness Progress Chart

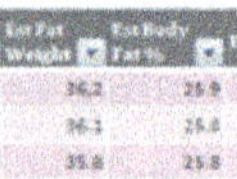

Height (feet)	5
Height (inches)	6.5

Date	Weight (pounds)	Chest (inches)	Waist (inches)	Hips (inches)	Wrist (inches)	Forearm (inches)	Est Lean Weight	Est Fat Weight	Est Body Fat %	Est BMI
1/1/2011	140.0	32.0	31.0	40.0	6.8	11.5	103.8	36.2	25.9	22.26
1/8/2011	140.0	32.0	31.0	39.5	6.7	11.5	103.9	36.1	25.8	22.26
1/15/2011	139.0	32.0	31.0	39.5	6.7	11.5	103.2	35.8	25.8	22.10
1/22/2011	139.0	32.0	28.0	39.0	6.2	11.0	103.4	35.6	25.5	22.10
1/29/2011	139.0	32.0	28.0	39.0	6.3	11.0	103.4	35.6	25.6	22.10

Used with permission from Microsoft Corporation

Real Life Independent Challenge

This Independent Challenge requires an Internet connection.

You are preparing to apply for job in your preferred field. Before you apply for a job with a company, learn as much as you can about that company, including its products or services, competition, corporate philosophy, and background. Create an informal report to your instructor with your findings, and explain why you want to pursue employment with this company or research other employment possibilities.

a. Using your favorite search engine, search for articles in business publications about the best companies to work for in America. You can also narrow your search to a particular city. Start with *Fortune* magazine, which conducts an annual survey of the 100 best companies to work for and publishes the results.

b. Select a company and then research company information on the Web. Be sure to review the following information about the company:
- Company Web site
- Basic facts about the company, such as location, number of employees, and products or services provided
- Articles about the company
- Type of employment opportunities
- Type of career paths

c. Write an informal informational report with the following sections:
- Introduction
- Body section presenting your findings
- Conclusion explaining whether you want to pursue employment with this company

d. Proofread the report carefully to fix any grammar or formatting errors.

e. Submit the report to your instructor as requested.

Team Challenge

This Team Challenge requires an Internet connection.

You work for Farley Worldwide, a company specializing in information services, and have been recently promoted. You now travel overseas with a small group and help your client companies install computers and software. You and your team have just returned from Thailand, where you attended a conference on high technology. You and your team need to prepare a conference report for Connie, describing your experience and what you learned at the conference.

a. Using your favorite search engine, search for information about a conference in Thailand that covered a topic in high technology such as wireless communications, networks, or future technology. Note the addresses of the Web sites that provide the most useful information.

b. Meet as a team to discuss your findings.

c. As a team, outline a five-paragraph conference report to Connie describing a conference.

d. Individually, write one paragraph of the report. Then assemble the paragraphs into a cohesive report as a group.

e. Submit the report to your instructor as requested.

Be the Critic

Review the poorly written report excerpt shown in Figure 3-15. Create an e-mail message that lists the weaknesses of the report and makes specific suggestions for improvement. Send the critique to your instructor.

FIGURE 3-15

Date: March 12, 2011

To: Ed Patterson

From: Allison Browne *AB*

Subject: Current State of Work from Home Program

Introduction

At your request, I prepared the following report on telecommuting.

Recommendations

- Allow employees who have worked for the company at least two years to work from home.
- Restrict telecommuting to two days per week.

Justifications

Telecommuting matches the company goal of flexible work options, such as flexible scheduling. Telecommuting seems to make employees more productive and efficient. This is especially true for salespeople. It also makes managing employees easier.

The purpose of this report is to evaluate the Work from Home program. By any criteria, it is quite successful.

Part 4

Writing for Employment

Files You Will Need:

WC4-Y26.docx
WC4-Y27.docx
WC4-Y28.docx
WC4-Y29.docx
WC4-Y30.docx
WC4-Y31.docx
WC4-Y32.docx
WC4-TechWork.docx
WC4-IC1.docx
WC4-IC2.docx
WC4-IC3.docx

Searching for employment opportunities effectively is one of the most important professional skills you can develop. Job hunting uses all of your communication skills, and most of the early steps involve written communication. Applicants that look good on paper by submitting professional documents on time are the finalists employers invite to interview. In this unit, you learn how to write effectively when presenting yourself as a job candidate—whether you are posting a message on a community site, writing an e-mail to inquire about a position, or writing a cover letter to accompany your résumé and application. case Kevin O'Brien is the manager of the New York office of Quest Specialty Travel and a friend of yours from college. He knows you are considering a move back to the East Coast, and mentions that Olympus Cruise Lines, one of Quest's travel partners, is hiring an assistant to the cruise sales manager in New York. Kevin doesn't know whether Olympus is advertising the job opening, but he suggests you contact Andrea Palis, the human resources director for Olympus Cruise Lines. Andrea can give you guidelines for applying to Olympus and general information about the company.

OBJECTIVES

25 Understand job searches
26 Write effective cover letters
27 Plan résumés
28 Write chronological résumés
29 Write functional résumés
30 Request letters of reference
31 Send follow-up messages
32 Accept or reject job offers

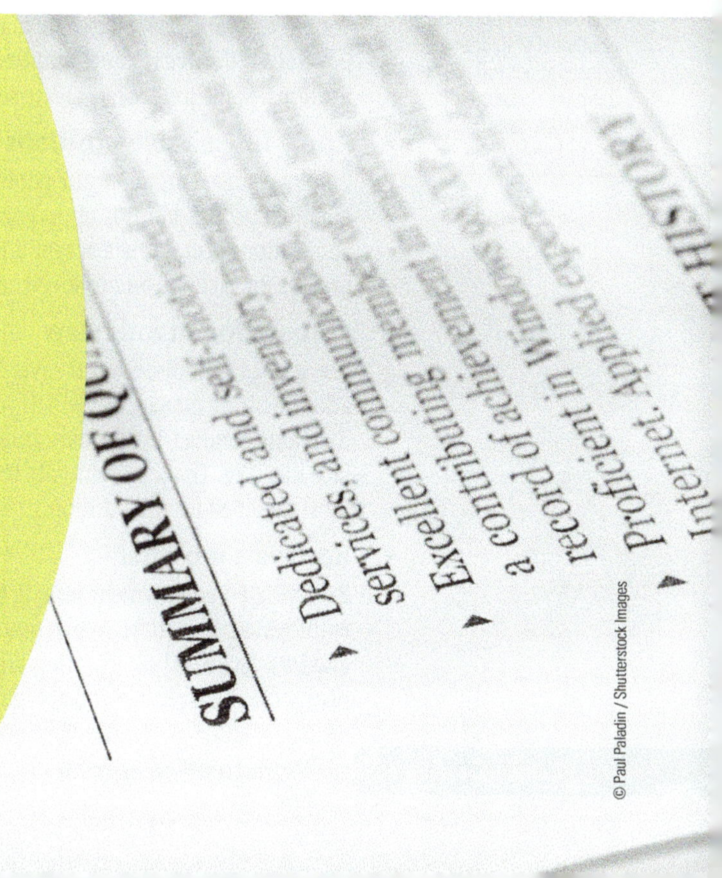

Objective 25
Part 4

Understanding Job Searches

The first step in finding appropriate employment is to evaluate your interests, goals, and qualifications and then identify corresponding jobs and employers. The job search continues until you reach the final step of accepting an offer. Because research suggests that the average person changes careers three to five times and has several jobs in each career, developing your job-search abilities provides you with a valuable life skill. The details of your search change for each job, but the general steps shown in Figure 4-1 remain the same. case Before getting in touch with Andrea Palis, you prepare for your job search by reviewing the following guidelines.

DETAILS

Most job searches involve the following steps:

- **Define your employment objective**
  Before you complete your first application, develop a clear idea of what you are seeking. Ask yourself questions such as the following: What are your professional skills, talents, and interests? What kind of position are you seeking now? How does that fit your long-term career goals? What are the characteristics of the job market in the fields of your interest? Where would you like to live? See Figure 4-2. Your answers will help you to develop your job-search strategy.

- **Identify potential employers**
  The number of job options you have depends on the number of employers you contact. To identify potential employers, take advantage of Web sites and print media that provide job information and post openings, but spend most of your time talking to people (friends, acquaintances, instructors, and family members, for example) about job opportunities. Communicating with a network of personal contacts—including those on social networking sites—is the most effective way to find job leads and yields valuable information about potential employers.

QUICK TIP
If you use a major online job board, keep in mind that you are competing with hundreds of others for an advertised position.

QUICK TIP
Visit the Web site of a potential employer to learn about the company's products or services, customers, and philosophy.

- **Develop a targeted résumé and cover letter**
  Your résumé and cover letter are marketing tools you can use to promote yourself as you apply for particular positions. Effective résumés and cover letters are customized for the job you want and highlight your qualifications. Some job seekers create several résumés and use them to apply for jobs in various industries.

- **Apply for suitable positions**
  Employers need an applicant pool from which they can fill a job opening. Most solicit applications from qualified people, but it is up to you to signal your interest. Some organizations require you to complete an application form. Others accept a résumé and letter of application. You should determine the application process for each job and follow it carefully.

- **Prepare for an interview**
  The goal of your résumé and cover letter are to arrange interviews. An **interview** is a meeting between you and the hiring manager in which you both discuss the job opportunity and your qualifications. Many organizations conduct preliminary interviews by telephone, but few make hiring decisions without a face-to-face meeting. The job often goes to the person who is best prepared for the interview—not always the one most qualified for the position.

- **Receive a job offer**
  Receiving an employment offer is the last step before achieving your ultimate goal—a job that meets your employment objectives. When you are offered a job, evaluate the offer to see if it corresponds to your needs and interests. The best job offers are a good fit for you and the employer. Carefully weigh the pros and cons of any offer you receive and accept only those that match your interests, talents, and goals.

FIGURE 4-1: Job search steps

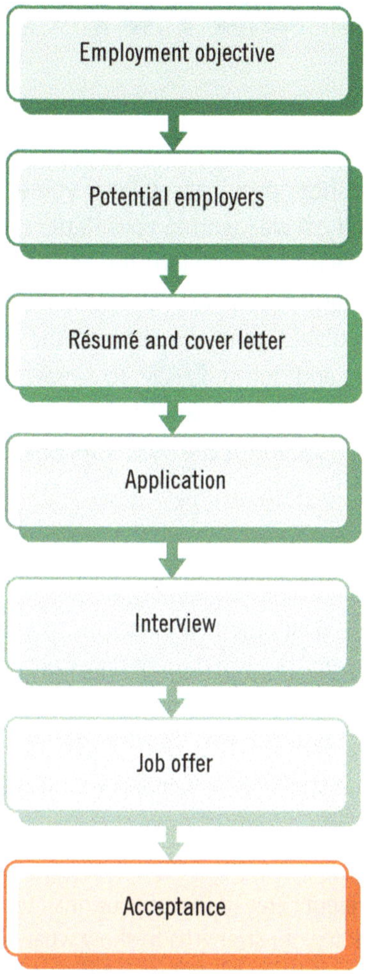

FIGURE 4-2: Defining your employment objective

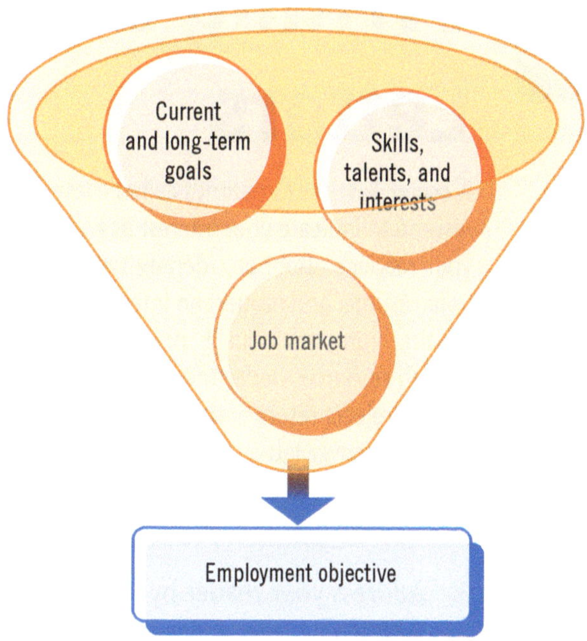

Written Communication

Searching for jobs on the Internet

Dozens of Web sites post job openings, but they are not a one-stop solution for job seekers. According to The Conference Board, a business research organization, over 4 million new job vacancies are posted online each month. However, job candidates report that listings are often outdated, misleading, or unproductive, generating few leads. Applicants have better results using online job listings at sites professional associations host and at corporate Web sites, which provide helpful information about potential employers. Instead of depending on large employment sites, successful job hunters are using them to find tips on the job market, salaries, and hiring trends, and turning to social networking sites such as LinkedIn and Facebook to make contacts. Be aware that employers also use social networking sites to screen applicants—often to eliminate candidates based on unprofessional videos, photos, or other information. In the end, the Internet provides tools that can help you meet potential employers face to face, which is where job offers are made.

Source: Tugend, Alina, "Shortcuts–Job Hunting Is, and Isn't, What It Used to Be," *New York Times*, September 26, 2008.

Objective 26 Part 4

Writing Effective Cover Letters

A **cover letter** (sometimes called a letter of application) is a short, personalized letter you send with your résumé to indicate your interest in an employment opportunity. A well-written cover letter should capture your reader's attention, identify which position you are applying for, highlight the key qualifications on your résumé, and request an interview. Send your cover letter and résumé to the person who is responsible for the hiring decision. If this contact information is not available, send the letter to the organization's human resources department. Table 4-1 lists cover letter do's and don'ts. case You know that Olympus usually rejects résumés that don't include a cover letter, so you start your application by writing the first draft of a cover letter to Andrea Palis about your interest in working for the New York office of Olympus Cruise Lines.

ESSENTIAL ELEMENTS

QUICK TIP
You can often find the name of the hiring manager by asking the organization's receptionist.

1. **Address your reader by name**

   To start your letter, address your reader by name. This grabs their attention and helps to personalize your application. Avoid generic salutations such as "Dear Sir/Madam" or "To Whom It May Concern".

2. **Identify the position**

   Your targeted organization might have several positions open when you apply. The first paragraph of your cover letter should identify which position you are seeking. If appropriate, mention who suggested that you apply or where you saw the job advertised.

QUICK TIP
You can send the cover letter via e-mail and include the résumé as an attachment.

3. **Highlight your most relevant skills**

   The second paragraph of your cover letter should briefly present three to five of your qualifications, accomplishments, or skills that relate to the open position. Promote your strengths to show what you can do for the employer, but don't go into detail. Your goal is to capture the reader's interest and motivate them to carefully read your résumé. As you describe your qualifications, suggest that your reader refer to your résumé for more information.

   Figure 4-3 shows the beginning of the cover letter to Andrea Palis, which is personalized and emphasizes reader benefits.

QUICK TIP
Be sure to include a telephone number where you can be reached.

4. **Conclude with a call to action**

   The immediate goal of your cover letter and résumé is to pass your application through the initial screening and secure an interview. Conclude your cover letter by directly requesting this meeting.

5. **Follow up with interesting prospects**

   Your initial application won't always reach the right person at the right time. Send your letter again if you don't receive a response within a couple of weeks. Following up shows the hiring manager that you take initiative and are enthusiastic about the job opportunity.

YOU TRY IT

Practice writing effective cover letters by revising a letter. Open the WC4-Y26.docx document and follow the steps in the worksheet. When you are finished, submit the document to your instructor as requested.

FIGURE 4-3: Beginning of revised cover letter

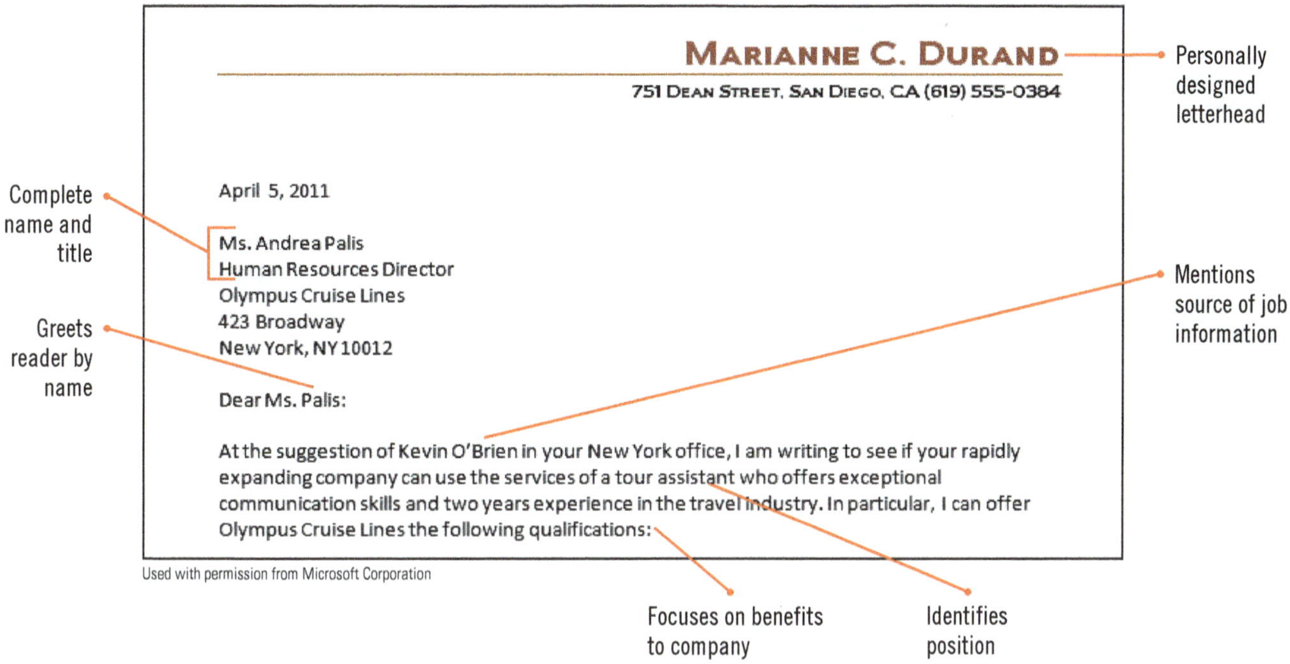
MARIANNE C. DURAND

751 DEAN STREET, SAN DIEGO, CA (619) 555-0384

April 5, 2011

Ms. Andrea Palis
Human Resources Director
Olympus Cruise Lines
423 Broadway
New York, NY 10012

Dear Ms. Palis:

At the suggestion of Kevin O'Brien in your New York office, I am writing to see if your rapidly expanding company can use the services of a tour assistant who offers exceptional communication skills and two years experience in the travel industry. In particular, I can offer Olympus Cruise Lines the following qualifications:

Used with permission from Microsoft Corporation

TABLE 4-1: Writing cover letters do's and don'ts

letter element	do	don't
Greeting (salutation)	• Address your reader by name	• **Don't** use a generic greeting, such as "Dear Hiring Manager"
Opening	• Identify the position you are applying for • Mention by name the person who suggested that you apply • Explain where you saw the job advertisement	• **Don't** refer to a position in general, as in "I am applying to fill the job vacancy at your company."
Qualifications	• Present three to five of your qualifications that directly relate to the position • Describe what you can do for the employer • Focus on how your strengths benefit the reader	• **Don't** list courses or previous job duties • **Don't** include skills or experiences you don't have • **Don't** describe your qualifications in detail or repeat résumé specifics
Conclusion	• Confidently request an interview • If you haven't referred the reader to your résumé, do so in this section • Provide your phone number	• **Don't** directly ask for the job • **Don't** sound insincere, demanding, or apprehensive • **Don't** provide elaborate contact instructions and the best times to call
Follow-up	• Resend the cover letter and résumé if you don't hear from a potential employer	• **Don't** ignore instructions or advice from the employer about following up

Objective 27
Part 4

Planning Résumés

A **résumé** is a one- or two-page summary of your education, employment history, skills, and accomplishments. Like a cover letter, you customize a résumé for each potential employer. A well-written résumé presents your background and promotes the qualities and achievements that are most likely to appeal to your targeted employer. Although résumés are short, structured documents, they demand careful planning, editing, and proofreading. Expect to create several versions of a résumé before it meets the goal of securing a job interview. Table 4-2 summarizes the do's and don'ts of creating a résumé. case After spending time on the Olympus Cruise Line Web site researching the company, you are ready to create a résumé emphasizing the qualifications and skills you have that match Olympus' corporate goals.

ESSENTIAL ELEMENTS

QUICK TIP
Don't list an unprofessional e-mail address on your résumé (such as *sugarpie1975@aol.com*); set up a separate account, if necessary.

1. **Main heading**
   Always start your résumé with your name, address, and other contact information, including a telephone number and e-mail address. Invest in voice mail, an answering machine, or a subscription answering service so that recruiters or employers can leave a message for you.

2. **Career objective or summary of qualifications**
   If you are responding to a posting or ad, you can include an "Objective" section after the main heading. The objective should be customized for the job opening to demonstrate how your career goals match the position requirements. A recent trend is to incorporate the objective into a summary of qualifications. To distinguish your résumé from the hundreds of others a hiring manager might receive, include a bulleted list of three to eight qualifications that demonstrate you are the ideal candidate for the position. Figure 4-4 shows a résumé with an objective section.

QUICK TIP
You can provide the GPA in only your major courses if your overall grades are weak.

3. **Education summary**
   If you have graduated recently, you can summarize your education next. List the names and locations of schools you have attended, your major or field of study, minors or secondary concentrations, and the dates of any degrees you have earned. Include your grade point average if you did well in your courses.

4. **Employment history**
   Your past work experience and professional accomplishments help to show hiring managers how you might fit into their organization. For each position you've had, list the organization name and location, job title or position, employment period (by year, as in 2008–2010, or by month, as in October 2008–March 2010), and a short description of your responsibilities and achievements.

QUICK TIP
Don't include activities or affiliations that might be controversial, such as memberships in political organizations.

5. **Skills, activities, and awards**
   List the special skills you can bring to a position, such as computer proficiency, languages spoken, and industry certifications. You can also list activities you performed, groups you joined, or awards you received, if you have several of these experiences.

YOU TRY IT

Practice planning résumés by creating and organizing one. Open the WC4-Y27.docx document and follow the steps in the worksheet. When you are finished, submit the document to your instructor as requested.

FIGURE 4-4: Résumé with an objective section

Marianne C. Durand

751 Dean Street, San Diego, CA 92107 (619) 555-0384 MDurand@msg.course.com

OBJECTIVE

Apply my organizational skills, training experience, program development, and customer service qualifications to a career in the travel industry

EDUCATION

2007 to 2011 • New Jersey State College • Paramus, NJ
Associate Degree in Communication and Public Relations

2006 to 2007 • Dover Business College • Dover, NJ
Courses in business administration and marketing

Used with permission from Microsoft Corporation

TABLE 4-2: Creating résumés do's and don'ts

résumé element	do	don't
Main heading	• Include your full name and complete address • Use a simple, professional format that highlights your name • Provide a personal e-mail address that looks and sounds professional • Check your messages and e-mail regularly while you are searching for a job	• **Don't** omit your contact information • **Don't** list out-of-date contact information • **Don't** include your work e-mail address • **Don't** use flashy or unconventional formatting • **Don't** indicate your age, marital status, or salary requirements
Objective or qualification summary	• Include a career objective if you have made a commitment to a career • List your most important qualifications instead of an objective	• **Don't** include an objective if it doesn't match the job description • **Don't** minimize your talents in an objective by identifying your goal as an entry-level position
Education summary	• Refer to specific courses if they relate to the position • Find a balance between too much and too little information • Include your grade point average if it is 3.0 or higher	• **Don't** list high school information if you have attended college • **Don't** list all the courses you took
Employment history	• Use short, concrete descriptions • Format your history in a bulleted list • Quantify your achievements	• **Don't** list every job duty or activity • **Don't** use passive verbs or emphasize personal pronouns (such as I, me, and my)
Skills, activities, and awards	• Focus on skills that show you are qualified for the position • Provide details that verify your claims • Use action verbs to describe skills and activities	• **Don't** list awards if they are minor or few (less than three) • **Don't** assume readers know the significance of an award or honor; provide a brief explanation

Objective
28
Part 4

Writing Chronological Résumés

The two most popular ways to organize your résumé are the chronological and functional formats. A **chronological résumé**, sometimes called a reverse-chronological résumé, presents your work experience and education sorted by date. Entries start with the most recent position held (or school attended) and work backwards. Include more detail for your most recent entries and less for those further in the past. The chronological style is the most popular with recruiters and hiring managers because it shows a clear time line of your employment. If you have a relatively steady work history and several relevant positions, the chronological format is usually your best choice. Table 4-3 summarizes the do's and don'ts of writing a chronological résumé. case Before sending your résumé and cover letter to Andrea Palis, you decide to create a revised version that uses a more detailed chronological format.

ESSENTIAL ELEMENTS

QUICK TIP
Instead of writing long job descriptions, emphasize the highlights to catch your reader's attention and hold their interest.

1. **Decide whether to list education or experience first**
   If you are a current student or a recent graduate with a limited employment history, list your education first. If you have held three or more positions related to your current job prospect, your work history is more interesting to your readers. As your portfolio of work experience grows, you should reduce the education section to a simple list of schools attended and degrees earned.
2. **Format your résumé for readability**
   Typically, recruiters and managers quickly scan a résumé for important highlights, and skip résumés that are hard to read. Summarize your experience and education entries in a line or two, and use bullets to present your responsibilities and achievements. (See Figure 4-5.) Use headings, lines, **white space** (areas without text or graphics), color, and bold and italic fonts to break up the page and call attention to your sections in a clear, uncluttered format.
3. **Use left-aligned headings**
   Organize the page using left-aligned headings (instead of centered). This reduces your line length, making the text easier to read. The uniform white space in the left margin draws your reader's eyes down the page, pausing at the headings, which signal the beginning of a new section.

QUICK TIP
Limit your use of personal pronouns (I, me, my) in your résumé and focus on the reader.

4. **Write powerfully**
   Carefully edit your résumé to make every sentence brief, accurate, and positive. Start your sentences with active verbs—*clarified*, *improved*, and *resolved* instead of *did*, *was*, and *had*. Use present-tense verbs for your current job and past tense for previous positions.
5. **Limit the length**
   If your employment history includes less than three positions, limit your résumé to a single page. Recruiters claim they prefer this short format because it allows them to quickly scan many résumés. However, as your work history grows, your résumé can expand to two pages.

YOU TRY IT

Practice writing chronological résumés by completing a partial résumé. Open the WC4-Y28.docx document and follow the steps in the worksheet. When you are finished, submit the document to your instructor as requested.

FIGURE 4-5: Chronological résumé

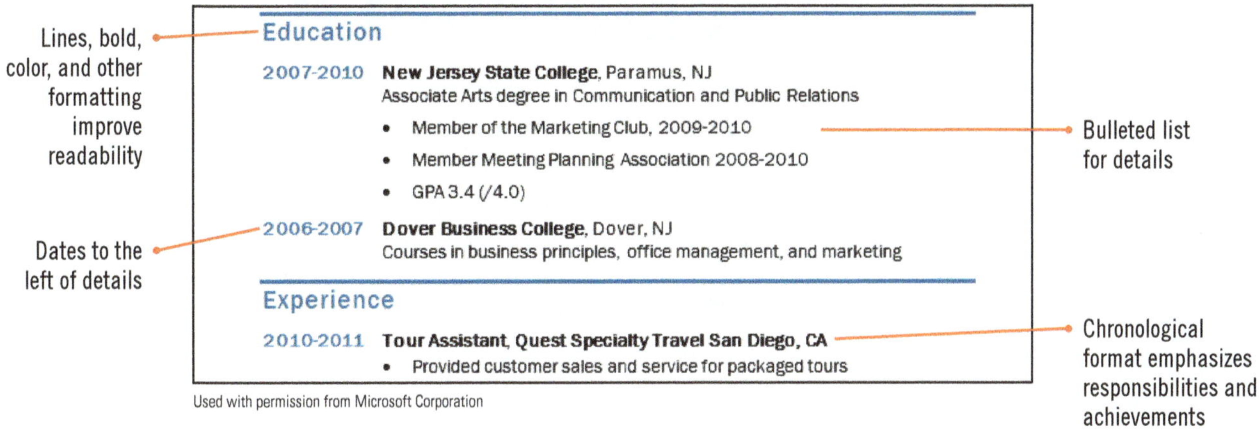

Used with permission from Microsoft Corporation

TABLE 4-3: Writing chronological résumés do's and don'ts

résumé element	do	don't
Employment or education history	• List education first if you are a recent graduate • List employment first if your work experience is significant	• **Don't** include all your experience if it is extensive
Format	• Follow an outline format with bulleted lists for details • Strive for order, clarity, and accessibility	• **Don't** provide long paragraphs of text • **Don't** use a standard, unmodified template that will be overly familiar to recruiters
Headings	• Start each section with a heading • Use standard text, such as *Summary of Qualifications*, Experience, and Education	• **Don't** use humorous or atypical headings • **Don't** overlook headings when proofreading
Writing	• Use concise, concrete language • Check for spelling and grammar mistakes • Start descriptions with action verbs	• **Don't** include vague or wordy descriptions • **Don't** include even one typo or mistake • **Don't** use passive verbs
Length	• Use one page if your experience is limited • Expand to two pages if your experience is extensive, more if you are applying for an executive position	• **Don't** make the résumé too long or too brief • **Don't** reduce the margins to fit the content on one or two pages

Avoiding ethical pitfalls

Do you think it's ethically acceptable to list a degree on your résumé that you haven't earned? What about stretching employment dates, inflating a salary, or embellishing a job title? A recent survey on CareerBuilder.com found that only 8 percent of workers admitted to padding their résumés, yet 49 percent of hiring managers reported they caught a lie on a résumé. Of these employers, 57 percent said they rejected the applicant. "Even the slightest embellishment can come back to haunt you and ruin your credibility," said Rosemary Haefner, vice president of human resources at CareerBuilder.com. Consider the high-profile cases of David J. Edmondson, former chief executive officer of Radio Shack, and Kenneth Lonchar, former chief financial officer of Veritas Software. On their résumés, they both claimed degrees they did not earn and subsequently lost their jobs, despite their executive positions. While you should certainly write your résumé to portray yourself in the best possible light, use facts and tell the truth.

Source: Staff, "Nearly Half of Employers Have Caught a Lie on a Résumé, CareerBuilder.com Survey Shows," CareerBuilder.com Web site, *www.careerbuilder.com*, July 30, 2008.

Objective 29

Part 4

Writing Functional Résumés

A **functional résumé**, also called a skills résumé, highlights your skills and abilities instead of your work history. The functional format breaks the résumé into several categories and showcases the talents, responsibilities, and accomplishments you can demonstrate through college classes, volunteer work, employment, hobbies, or other means. The functional résumé is appropriate for students with limited work experience, career changers, or people with irregular work histories. Functional résumés are also popular in certain industries, such as the arts, graphic design, and Web development. Table 4-4 compares chronological and functional résumés. case Besides creating a revised chronological résumé, you decide to develop a functional résumé to highlight your skills. You'll send the best résumé to Andrea Palis.

ESSENTIAL ELEMENTS

QUICK TIP
Search the Internet for "functional résumé" to see other examples of categories.

1. **Use three to five categories**

   Identify several categories to describe your experience or abilities and create a heading for each. Choose the categories that best reflect your skills, such as *Customer Service Skills* and *Technology Skills*. Develop a bulleted list of examples for each category. Ask someone you trust to read your résumé thoroughly and share their impression of what it communicates about you.

2. **List categories by importance**

   Sort your functional categories in order of their importance to a prospective employer. Also organize the bulleted entries within each category to present your most relevant skills and abilities first. To customize the résumé, change the order of the categories to suit each job.

3. **Start each entry with an action verb**

   The entries in each of your bulleted lists should be short, active, and memorable. Starting each of these entries with an action verb makes them more interesting and easier to read. Search the Internet for "résumé action verbs" to find examples that you can use.

QUICK TIP
In an employment synopsis, list only the years that you worked with each organization.

4. **Provide a synopsis of your work experience**

   Even if you are trying to sell yourself on the basis of your skills and abilities, recruiters and hiring managers still want to know where you've worked. Omitting references to your job history is not recommended. Instead, summarize your work history in a brief list at the end of the résumé. Indicate the employer, time period, and position held for each job. See Figure 4-6.

YOU TRY IT

Practice writing functional résumés by creating one from a rough draft. Open the WC4-Y29.docx document and follow the steps in the worksheet. When you are finished, submit the document to your instructor as requested.

Including keywords in your résumé

Large to midsized companies sometimes use applicant-tracking software to scan résumés, searching for keywords to determine if you are qualified for the position. This is especially true for employers that accept résumés electronically. The *Occupational Outlook Handbook* (2008–2009) defines keywords as nouns or phrases related to the expertise required to perform a job. They include technical terms, industry buzzwords, job titles, and names of products and services. To make sure that tracking software does not reject your résumé, be sure to include keywords that reflect skills employers seek, such as *networking, customer service*, and *problem-solving ability*. Study the job description or advertisement, and add the same language or terms to your résumé. Do the same with other job ads in your field. If you are sure your résumé will be scanned, e-mail an electronic version of the résumé. Make sure the format uses a common font and plain text, which means no bold, italic, or underlining.

Source: Occupational Outlook Handbook, 2008–09 Edition, www.bls.gov/oco/oco20043.htm, accessed December 9, 2008.

FIGURE 4-6: Work synopsis in a functional résumé

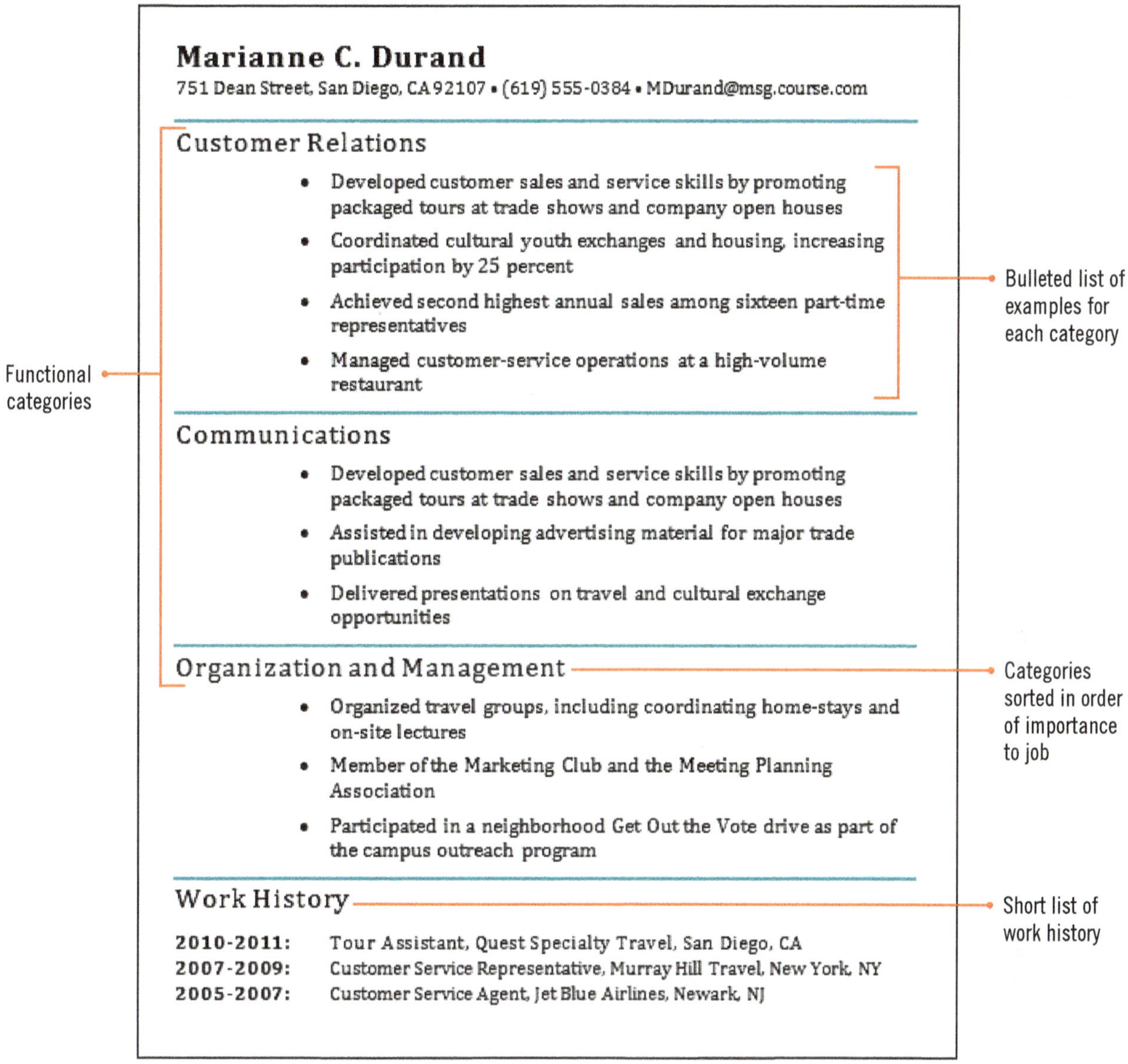
Marianne C. Durand
751 Dean Street, San Diego, CA 92107 • (619) 555-0384 • MDurand@msg.course.com

Customer Relations

- Developed customer sales and service skills by promoting packaged tours at trade shows and company open houses
- Coordinated cultural youth exchanges and housing, increasing participation by 25 percent
- Achieved second highest annual sales among sixteen part-time representatives
- Managed customer-service operations at a high-volume restaurant

Communications

- Developed customer sales and service skills by promoting packaged tours at trade shows and company open houses
- Assisted in developing advertising material for major trade publications
- Delivered presentations on travel and cultural exchange opportunities

Organization and Management

- Organized travel groups, including coordinating home-stays and on-site lectures
- Member of the Marketing Club and the Meeting Planning Association
- Participated in a neighborhood Get Out the Vote drive as part of the campus outreach program

Work History

2010-2011: Tour Assistant, Quest Specialty Travel, San Diego, CA
2007-2009: Customer Service Representative, Murray Hill Travel, New York, NY
2005-2007: Customer Service Agent, Jet Blue Airlines, Newark, NJ

Used with permission from Microsoft Corporation

Written Communication

TABLE 4-4: Choosing a chronological or functional style

scenario	chronological	functional
Your employment history includes many gaps.		•
You have changed jobs frequently.		•
Most of your experience has been in one field.	•	
Your work history follows a clear career path.	•	
You want to enter a new field of employment.		•
Your new field traditionally does not accept functional résumés.	•	
You are a college student with little experience in your chosen field.		•
You plan to submit your résumé to an online job board or recruiting firm.	•	

Objective 30
Part 4

Requesting Letters of Reference

Before offering a job, most employers expect you to provide the names of people who can discuss your qualifications. Prepare a list of references separate from your résumé, and then offer the list during the interview. Former employers, supervisors, and college professors are routinely listed as references. Always ask someone, ideally in person or by telephone, before you list that person as a job reference. Don't use friends, neighbors, or family members as references or anyone who seems doubtful or hesitant about your request. A weak or mixed message from a reference might eliminate you from further consideration. You can also ask recommenders to write a letter of reference that you can give to prospective employers. Be sure to provide information about yourself and the positions you are seeking so recommenders can write knowledgably about your qualifications. case After sending Andrea Palis your résumé, she suggests you meet for an interview at an upcoming trade show for the travel industry in New York. You need to prepare a list of references and review their letters of recommendation.

ESSENTIAL ELEMENTS

QUICK TIP
Ask for a letter of reference from a professor or employer while you are working with them.

1. **Establish your references early**
   Ask prospective recommenders to serve as references before you start to apply for jobs. If a potential employer requests your references, you should be able to immediately provide a list of names and contact information, similar to the list in Figure 4-7.

2. **Ask for a letter of reference**
   Besides asking someone to serve as a reference for you, request each recommender to write a general letter of reference. They can address the letter to "Whom It May Concern." Provide a self-addressed stamped envelope so your references can return their letters to you. Let recommenders know that you will send a copy of their letter to prospective employers.

QUICK TIP
Providing several letters of reference is more impressive than supplying a list of names and telephone numbers.

3. **Provide information for your recommenders**
   Help your recommenders by providing them with specific information about you and your job search, including a copy of your résumé, descriptions of the types of positions and locations you are targeting, and a letter outlining your qualifications and summarizing their relationship to you. See Figure 4-8. Recommenders often use some of this content in the letters they write.

4. **Communicate with your references**
   Keep in touch with your references, such as by e-mail, to let them know how your job search is progressing. Mention the names of the companies that have interviewed you so recommenders can prepare for possible phone calls and reference checks. If you accept a position, send each of your references a formal thank-you letter and tell them about your success.

YOU TRY IT

Practice requesting letters of reference by analyzing a job candidate's experience and then writing a request letter. Open the WC4-Y30.docx document and follow the steps in the worksheet. When you are finished, submit the document to your instructor as requested.

FIGURE 4-7: List of references

References for Marianne C. Durand

751 Dean Street, San Diego, CA 92107
Home: (619) 555-0384 • Cell: (619) 555-0075 • E-mail: MDurand@msg.course.com

Dr. John Peterson
Business and Communications Chair
Dover Business College
15 East Blackwell Street
Dover, NJ 07801
973-555-6700

Ms. Irene Guelden
Communications and Public Relations Advisor
New Jersey State College
515 Administration Hall
2960 State Parkway
Paramus, NJ 07652
201-555-1851

Ms. Valerie Slater
Owner
Murray Hill Travel Agency
6751 West Fifth Avenue
New York, NY 10012
212-555-1200

Heading and style should match résumé

References are all professional contacts

Format for each reference is identical

Used with permission from Microsoft Corporation

FIGURE 4-8: Letter requesting a recommendation

Marianne C. Durand

751 Dean Street, San Diego, CA 92107
Home: (619) 555-0384 • Cell: (619) 555-0075 • E-mail: MDurand@msg.course.com

April 20, 2011

Dr. John Peterson
Business and Communications Chair
Dover Business College
15 East Blackwell Street
Dover, NJ 07801

Dear Dr. Peterson,

I would appreciate your help with my job search. I graduate this spring and am beginning to look for a job. My goal is to secure an entry-level position in the travel industry.

With your permission, I would appreciate being able to use you as a reference who can discuss my qualifications, skills, and abilities. If you would be willing to provide a reference for me I would be most grateful if you could write a letter on my behalf. I will include the letter with my job applications as part of my portfolio.

I was a student in your Introduction to Business Management 103 class in the spring of 2007 and earned an A. My final project was a specialty Web site for

Ask permission

Solicit a letter of reference

Provide relevant background information

Used with permission from Microsoft Corporation

E-portfolios and video résumés

In fields such as advertising and acting, video portfolios of completed projects have long been the norm. Job candidates in other professional fields are also using electronic portfolios, or e-portfolios, to showcase their talents and accomplishments. Some e-portfolios are online presentations that include images or links to reference letters, awards, work samples, photographs, and videos. E-portfolios are usually posted online, where employers can view them when it is convenient. Your e-portfolio can be part of a video résumé, which is a suitable option if you want to work for a distant company or distinguish yourself from the pack of applicants. However, video résumés have been slow to catch on, primarily because they are more difficult and costly to produce than written résumés. They can be effective if they are short, professional, and designed to set up an interview when other more traditional techniques have failed.

Objective 31 Part 4

Sending Follow-Up Messages

Although your cover letter and résumé are your primary job-search tools, you can set yourself apart from other applicants by sending follow-up e-mail messages or letters during your search. This correspondence improves your visibility with the hiring manager, demonstrates your professionalism, and shows your interest in the position. Create basic templates of the different types of follow-up messages and letters, and then adapt them to each job application. As with other professional documents, carefully edit and proofread all job-related correspondence before you send it. case Your interview in New York with Andrea Palis was productive, and you are excited about the possibility of working for Olympus Cruise Lines. Now that you are back in San Diego, you want to follow up with Andrea and thank her for the interview.

ESSENTIAL ELEMENTS

QUICK TIP
A thank-you letter is more memorable than a thank-you e-mail message.

1. **Application follow-up**
   If your initial application does not generate a response after a couple of weeks, send a follow-up e-mail message with your résumé to the hiring manager. Express your continued interest in the position, describe your best talent or skill, and briefly explain how it relates to the job description. Close positively by requesting an interview. Figure 4-9 shows an example of an application follow-up message. Avoid using an accusing tone or expressing disappointment in the lack of a response.

QUICK TIP
If you do send a follow-up message by e-mail, be sure it is professional and free of shorthand slang and emoticons.

2. **Interview follow-up**
   Send a thank-you message or letter after every interview, the same day if possible. Send a note of thanks even if the interview didn't seem to go well. Express your appreciation for the opportunity to meet with the hiring manager and summarize the important points you discussed. Following up after the interview is another chance to demonstrate your interest in the position and explain why you are the most qualified applicant. Figure 4-10 shows an example of an interview follow-up e-mail message.

3. **Rejection follow-up**
   If you receive a rejection letter for a job that you are particularly interested in, don't assume that it is the final word. The company's first choice might not work out or another position at that company might become available. Take advantage of the contacts you've developed and send a follow-up message or letter to the hiring manager. Emphasize your interest in the company and ask them to reconsider you if this or a similar position becomes available.

YOU TRY IT

Practice sending follow-up messages by reading about an interview and then writing a follow-up message. Open the WC4-Y31.docx document and follow the steps in the worksheet. When you are finished, submit the document to your instructor as requested.

FIGURE 4-9: Application follow-up message

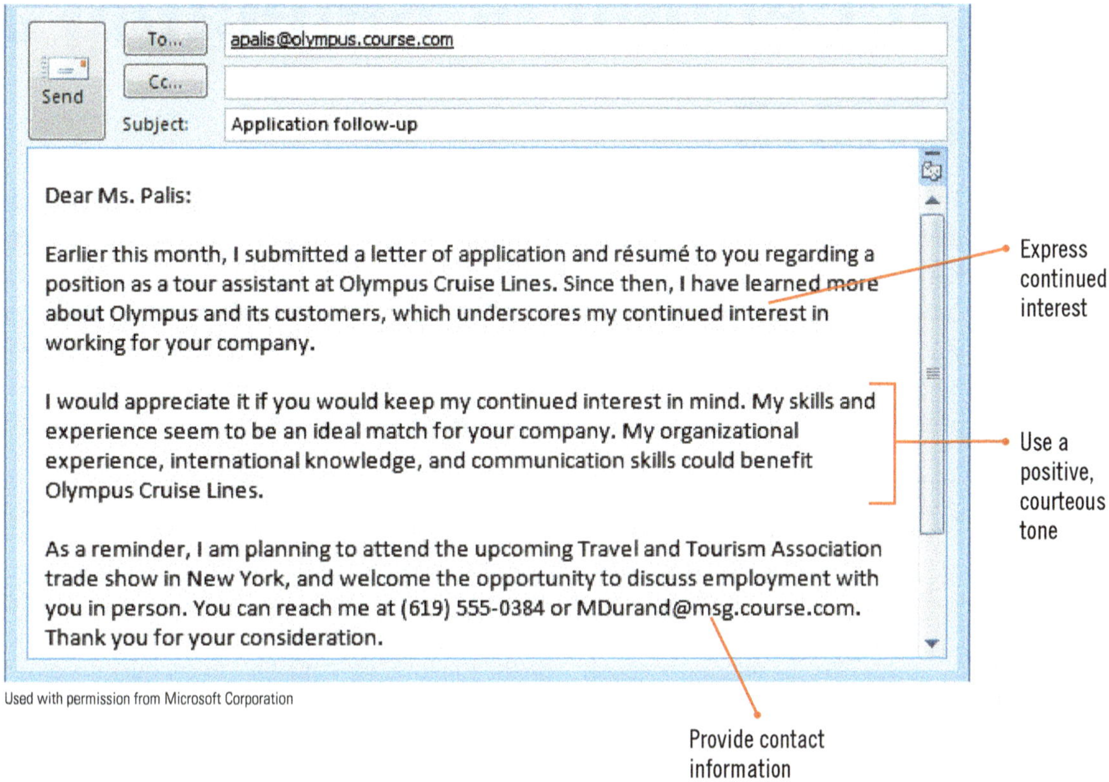

To... apalis@olympus.course.com

Cc...

Subject: Application follow-up

Dear Ms. Palis:

Earlier this month, I submitted a letter of application and résumé to you regarding a position as a tour assistant at Olympus Cruise Lines. Since then, I have learned more about Olympus and its customers, which underscores my continued interest in working for your company.

I would appreciate it if you would keep my continued interest in mind. My skills and experience seem to be an ideal match for your company. My organizational experience, international knowledge, and communication skills could benefit Olympus Cruise Lines.

As a reminder, I am planning to attend the upcoming Travel and Tourism Association trade show in New York, and welcome the opportunity to discuss employment with you in person. You can reach me at (619) 555-0384 or MDurand@msg.course.com. Thank you for your consideration.

Used with permission from Microsoft Corporation

FIGURE 4-10: Interview follow-up message

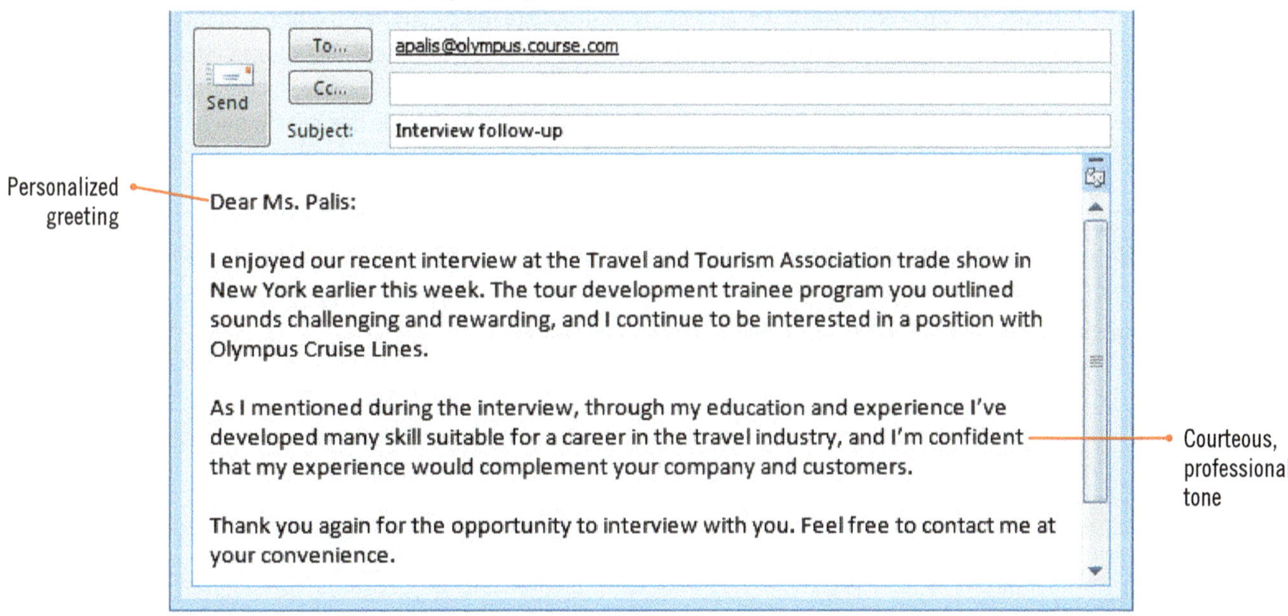

To... apalis@olympus.course.com

Cc...

Subject: Interview follow-up

Dear Ms. Palis:

I enjoyed our recent interview at the Travel and Tourism Association trade show in New York earlier this week. The tour development trainee program you outlined sounds challenging and rewarding, and I continue to be interested in a position with Olympus Cruise Lines.

As I mentioned during the interview, through my education and experience I've developed many skill suitable for a career in the travel industry, and I'm confident that my experience would complement your company and customers.

Thank you again for the opportunity to interview with you. Feel free to contact me at your convenience.

Used with permission from Microsoft Corporation

Objective 32 Part 4

Accepting or Rejecting Job Offers

The goal of any job search is to earn one or more suitable job offers. When you receive a job offer, be sure you carefully evaluate it and make an educated decision to accept or reject it. Don't let the emotion of the moment lead to a hasty choice that you may regret later. When an organization makes you an offer of employment, conclude the process by sending either a letter of acceptance or a polite rejection. case Andrea Palis called you this morning offering you a job as a tour assistant in the New York office of Olympus Cruise Lines. She suggested you take a day to consider the offer, and agreed to call you later. You are fairly sure you will accept the offer over the phone, and begin to prepare a formal acceptance letter.

ESSENTIAL ELEMENTS

1. **Consider the offer**

   Before you make a decision, carefully consider how the position and offer fit into your personal goals and plans. Evaluate the entire package, including salary, benefits, work environment, opportunity for growth, and your potential colleagues and bosses. Compare the offer to others you received. Most job offers are made over the phone; if necessary, ask the employer for some time to consider the offer before making a decision.

2. **Accept the position**

   If you decide to accept the job offer, immediately send a formal letter of acceptance, even if you already accepted the job offer in person or on the phone. A letter establishes a written record of your employment and your understanding of its terms. Table 4-5 lists the details to include in an acceptance letter, and Figure 4-11 shows a typical sample.

3. **Reject the position**

   You might turn down a job offer if the company or position isn't what you are seeking, or if the details of the offer are not acceptable. If you are willing to negotiate the details, tell the hiring manager what is agreeable to you. Sometimes you can negotiate an acceptable solution. If you are not interested in the position, politely decline the offer. Be sure to do so in a professional, courteous manner in case the employer returns with a better offer or different position. Table 4-5 lists details to include in a rejection letter, and Figure 4-12 shows a typical sample.

QUICK TIP

If you accept a job, let other companies that you've applied to know you are no longer available.

YOU TRY IT

Practice accepting a job offer by revising a rough draft of an acceptance letter. Open the WC4-Y32.docx document and follow the steps in the worksheet. When you are finished, submit the document to your instructor as requested.

FIGURE 4-11: Typical acceptance letter

Verify verbal job offer in writing

> As we discussed on the phone, I am very pleased to accept the position of tour assistant at Olympus Cruise Lines. Thank you so much for this exciting opportunity. I am eager to make a positive contribution to the company and to work with everyone on the Olympus team.
>
> As we discussed, my starting salary will be $30,000, and health and life insurance benefits will become available after 60 days of employment.

Confirm the job title or position

Used with permission from Microsoft Corporation

Summarize the compensation package

FIGURE 4-12: Typical rejection letter

Clearly indicate that you are rejecting the offer

> Thank you very much for offering me the position of tour assistant at Olympus Cruise Lines. After careful consideration, I regret that I must decline your offer. I have decided to accept a position elsewhere that is well suited to my qualifications and skills.
>
> Again, thank you for your consideration and best wishes to you.

Provide a brief explanation for your decision

Used with permission from Microsoft Corporation

Use polite and appreciative language

Written Communication

TABLE 4-5: Accepting or rejecting job offers do's and don'ts

follow-up type	do	don't
Consider the offer	• Objectively consider how the offer matches your goals • Evaluate the entire package	• **Don't** wait more than a day or two to respond • **Don't** talk yourself into a job you don't really want
Acceptance	• Address a letter to the person who offered you the position • Start by accepting the position with positive and enthusiastic language • Confirm your position or title • Verify your start date, compensation, and any other special terms • Express appreciation for the opportunity to join the organization	• **Don't** back out after you have accepted, which is considered unethical • **Don't** continue the job search to see if you can find a better position
Rejection	• Be tactful, positive, and polite • Express appreciation for the offer, even if you find part of it disagreeable	• **Don't** list specific reasons for rejecting the offer • **Don't** hide the rejection—explain briefly and directly that you are turning down the offer

Technology @ Work: Professional Networking Sites

A **professional networking site** is a Web site you use to connect with employers and colleagues with a variety of online methods, such as e-mail and text messages. Some social networking sites such as LinkedIn are designed to communicate and share professional information, including information about jobs and careers. Social networks connect people with minimal expense, which is particularly beneficial to small businesses and job seekers. To learn more about LinkedIn, visit their What Is LinkedIn? Web page (*http://learn.linkedin.com/what-is-linkedin*) shown in Figure 4-13. Similar to a network of colleagues, in a virtual community such as LinkedIn, you can interact with others that share your career and business interests and employment objectives, learn about suitable positions and employers, and prepare for interviews and other meetings by reading articles, watching slide shows and videos, asking questions, and searching for job information. Figure 4-14 shows responses to a question about travel jobs on LinkedIn. case Kevin O'Brien suggests you learn about the advantages and disadvantages of professional social networking sites, which are becoming increasingly popular. You are considering setting up an account on a site so you can maintain your contacts at Quest Specialty Travel and keep track of new contacts at Olympus Cruise Lines.

ESSENTIAL ELEMENTS

QUICK TIP

On LinkedIn, you can build a network from people in your e-mail address book, current and past colleagues, and former classmates.

1. **Provide two-way communication**
   Professional networking sites allow you to communicate with contacts and allow contacts to communicate with you. Businesses can take advantage of this type of communication by keeping in touch with customers and suppliers and letting customers and suppliers contact them.

2. **Stay in touch while mobile**
   You can use professional networking sites to identify and contact colleagues, employers, and customers even while you are traveling or moving from one job to another. As the popularity of networking sites continues to grow, you can reconnect with contacts you lost touch with in the past.

3. **Use with in-person networking**
   Setting up contacts with people you meet face-to-face can be an effective way to prepare for interviews, meetings, and conferences, for example. You can also research companies and job trends. However, professional networking sites don't take the place of in-person meetings.

4. **Manage your time on networking sites**
   One caution is that building a network takes time, which can detract from other job-seeking or career-building activities. Many employers frown on online conversations that take too much time. They also object to using the computer to deliver messages that are better delivered in person. As with all forms of communication, make sure the audience and purpose of your message are suitable for online networking sites.

YOU TRY IT

Practice using a professional networking site. Open the WC4-TechWork.docx document and follow the steps in the worksheet. When you are finished, submit the document to your instructor as requested.

FIGURE 4-13: What Is LinkedIn page

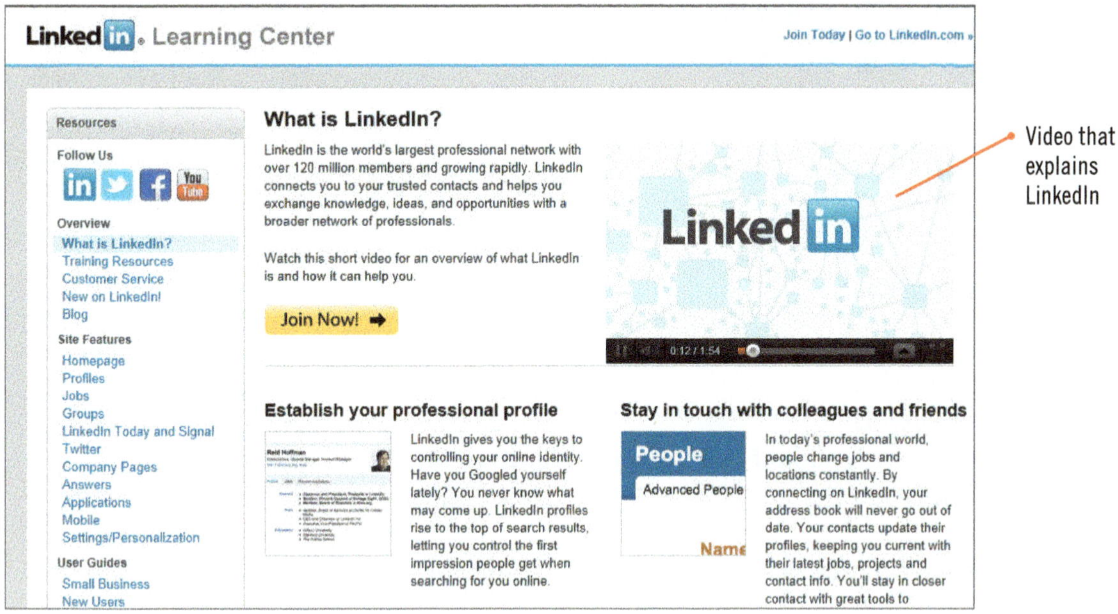

LinkedIn Corporation © 2012

FIGURE 4-14: LinkedIn job search results

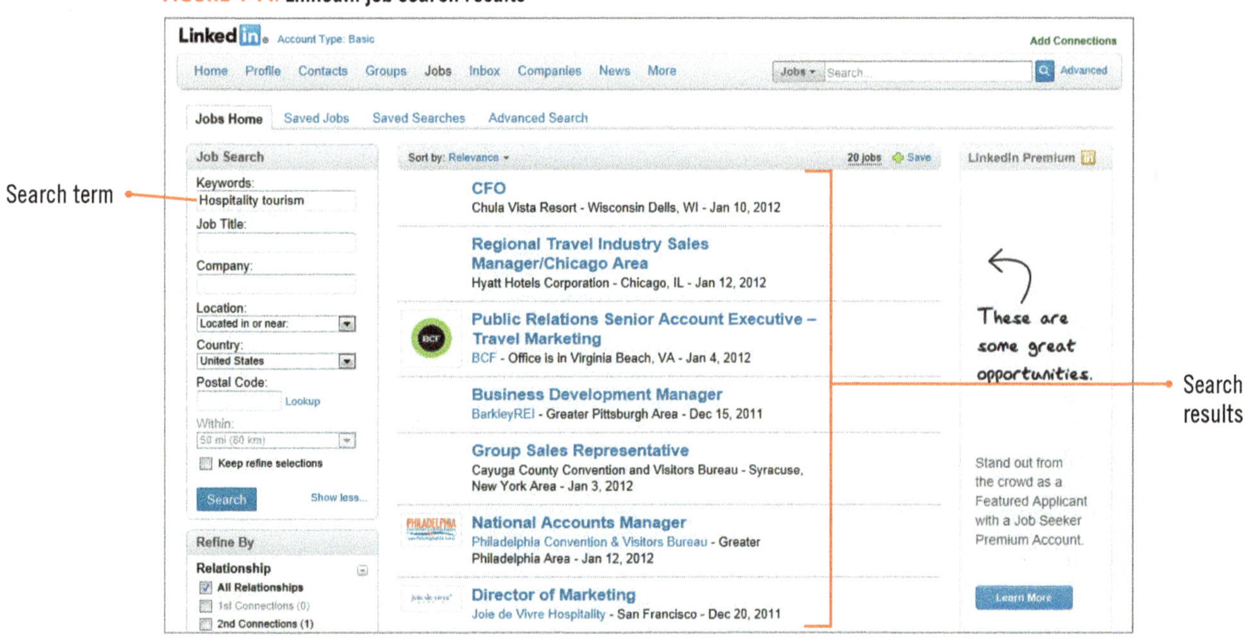

LinkedIn Corporation © 2012

Practice

Soft Skills Review

Understand job searches.

1. **Which one of the following steps should you perform before submitting your first application?**
   - **a.** Prepare for an interview
   - **b.** Write a follow-up letter
   - **c.** Write a cover letter
   - **d.** Define your employment objective
2. **Which of the following should you *not* do to identify potential employers?**
   - **a.** Visit employment Web sites
   - **b.** Communicate with a network of contacts
   - **c.** Send copies of the same e-mail message addressed to "Dear Hiring Manager"
   - **d.** Take advantage of social networking sites

Write effective cover letters.

1. **A cover letter is a short, personalized letter you send with a:**
   - **a.** follow-up letter
   - **b.** résumé
   - **c.** list of references
   - **d.** formal acceptance
2. **Which of the following is an effective way to end a cover letter?**
   - **a.** Suggest a time for a conference call
   - **b.** Request an interview
   - **c.** List your degree and date of graduation
   - **d.** Describe your strengths

Plan résumés.

1. **Which of the following statements best describes a résumé?**
   - **a.** Long, unstructured document describing your talents and goals
   - **b.** Customized summary of your education, employment history, skills, and accomplishments
   - **c.** Detailed list of your education, preferably organized by month
   - **d.** Basic template for professional correspondence
2. **Which of the following should you *not* provide in the main heading, or contact information section, of your résumé?**
   - **a.** Work e-mail address
   - **b.** Full name and phone number
   - **c.** Simple formatting that highlights your name
   - **d.** Personal e-mail address

Write chronological résumés.

1. **Which of the following should you include to separate résumé sections?**
   - **a.** Centered employment dates
   - **b.** Photos
   - **c.** Contact information
   - **d.** Standard headings
2. **Which of the following is considered ethically acceptable in a chronological résumé?**
   - **a.** Shortening your education section
   - **b.** Stretching employment dates
   - **c.** Enhancing job titles
   - **d.** Listing degrees you plan to earn, but haven't yet

Write functional résumés.

1. **In contrast to a chronological résumé, a functional résumé highlights your:**
   - **a.** work history
   - **b.** employment objective
   - **c.** references
   - **d.** skills
2. **In which of the following circumstances should you consider creating a functional résumé?**
   - **a.** Most of your experience is in one field
   - **b.** Your work history follows a clear career path
   - **c.** You have changed jobs frequently
   - **d.** You plan to submit your résumé to a recruiting firm

Request letters of reference.

1. **Who should you *not* ask for a letter of reference?**
   - **a.** Former neighbor
   - **b.** Former employer
   - **c.** College professor
   - **d.** Supervisor
2. **What should you provide to your recommenders?**
   - **a.** Letters from other recommenders
   - **b.** Link to your social networking site
   - **c.** Copy of your résumé
   - **d.** Unedited cover letter

Send follow-up messages.

1. **Which of the following should you *not* do when following up an application?**
   - **a.** Express disappointment in the lack of response
   - **b.** Express continued interest in the position
   - **c.** Request an interview
   - **d.** Describe your skills
2. **Which of the following should you *not* do when following up an interview?**
   - **a.** Send a written response
   - **b.** Send an e-mail message
   - **c.** Send a text message from a mobile phone
   - **d.** Send a personalized note

Accept or reject job offers.

1. **Which of the following is the goal of any job search?**
   - **a.** Scheduling an interview
   - **b.** Contacting a hiring manager
   - **c.** Rejecting many job offers
   - **d.** Receiving a job offer
2. **Address an acceptance letter to:**
   - **a.** the head of the department
   - **b.** the person who offered you the position
   - **c.** the president of the company
   - **d.** the recruiter who found the job

Technology @ work: Professional networking sites.

1. **A professional networking site is:**
   - **a.** a centralized job fair
   - **b.** restricted to company owners
   - **c.** a place to learn about computer networks
   - **d.** a Web site you use to connect with employers and colleagues
2. **Which of the following is a disadvantage of using professional networking sites?**
   - **a.** It takes time to develop a network
   - **b.** It provides two-way communication
   - **c.** It lets you stay in touch while mobile
   - **d.** It complements face-to-face networking

Critical Thinking Questions

1. **You can easily find résumé-writing services on the Web. What are the pros and cons of using such a service?**
2. **Suppose you are applying to two companies: one that publishes online magazines, and another located outside the United States that provides financial services. Describe the résumés you send to each company. What are their similarities and differences?**

Critical Thinking Questions (continued)

3. A close friend is taking initiative and preparing his résumé months before he completes his coursework. When the semester ends, he'll only be two credits short of his degree. He's planning to list the degree on his résumé anyway because he already did most of the work and he'll earn the two credits quickly. What do you say to your friend?

4. Some companies are saving time and resources by scanning résumés for keywords. What are the advantages and disadvantages of this practice for employers? For job applicants?

5. The Web is changing the way people find and apply for jobs. Which online job tools seem promising to you? Which seem unproductive or even unscrupulous? Research job searches online, if necessary.

Independent Challenge 1

You are interested in applying for a job in the marketing department of a small Web design company named Overland Designs. You want to revise your résumé so that it showcases the skills and experience a Web design firm is likely to want. You need to customize your résumé, shown in Figure 4-15, before sending it to Overland Designs.

FIGURE 4-15

Memberships: Alpha Gamma Rho 2007-2012
National Business Honor Society 2010-2012
Certificate of Achievement for Outstanding Business Students
Varsity Tennis 2009-2012
GPA 3.6 (/4.0)

EDUCATION

Emory University, Atlanta, GA
B.S. in Business Administration – Marketing major, 2010

I am highly motivated to work in a career in Web design, seeking to use formal training in design, personnel management, data analysis, and marketing, where I can use my experience to enhance my skills.

WORK HISTORY

2008 Suwanee Business Alliance
Intern in the tourism office (community events and tourist awareness)

Used with permission from Microsoft Corporation

a. Open the **WC4-IC1.docx** document and follow the steps in the worksheet.
b. Proofread the document carefully to fix any grammar or formatting errors.
c. Submit the document to your instructor as requested.

Independent Challenge 2

You are applying for a position as manager of the flagship Four Winds Apparel store in Minneapolis, Minnesota. Four Winds Apparel specializes in affordable active wear for men, women, and children and has five other stores in the Minneapolis-St. Paul area. You have prepared a suitable résumé and the first draft of a cover letter, shown in Figure 4-16. You need to revise the cover letter before sending it to Allison Crandall, the regional manager of Four Winds Apparel at 1210 Red Wing Way in Minneapolis.

a. Open the **WC4-IC2.docx** document and follow the steps in the worksheet.
b. Proofread the document carefully to fix any grammar or formatting errors.
c. Submit the document to your instructor as requested.

Independent Challenge 2 (continued)

FIGURE 4-16

Dear Hiring Manager:

I am writing to see if you have any openings for a junior manager. I recently graduated from Carroll College, and I am pursuing full-time employment. I enjoy fashion and have some experience in the retail industry.

My qualifications include:

- My four-year degree in fashion merchandising
- My area of concentration is fashion retail
- I have experience in fashion design
- I was the vice president of the local chapter of the Council of Fashion Designers of America (student division)

Let me know, I can send you anything you need. The ad I saw in the Minneapolis Star Tribune mentioned that you will be interviewing at the Minneapolis Career Fair. I would love to meet you there!

Sincerely,

Student Name

Real Life Independent Challenge

This Independent Challenge requires an Internet connection.

To prepare for full-time employment along a satisfying career path, research a field that interests you, and then write a résumé you could use to apply for a job in that field.

a. Prepare for your job search by identifying your employment interests, evaluating your qualifications, and identifying fields in which you'd like to work.
b. Using your favorite search engine, research a field that interests you. The online *Occupational Outlook Handbook* (*www.bls.gov/oco*) is also a good resource for information about occupations.
c. Research an organization or company where you might work.
d. Open the **WC4-IC3.docx** document and follow the steps in the worksheet.
e. Proofread the document carefully to fix any grammar or formatting errors.
f. Submit the document to your instructor as requested.

Team Challenge

You are working for Farley Worldwide, a company specializing in information services, and you are part of a new group that interviews job applicants. To prepare for this job responsibility, you and your team decide to review your own résumés and offer suggestions for improvement.

a. Select a résumé you have created for this lesson or for another purpose.
b. Meet as a team and exchange résumés.
c. Review your teammate's résumé, and list two strengths. Also list two concrete suggestions or examples of how to improve the résumé.
d. Return the résumé to its author. Review the comments your teammate provided for your résumé.
e. As a team, meet to discuss the suggestions you found most useful.

Be the Critic

Review the poorly written follow-up message shown in Figure 4-17. Create an e-mail message that lists the weaknesses of the follow-up message and makes specific suggestions for improvement. Send the critique in an e-mail message to your instructor.

FIGURE 4-17

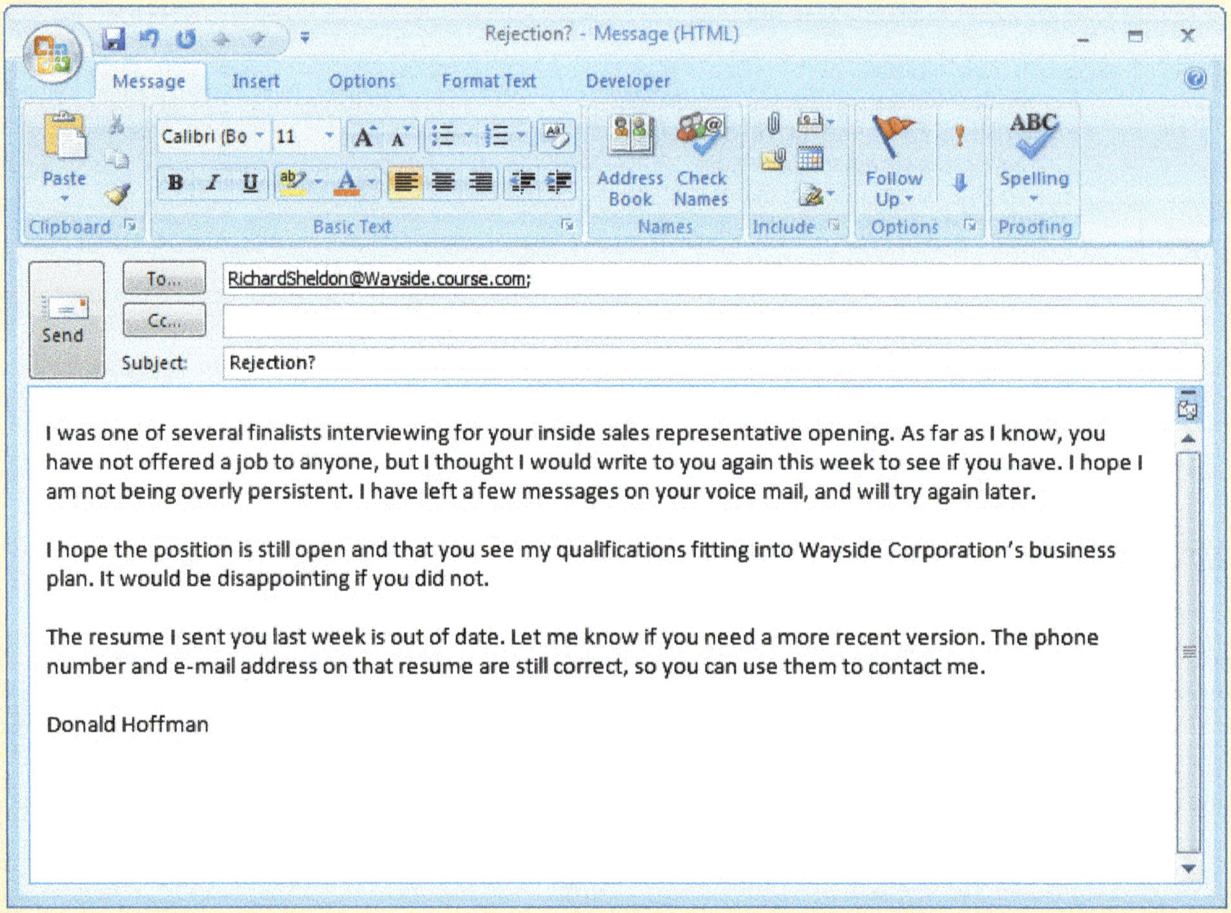

Used with permission from Microsoft Corporation

Part 5

Writing Professional Letters

Files You Will Need:

- WC5-Y34.docx
- WC5-Y35.docx
- WC5-Y36.docx
- WC5-Y37.docx
- WC5-Y38.docx
- WC5-Y39.docx
- WC5-Y40.docx
- WC5-TechWork.docx
- WC5-IC1.docx
- WC5-IC2.docx

Business letters are powerful ways to deliver formal or persuasive information, establish permanent records, or send significant, sensitive, or confidential messages. Although e-mail has become the most popular way to exchange written messages, business letters are still a necessary communication tool. You usually write letters to communicate with people outside of your organization, though you can also use letters to send formal messages to colleagues. Besides the words you write on the page, your letter's design and format tell your reader about you, your attention to detail, and your level of professionalism. In this unit, you learn about the common guidelines to follow when you compose and format your letters. You also learn how to write business letters that respond to requests, convince readers to take action, and express goodwill. **case** Ron Dawson, vice president of marketing at Quest Specialty Travel, has received a few customer inquiries recently, and he asks you to write letters responding to their requests. In addition, Ron wants you to work on a marketing letter to send to anyone who has enrolled on a Quest tour.

OBJECTIVES

33 Understand professional letter writing
34 Write business letters
35 Use salutations
36 Close business letters
37 Write routine letters
38 Answer request letters
39 Write persuasive letters
40 Write for goodwill

Objective 33
Part 5

Understanding Professional Letter Writing

A **business letter** is a professional communication tool for delivering messages outside of an organization. Although business letters are used less frequently than other communication media such as electronic mail and faxes, when you need to communicate with suppliers, other businesses, and most importantly, customers, a business letter is the most appropriate choice. Figure 5-1 shows examples of typical business letters. case Before you start working on the letters Ron Dawson asked you to write, you want to review the guidelines for composing business letters.

DETAILS

QUICK TIP
You usually send business letters to people outside of your organization. Send memos to people within your company.

QUICK TIP
You can send a letter using certified mail with a return receipt to document the date your message was delivered.

Use a business letter when you need to:

- **Communicate with someone you don't know**
  If you need to comunicate with someone you haven't met or don't know personally, send a business letter to establish a professional relationship. Although an e-mail message is easier to write and faster to send, its informal, spontaneous nature can make your message seem too personal or bold.
- **Document your communication**
  If you need to maintain a written record of formal communication with someone outside your company, a business letter is often the best choice. Business letters produce a permanent record, especially when they accompany contracts, terms of agreement, or special offers.
- **Deliver bad news or discuss a sensitive matter**
  A business letter printed on company stationery conveys more formality and respect than channels such as e-mail. Composing a written letter shows your reader that you take its subject seriously. In addition, business letters can be confidential and are more private than digital forms of communication.
- **Develop goodwill**
  A written letter is appropriate when you want to offer thanks, congratulations, sympathy, or apologies. In each case, a letter—including the stationery, typeface, and signature—expresses emotion more effectively than an informal message.

Use a telephone call, personal visit, or e-mail message when you need to:

- **Deliver a message as quickly as possible**
  Business letters are typically sent via first-class mail, which can take several days to be delivered. Overnight express services are an option, though delivery costs are high.
- **Contact someone with whom you have a good working relationship**
  For day-to-day communication with someone you know, a letter is generally too formal. Exceptions are when you are writing to develop goodwill or need to produce a written record.
- **Write about a routine subject**
  E-mail is popular because it's efficient, and phone calls and visits are more personal than written messages. For routine communication such as requests and responses that do not need to create permanent records, maintain confidentiality, express formality, or deliver persuasive arguments, use e-mail or phone calls.

FIGURE 5-1: Examples of business letters

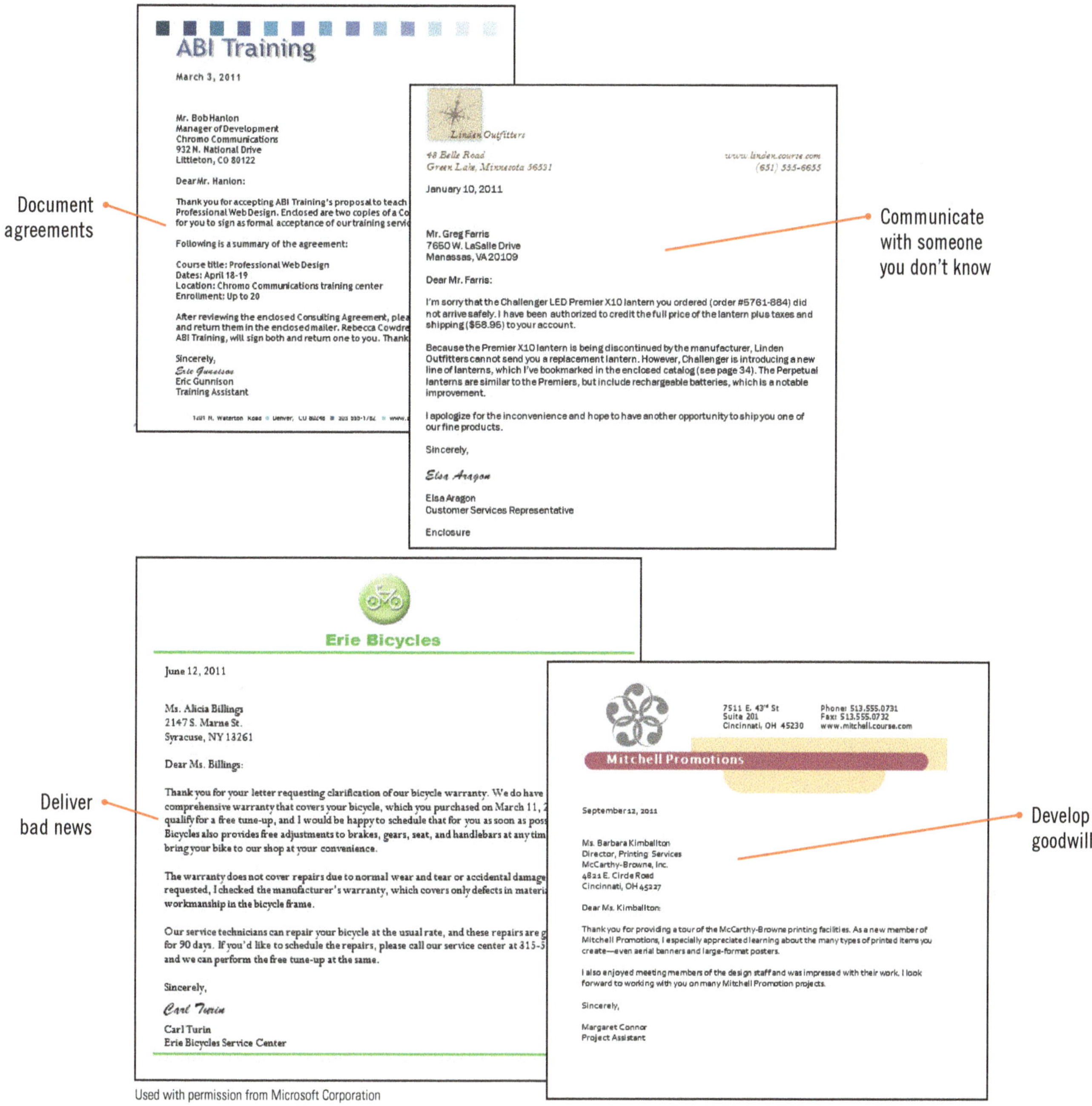

Used with permission from Microsoft Corporation

The world's most effective business letter?

In 1975, Martin Conroy, an advertising executive, wrote a letter as a subscription pitch for the *Wall Street Journal*. The letter was so effective, the *Journal* used it continuously for 28 years, making it the longest running direct response letter ever written. "It's the 'Hamlet,' the 'Iliad,' the 'Divine Comedy' of direct-mail letters," said James R. Rosenfield, a direct-marketing consultant. What makes this simple, two-page letter so successful? In a nutshell, it uses plain language to tell an engaging story. The letter begins with the lines, "On a beautiful late spring afternoon, twenty-five years ago, two young men graduated from the same college. They were very much alike, these two young men." The letter describes how the men return to their college for a reunion. They are still very much alike and even work for the same company, except one is the manager of a small department and the other is the company president. The letter asks, "What made the difference?" implying that the answer involves reading the *Wall Street Journal*. Millions of readers responded to the letter by buying subscriptions, making it one of the most effective business letters in the world.

Sources: Fox, Margalit, Martin Conroy obituary, *The New York Times*, December 22, 2006, and "Brand Story," *Wall Street Journal*, December 26, 2006.

Objective
34
Part 5

Writing Business Letters

Before you write a business letter, establish the goal or purpose of the communication. Are you making a request, responding to an inquiry, documenting a decision, or acknowledging an action? Next, consider your audience and anticipate the reaction to your message. When you start to write, follow the standard conventions for business letters shown in Figure 5-2. Using the correct form, or **block style**, shows your professionalism and simplifies your task as a writer. case Ron gives you a letter from a customer inquiring about ecotours to the Caribbean and Central America. You begin a letter in response using the block style on Quest stationery.

ESSENTIAL ELEMENTS

1. **Letterhead**

   Most business letters are written on letterhead stationery that includes the company name, street address, telephone and fax numbers, and Web site address. A logo usually identifies the organization. Figure 5-3 shows the letterhead for Quest Specialty Travel.

2. **Dateline**

   Start with today's date. Spell the name of the month and use all four digits in the year. Always use the current date for your letters. Don't pre- or postdate business letters.

3. **Inside address**

   The inside address includes basic information about the recipient: name, title, and the organization's name and mailing address.

4. **Salutation**

   A business letter is considered formal communication and should always start with a salutation. This is usually the word *Dear* followed by the reader's name, as in *Dear Ms. Alvarez*.

5. **Introduction**

   Your first paragraph should directly express the purpose of your letter. Explain why you are writing so that your reader can anticipate and better understand your message. Use a polite and conversational tone. Avoid canned introductory statements.

6. **Body**

   The bulk of your letter should contain one or more paragraphs that provide your reader with information, an explanation, or other details related to your message. These paragraphs should all directly support the main idea presented in your introduction.

7. **Closing**

   Include a closing paragraph that gracefully concludes the letter. Don't abruptly end a business letter. Instead, end with an expression of goodwill, a polite comment or observation, or a request to take a specific action.

8. **Complimentary close and signature**

   End the letter with a complimentary close such as *Sincerely*, *Respectfully*, or *Cordially*. Insert your name four lines below the complimentary close to leave room for your handwritten signature.

QUICK TIP
When you are writing a business letter, use a colon (:) after the name.

QUICK TIP
The closing statement can express goodwill, make a polite comment, or ask your reader to take a specific action.

YOU TRY IT

Practice writing business letters by revising a letter. Open the WC5-Y34.docx document and follow the steps in the worksheet. When you are finished, submit the document to your instructor as requested.

FIGURE 5-2: Standard business letter format

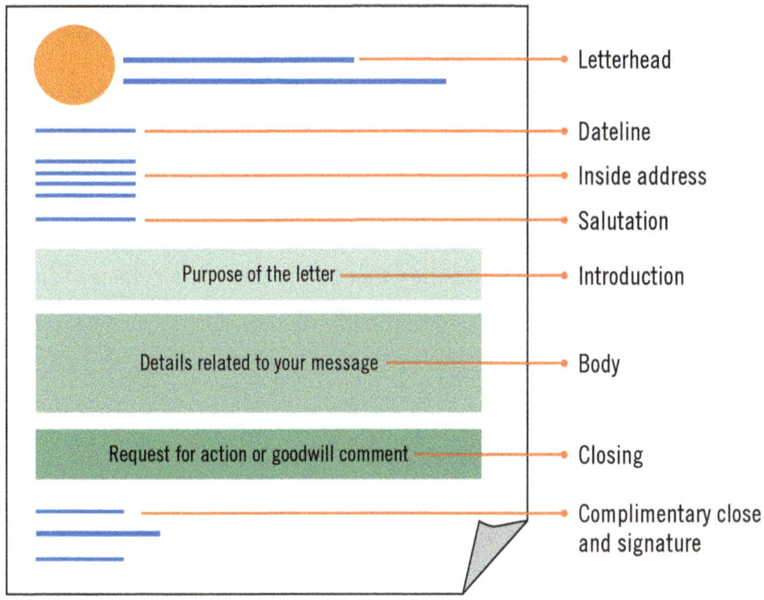

Used with permission from Microsoft Corporation

FIGURE 5-3: Customer letter and response on Quest letterhead

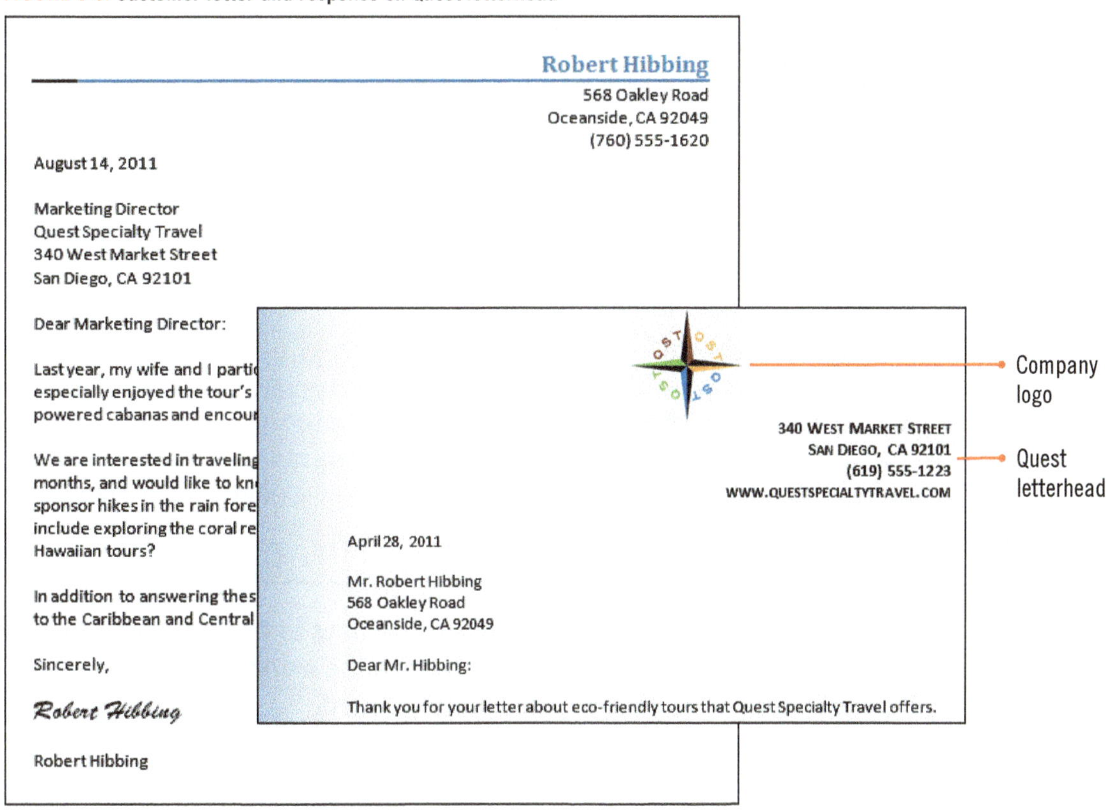
Robert Hibbing
568 Oakley Road
Oceanside, CA 92049
(760) 555-1620

August 14, 2011

Marketing Director
Quest Specialty Travel
340 West Market Street
San Diego, CA 92101

Dear Marketing Director:

Last year, my wife and I parti
especially enjoyed the tour's
powered cabanas and encou

We are interested in traveling
months, and would like to kn
sponsor hikes in the rain fore
include exploring the coral re
Hawaiian tours?

In addition to answering thes
to the Caribbean and Central

Sincerely,

Robert Hibbing

Robert Hibbing

340 WEST MARKET STREET
SAN DIEGO, CA 92101
(619) 555-1223
WWW.QUESTSPECIALTYTRAVEL.COM

April 28, 2011

Mr. Robert Hibbing
568 Oakley Road
Oceanside, CA 92049

Dear Mr. Hibbing:

Thank you for your letter about eco-friendly tours that Quest Specialty Travel offers.

Used with permission from Microsoft Corporation

Objective 35 Part 5

Using Salutations

When you write a business letter, you are establishing an image of yourself and the organization that you represent. Often, your letter is the first contact someone has with you and the impression can be lasting. Starting your business letter with a proper salutation and introduction establishes a friendly tone and helps to make a positive impression on your reader. See Figure 5-4. case In addition to writing a letter about Quest ecotours in the Caribbean and Central America, you need to send similar letters to other customers, including one in France and the other to the dean of a college. You plan to use the same letter with slight adjustments such as revised salutations.

ESSENTIAL ELEMENTS

QUICK TIP Avoid using "Miss" and "Mrs." in your salutations because they make assumptions about the age and marital status of your reader.

QUICK TIP In the inside address, include your reader's first and last names regardless of the salutation format.

1. Salutation format

The format Dear *Title Name* is always correct and should be used in all of your business letters. Use either Mr. or Ms. for the courtesy title, unless you are addressing someone with a formal title such as Dr. or Reverend.

2. Punctuation

The punctuation in your salutation signals the intent of your letter. Follow salutations in business correspondence with a colon (:), and follow salutations in personal letters with a comma (,).

3. First names

When writing a formal letter, do not include the reader's first name in the salutation (as in *Dear Ms. Louisa Jones* or *Dear Mr. Carl Roberts*). However, if you have a friendly relationship with your recipient, you can use their first name only (as in *Dear Bob*).

4. Impersonal salutations

If you don't know the name of your recipient, use an impersonal salutation, such as the reader's title (*Dear Operations Manager*) or the name of their department or unit (*Dear Human Resources Department*). Avoid salutations such as "Dear Sir/Madam" and "To Whom It May Concern," if possible.

5. Titles of rank and honor

When writing particularly formal business letters, you might need to include job titles, rank, or titles of honor in your salutation (such as *Dear President Cunningham*, *Dear Dr. Smith*, or *Dear Ambassador Wharton*). Letters sent to political dignitaries can include terms such as *Honorable* or *Excellency*. Figure 5-5 lists titles used in typical salutations.

6. Writing internationally

Titles and salutations are taken more seriously in some countries than they are in the U.S. However, the rules for their use vary from place to place and using the wrong form of address can be embarrassing. If you are writing to someone internationally, the safest approach is to use the traditional Dear *Title Name* salutation and write your letter with a formal tone. Table 5-1 summarizes the do's and don'ts for writing salutations.

YOU TRY IT

Practice using salutations by writing appropriate ones to begin letters. Open the WC5-Y35.docx document and follow the steps in the worksheet. When you are finished, submit the document to your instructor as requested.

FIGURE 5-4: Salutations in Quest business letters

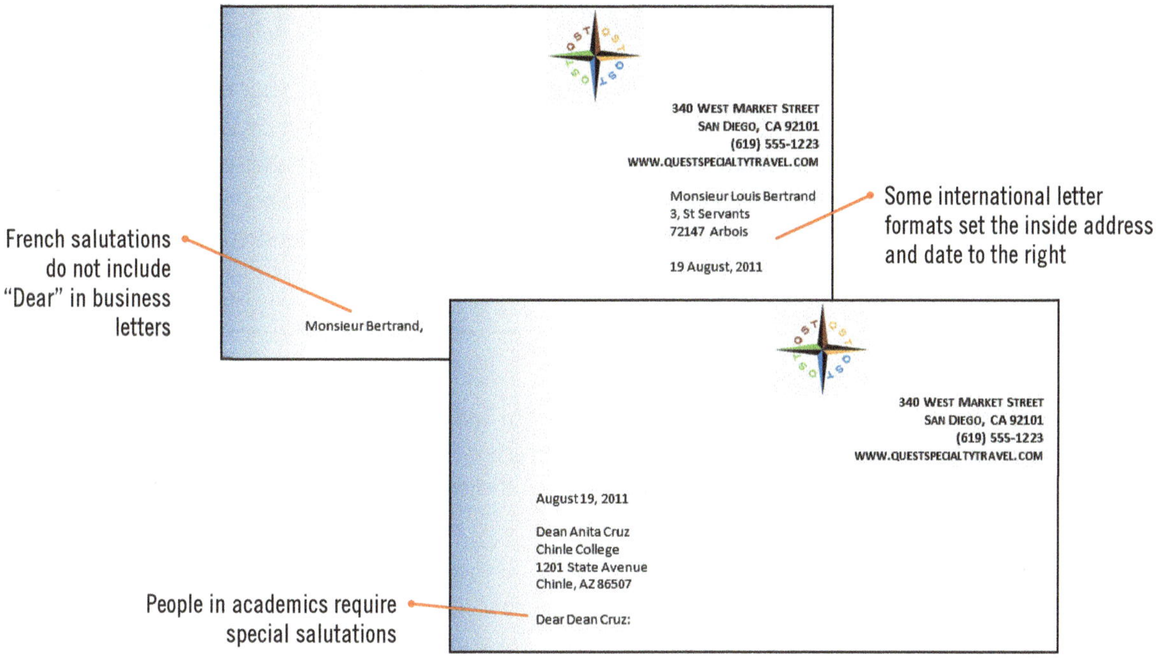

Used with permission from Microsoft Corporation

FIGURE 5-5: Typical titles in salutations

Academics	Armed Services
Professor *First Name Last Name* (inside address) Dear Professor *Last Name*: **Example:** Dear Professor Cleary:	Dear *Full Rank Last Name*: **Example:** Dear Admiral Williams:
Professions	**Social**
First Name Last Name, M.D. (inside address) Dear Dr. *Last Name*: **Example:** Dear Dr. Franke:	Dear Mr./Ms. *Last Name*: **Example:** Dear Ms. Prescott:

TABLE 5-1: Salutation do's and don'ts

salutation element	do	don't
Format	• Use the format Dear *Title Name* • Include a colon (:) at the end for business letters	• **Don't** omit the "Dear" • **Don't** use comma at the end except in personal letters
Name	• Include the reader's last name • Use only the reader's first name for a letter with a personal message	• **Don't** use "Miss" or "Mrs." as a title • **Don't** include the reader's first name in a formal letter
International readers	• Become familiar with letter customs in your reader's country • Use formal salutations	• **Don't** assume you can be personal • **Don't** use an informal greeting, even if you have a personal relationship with your reader

Objective 36
Part 5

Closing Business Letters

The way you close your business letters affects your readers' understanding of your message, their willingness to act on your requests, and their impression of you. Business letters always end with a complimentary close, such as *Sincerely*. Your signature block appears at the end of the business letter and consists of your signature, typed name, and title (if you are writing a formal letter). Figure 5-6 shows examples of closings for a formal business letter. case Before sending your response letters to Quest customers, you need to write a closing, insert a complimentary close, and add a signature block.

ESSENTIAL ELEMENTS

1. **End with a call to action**
   Readers typically scan the last paragraph in your letter to find action requests, deadlines, and activities that you are asking them to complete. Due dates are especially helpful. Remember to be courteous in your requests because people respond more favorably when treated with respect. Table 5-2 summarizes the do's and don'ts of ending a business letter.

2. **Express appreciation**
   Express appreciation when asking for something. You can include your appreciation directly in your request, as in "I appreciate your help in completing this report by March 15."

3. **Maintain goodwill**
   If you are not making a specific request, you can close with a positive statement, observation, or desire for a continued relationship. Even when you are writing about a negative subject, try to end your business letter on a positive and professional note.

QUICK TIP
Only the first word of the complimentary close begins with an uppercase letter.

4. **Use a traditional close for formal business letters**
   The most common complimentary close in business correspondence is *Sincerely*. Others are variations on that close, such as *Sincerely yours*. Closings built around the word *Respectfully* typically show deference to your recipient, so use this close only when deference is appropriate.

QUICK TIP
Complimentary closes end with a comma.

5. **Use a personal close for informal letters**
   For personal or informal letters to friends and acquaintances, you can use complimentary closes such as *Cordially*, *Warm regards*, and *Best wishes*.

6. **Insert your position in the signature block**
   In a formal business letter, include your title or job position next to your printed name. A good rule of thumb is to list your position if you also included one for your recipient.

7. **Include your company name in the signature block**
   If you are acting as an agent of your company, such as when you submit a proposal or contract, include the company's full legal name one line below the complimentary close and four lines above your signature. This shows that you are acting on behalf of the company, not individually.

8. **Provide additional notations**
   When appropriate, include *Enclosure* (or *Enc*) to indicate you are sending material with the letter. Include reference initials if you wrote the letter but someone else typed it. For example, *KL:mcd* shows that KL wrote the letter and MCD typed it.

YOU TRY IT

Practice closing business letters by writing a closing paragraph, complimentary close, and signature block. Open the WC5-Y36.docx document and follow the steps in the worksheet. When you are finished, submit the document to your instructor as requested.

FIGURE 5-6: Sample closings

Action

We plan to send you the proposal by March 15. Can you then send me the production estimates by April 30? That allows plenty of time to calculate the final estimate.

Sincerely,

John Robertson

Appreciation

Thank you so much for volunteering to represent our department at the fall trade show. If you need additional resources to prepare for the show, please let me know.

Sincerely,

John Robertson

Goodwill

Congratulations on your promotion, and good luck in the future.

Sincerely,

John Robertson

TABLE 5-2: Closing and signature block do's and don'ts

closing element	do	don't
Closing paragraph	• Be specific and courteous when making a request • Include a deadline • Provide a reason for the request and deadline • Make it easy to respond by providing contact information	• **Don't** command the reader, as in "Respond with an answer as soon as possible" • **Don't** close with a cliché such as "Thank you for your attention to this matter"
Complimentary close	• Use the traditional *Sincerely* for most of your business letters • Close with an alternative such as *Cordially* for personal letters • Use *Respectfully* to communicate deference, such as in letters sent abroad	• **Don't** use a close that reflects a negative emotion, such as *Angrily* or *Disappointedly* • **Don't** omit the complimentary close or the comma that follows it in formal letters
Signature block	• In formal letters, print and sign your full name • Include your title if the inside address includes your recipient's title • Insert the name of your company if you are acting on its behalf	• **Don't** sign your first name only in a formal letter • **Don't** sign with your initials only (as you do in a memo) • **Don't** use a computer-generated signature

Objective 37

Part 5

Writing Routine Letters

ESSENTIAL ELEMENTS

Although you use the block style for formal business letters, you can use a more direct, informal style called the **simplified letter format** for routine letters sent as mass mail, such as sales letters and announcements sent to customers, shareholders, suppliers, or employees. The simplified letter format omits the salutation, complimentary close, and signature, while focusing on the opening line and the body of the letter. See Figures 5-7 and 5-8. case Ron Dawson wants to send a sales letter to current and past Quest customers offering a discount on selected tours. You start by outlining this letter using the simplified letter format.

1. **Replace the salutation with a subject line**
   Starting a letter with the subject emphasizes your purpose so readers can immediately anticipate and understand the rest of the letter.
2. **State your purpose in the first line**
   Present a clear statement of your offer, request, answer, problem you propose to resolve, or action you are taking.
3. **Provide specifics in the body paragraphs**
   In the body paragraphs, explain the details that support your statement of purpose in the first line. These details might provide specifics about your offer or request, list the benefits of your ideas, or provide related facts. Arrange information logically, such as chronologically or from most important topic to least important. Address readers directly as "you," and focus on how the content of your letter can benefit them.
4. **Format the body paragraphs for readability**
   Minimize the use of paragraphs whenever possible. Instead, use numbered or bulleted lists, tables, and graphics to make your letter easier to read.
5. **Omit the complimentary close**
   The simplified letter format is not for formal letters and does not require a complimentary close. Instead, you should conclude the letter with your closing paragraph.
6. **Forgo the signature**
   A handwritten signature is not required with the simplified style. In many cases, you are sending numerous copies of the letter and signing each one would be impractical. If you are using a color printer to produce your letters, you have the option of printing your signature in blue ink.

QUICK TIP
Lack of clarity is a big problem in business letters. Avoid this problem by reading the letter as if you are the recipient.

QUICK TIP
As in formal business letters, the closing paragraph can politely request action, provide a deadline, or summarize your offer.

YOU TRY IT

Practice writing routine letters by composing a letter in the simplified letter format. Open the WC5-Y37.docx document and follow the steps in the worksheet. When you are finished, submit the document to your instructor as requested.

FIGURE 5-7: Outline of the simplified letter format

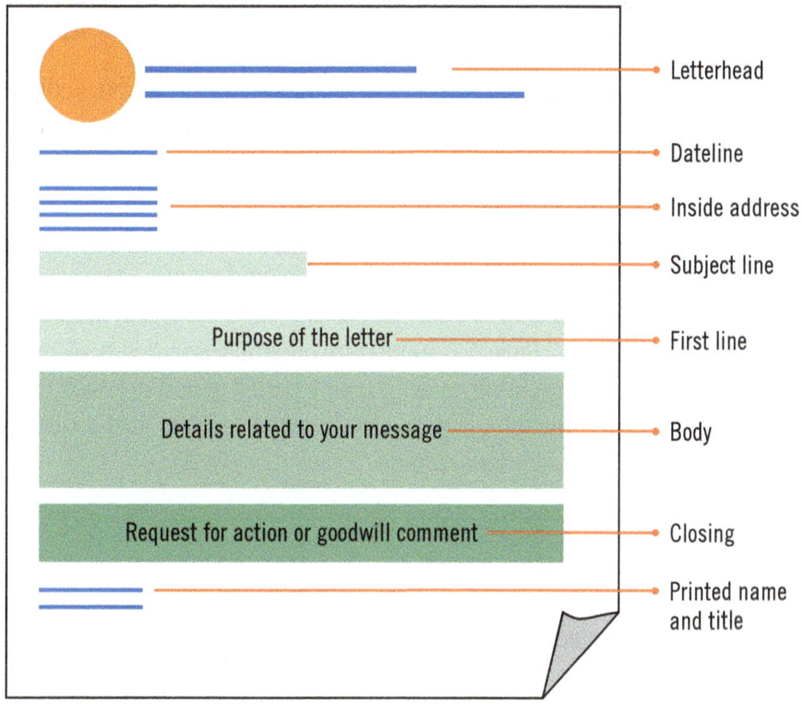

Used with permission from Microsoft Corporation

FIGURE 5-8: Quest letter in simplified format

340 West Market Street
San Diego, CA 92101
(619) 555-1223
www.questspecialtytravel.com

August 20, 2011

Ms. Helene Diaz
1268 Westport Drive
Carlsbad, CA 92008

Subject: Discount on upcoming Quest Specialty Travel tours

Quest Specialty Travel is offering a discount to travelers who enroll in the following tours by September 30, 2011:

- Cultural tour of Indonesia
- Adventure in Argentina
- Active Australia
- Spain by the back roads
- Yucatan highlights

Used with permission from Microsoft Corporation

Objective 38
Part 5

Answering Request Letters

When you receive written requests asking for information or action, your response is determined by whether you choose to comply. If you are responding favorably, tell your reader that you can accommodate their request in the opening line. If you are not agreeable to the request, you can respond directly or indirectly. A direct response is appropriate if you know your reader prefers directness or reasonably expects that you might deny the request. If your reader is likely to react negatively to your response, opt for an indirect approach. Start your response letter by establishing goodwill, then explain the circumstances of your decision, and gradually build up to your response. In either case, you should be tactful, polite, and careful about the language you use. Table 5-3 summarizes the do's and don'ts of response letters. case Ron Dawson received a letter from a customer requesting a partial refund of a tour throughout eastern Canada. Because you helped develop the tour, Ron discusses how to respond to the customer, and then asks you to write a letter answering the customer's request.

ESSENTIAL ELEMENTS

1. **Use a subject line**
   Instead of starting your letter by summarizing the original request, insert a subject line after the salutation. The subject should remind your reader about the original request letter and provide a context for your reply. Figure 5-9 shows a response letter with a subject line.

2. **Respond directly**
   Unless an indirect approach is more appropriate, provide your reader with an answer in the first sentence of your letter.

3. **Clarify your commitment**
   Follow your introduction with additional details and information to support your answer. When you agree to someone's written request, your response might have legal implications. Be sure to review your letter carefully before you send it.

4. **Write for readability**
   If you are responding to multiple questions or providing a detailed reply, use tables, graphics, lists, headings, and other visual cues to make your response easier to read.

5. **Present the good before the bad**
   If you can comply with only part of your reader's request, start with the good news. Explain the bad news clearly in the body of your letter, but don't dwell on it.

6. **Conclude on a positive note**
   If you can't accommodate a request, offer your reader an alternative solution, if possible. Reinforce the ideas that you value their relationship and want to continue doing business with them.

QUICK TIP
If you think your response might have legal implications, ask your manager to review your letter before you send it.

QUICK TIP
Starting with the good news establishes a positive tone for your letter.

YOU TRY IT

Practice answering request letters by responding to a request. Open the WC5-Y38.docx document and follow the steps in the worksheet. When you are finished, submit the document to your instructor as requested.

FIGURE 5-9: Response to customer request

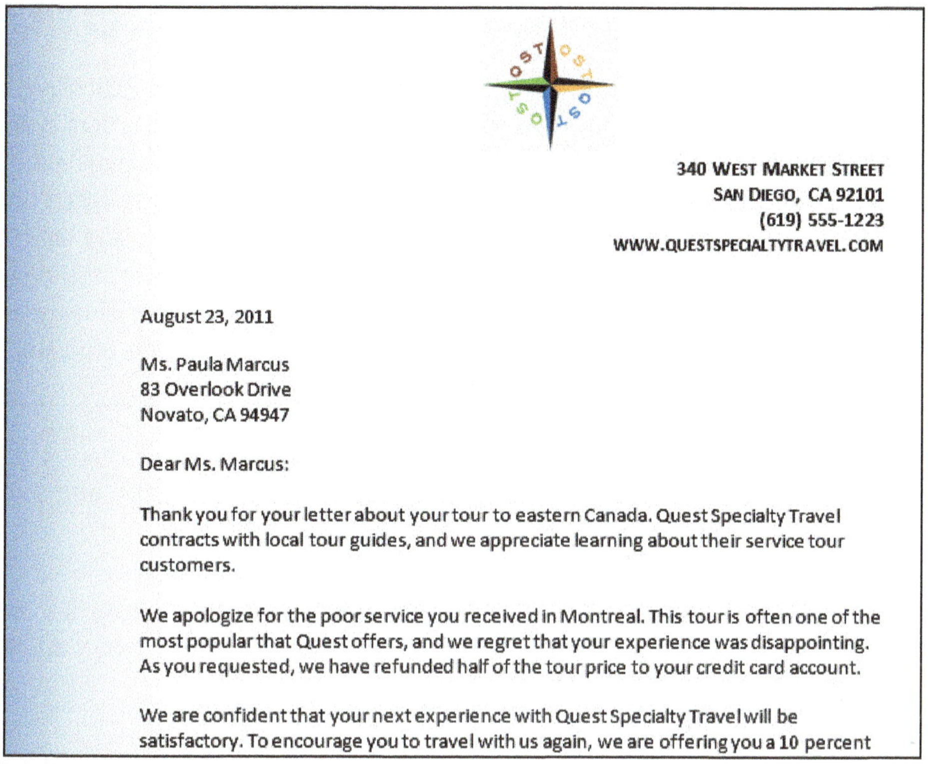

340 WEST MARKET STREET
SAN DIEGO, CA 92101
(619) 555-1223
WWW.QUESTSPECIALTYTRAVEL.COM

August 23, 2011

Ms. Paula Marcus
83 Overlook Drive
Novato, CA 94947

Dear Ms. Marcus:

Thank you for your letter about your tour to eastern Canada. Quest Specialty Travel contracts with local tour guides, and we appreciate learning about their service tour customers.

We apologize for the poor service you received in Montreal. This tour is often one of the most popular that Quest offers, and we regret that your experience was disappointing. As you requested, we have refunded half of the tour price to your credit card account.

We are confident that your next experience with Quest Specialty Travel will be satisfactory. To encourage you to travel with us again, we are offering you a 10 percent

TABLE 5-3: Response letter do's and don'ts

response letter element	do	don't
Subject line	• Summarize the original request, as in "Subject: Your March 10 inquiry about shipping dates"	• **Don't** repeat the request in detail
Direct approach	• Use a direct approach if you can comply with the request • If you cannot comply with the request, use a direct approach only if your reader expects directness	• **Don't** use a direct approach if your reader might respond negatively
Indirect approach	• Use an indirect approach if you need to soften your response • Establish goodwill • Explain the reason for your decision • Deliver the bad news clearly, then end on a positive note	• **Don't** overlook the legal implications of your response • **Don't** use negative language or make promises you can't keep

Objective 39
Part 5

Writing Persuasive Letters

Persuasion is the process of convincing others to change their beliefs or actions. Although you might not be aware of it, you frequently need to persuade other people to take action, change their opinion, authorize a request, purchase goods or services, or do a favor for you. Persuasion is not only an art for salespeople—it is an important skill for all professionals. Unlike other business letters that start by directly making their point, persuasive communication requires careful planning and an in direct approach. Figure 5-10 outlines the elements of persuasive letters. case You have been assisting Ron Dawson as he develops an incentive program corporate customers can use to reward their employees. Ron asks you to write the first draft of a persuasive letter encouraging companies to join the program.

ESSENTIAL ELEMENTS

QUICK TIP
You can also grab attention with visual persuasion by highlighting key words with bold, color, or italics.

1. **Capture your reader's attention**
   Your letter can only change readers' opinions if they carefully read it. Open with an engaging question, problem statement, unexpected declaration, or other attention grabber.
2. **Develop your reader's interest**
   Your readers are interested in information that is relevant to them, helps to solve their problems, or benefits them directly or indirectly. Approach your message from your reader's perspective to identify their interests and understand what is beneficial to them.
3. **Introduce your request**
   Let your reader know why you are writing and what you are requesting. Your request should be a logical conclusion to your opening paragraph, as shown in Figure 5-11.
4. **Answer your reader's questions**
   In many cases your reader will have questions and concerns about your message. It's human nature to resist new ideas and to be skeptical of offers and requests. Anticipate your reader's questions and answer them using examples, data, research, or other evidence to support your position and enhance your credibility.
5. **Call your reader to action**
   Decide what you specifically want from your reader and ask for it in your final paragraph. Maintain a positive attitude when making your request. Avoid the extremes of sounding too aggressive or too timid.

YOU TRY IT

Practice writing persuasive letters by writing a letter based on an outline. Open the WC5-Y39.docx document and follow the steps in the worksheet. When you are finished, submit the document to your instructor as requested.

FIGURE 5-10: Elements of a persuasive letter

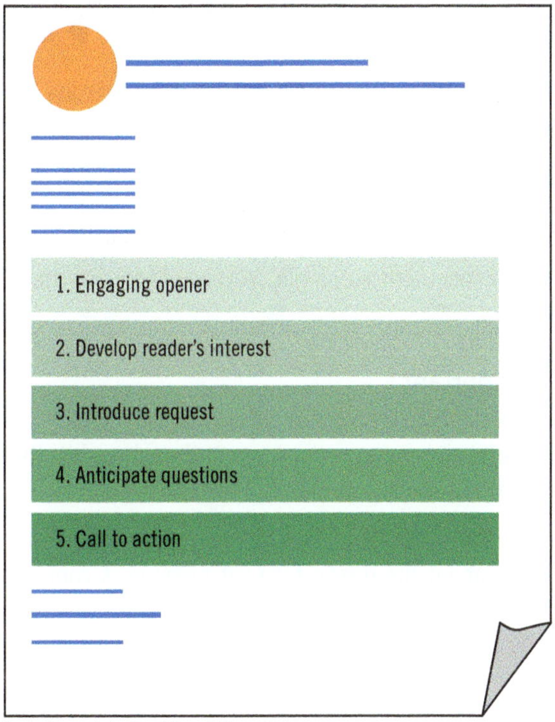

Used with permission from Microsoft Corporation

FIGURE 5-11: Persuasive letter to Quest customers

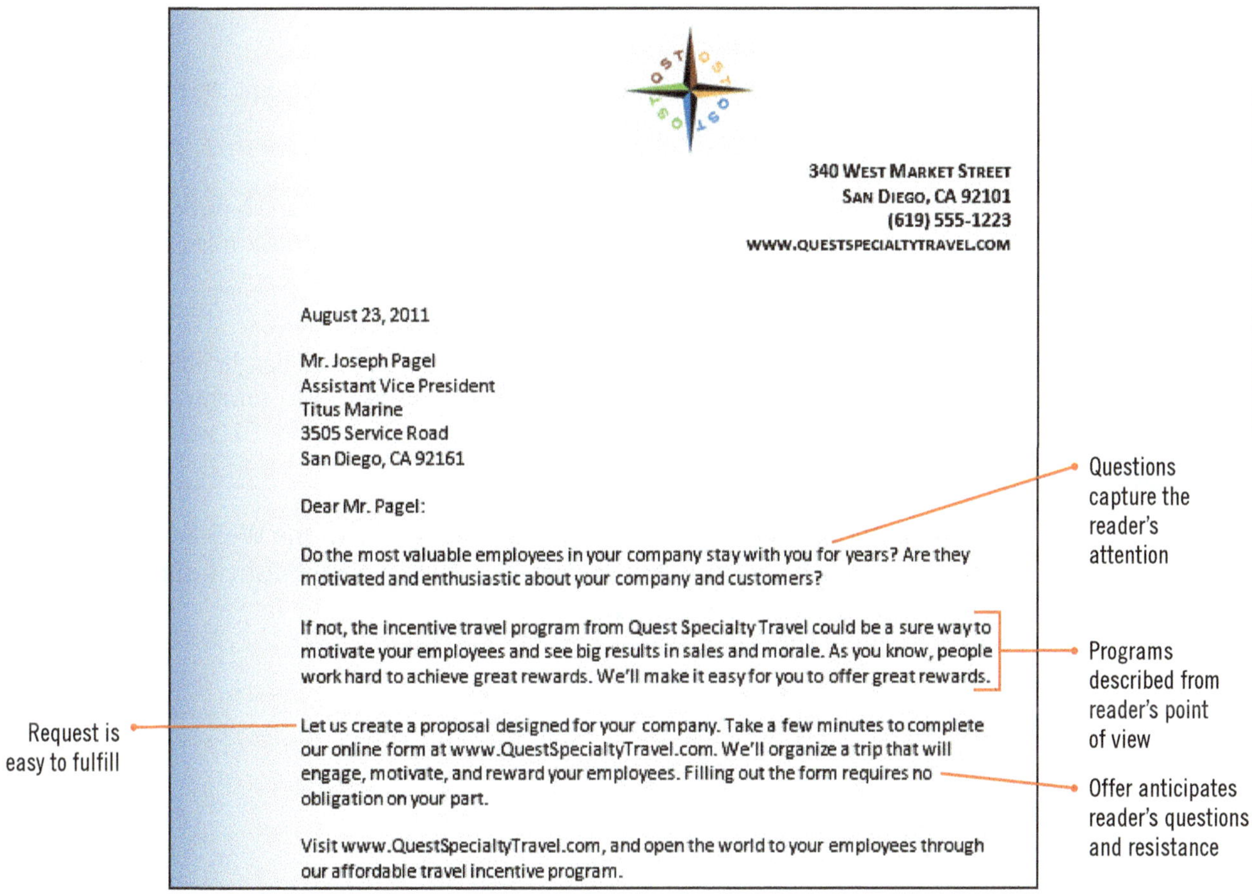

340 West Market Street
San Diego, CA 92101
(619) 555-1223
www.questspecialtytravel.com

August 23, 2011

Mr. Joseph Pagel
Assistant Vice President
Titus Marine
3505 Service Road
San Diego, CA 92161

Dear Mr. Pagel:

Do the most valuable employees in your company stay with you for years? Are they motivated and enthusiastic about your company and customers?

If not, the incentive travel program from Quest Specialty Travel could be a sure way to motivate your employees and see big results in sales and morale. As you know, people work hard to achieve great rewards. We'll make it easy for you to offer great rewards.

Let us create a proposal designed for your company. Take a few minutes to complete our online form at www.QuestSpecialtyTravel.com. We'll organize a trip that will engage, motivate, and reward your employees. Filling out the form requires no obligation on your part.

Visit www.QuestSpecialtyTravel.com, and open the world to your employees through our affordable travel incentive program.

Used with permission from Microsoft Corporation

Objective
40
Part 5

Writing for Goodwill

You can develop and foster the professional relationships that are crucial to your career success through **goodwill communication**, which includes messages of appreciation, recognition, condolence, and apology. Finding the appropriate words to express your goodwill can be more difficult than writing a standard business letter, but they can be meaningful and memorable if they are specific, sincere, and short, as shown in Figure 5-12. case To acknowledge your extra efforts in helping to organize an adventure tour to Hawaii, a pair of customers sent you a gift. You want to write them a letter to express your thanks.

ESSENTIAL ELEMENTS

QUICK TIP
A prompt goodwill letter conveys the message that you consider the reader as important.

1. Promptness is important

If you want to thank someone for a gift or favor, express sympathy, or offer congratulations, write a goodwill letter as soon as possible so you can compose your thoughts while the idea is fresh. A prompt message is also more meaningful to your reader.

2. Explain why you are writing

Provide brief details about the reason for your message. A common problem with goodwill messages is they don't explain why they are offering thanks or encouragement. Instead of writing *Congratulations on a job well done*, be specific, as in *Congratulations on your promotion to assistant manager. That is quite an accomplishment.*

QUICK TIP
One way to focus on the reader is to address him or her by name.

3. Focus on your reader

Goodwill messages should focus on your reader, not on you. Avoid starting sentences with "I" or making yourself the subject of the sentence. In most cases, you can rewrite these sentences to focus attention on your reader.

4. Keep your message short

Goodwill messages should communicate a single idea and do not need to fill an entire page. Most can accomplish their purpose in a single paragraph.

5. Handwrite when appropriate

A handwritten note is more memorable and personal than a typed letter and is particularly well suited for appreciation messages. Short thank-you and recognition notes are often handwritten on note cards or personal stationary.

6. Write the way you speak

Goodwill messages are personal communication and should be written as though two people were having a conversation. Use a friendly, informal tone and choose words that reflect sincerity. Figure 5-13 shows a goodwill message written to a group of Quest customers.

YOU TRY IT

Practice writing for goodwill by writing a goodwill letter. Open the WC5-Y40.docx document and follow the steps in the worksheet. When you are finished, submit the document to your instructor as requested.

FIGURE 5-12: Examples of goodwill messages

> Thank you, Alice, for the welcome gift of a potted plant. The shape of the vine is beautiful, and the ceramic pot is perfect for my office. More than anything, however, I appreciate your thoughtfulness in welcoming me to the department.

Thank you message

> I'm so sorry to hear about the loss of your aunt. I recall how warmly you spoke of her and how special she was to you. Please know you're in my thoughts.

Sympathy message

FIGURE 5-13: Thank-you letter to Quest customers

340 WEST MARKET STREET
SAN DIEGO, CA 92101
(619) 555-1223
WWW.QUESTSPECIALTYTRAVEL.COM

August 25, 2011

Mr. Warren Schroeder
Ms. Teresa Woodbury
1144 Yakima Avenue South
Tacoma, WA 98401

Dear Mr. Schroeder and Ms. Woodbury:

Thank you both for your Hawaiian gift basket, which I received this morning. The Kona coffee, macadamia nuts, and chocolates are delicious indulgences I'll share with others here at Quest.

I'm so glad you enjoyed your adventure tour to Hawaii, and I appreciate you thinking of me while you were snorkeling and parasailing in Maui.

Sincerely,

Explains reason for writing

Focuses on reader

Keeps message short

Used with permission from Microsoft Corporation

Written Communication

Respond to complaints with goodwill messages

If you receive a complaint from a customer about your company's goods or services, what's your first response? If you dismiss the complaint or act defensive, the customer is likely to leave your business dissatisfied and voice their displeasure to people they know. Instead, according to Janelle Barlow and Claus Moller, authors of *A Complaint Is a Gift*, your first response should be to thank the customer. "Complaints are one of the most direct and effective ways for customers to tell businesses that there is room for improvement," the authors state. Apply your skills in writing goodwill messages to thank the customer for the comment, explain why you appreciate it, apologize for the mistake, and then correct it promptly. Southwest Airlines takes a step beyond this approach by anticipating complaints though a management position dedicated to overseeing proactive communications with customers, held in 2008 by Fred Taylor. After a flight was delayed many times because of weather and pilot schedules, Taylor sent letters to the travelers along with ticket vouchers. "It's not something we had to do," Taylor said. "It's just something we feel our customers deserve." It's also a surefire way to build customer loyalty.

Sources: Barlow, Janelle and Moller, Claus, *A Complaint Is a Gift*, Berrett-Koehler Publishers; 2nd edition (August 1, 2008), and Editors, "25 companies where customers come first," *BusinessWeek*, April 1, 2008.

Technology @ Work: Instant Messaging

Instant messaging (IM) is a technology that involves communication between two people who type text messages to one another using a computer, mobile phone, tablet, or other device connected to the Internet. See Figure 5-14. Because they are short, informal, and impermanent, instant messages are the opposite of letters, which are longer, more formal, and more permanent. IM and e-mail are more similar because both technologies send messages across the Internet. IM, however, is like an electronic conversation—you see a message and respond to it immediately. IM software for business use is considered enterprise instant messaging (EIM). case Ron Dawson is considering using IM at Quest Specialty Travel for communication among travel tour developers and the office. He asks you to research IM, including its pros and cons.

ESSENTIAL ELEMENTS

1. **Organize contacts into categories**

   Instant messaging software lets you separate contacts into business, friends, and family categories, for example. This means you can easily keep your professional IMs separate from personal IMs. However, to participate in any type of instant messaging, you sign on to the software. Your friends and family can see when you are signed on, even at work. Make sure they know you need to concentrate on professional conversations when you are working.

   So that employees keep personal text messages separate from business messages, some organizations provide EIM software. For example, Brosix is an instant messenger designed for businesses. Brosix is popular because it runs on Windows, Mac OS X, and other operating systems. To tour the features of Brosix, use your browser to go to *www.brosix.com*. Click the Screenshots link, and then click the thumbnails to see larger screenshots.

2. **Send and reply to messages instantly**

   The instantaneous feature of IM is both an advantage and disadvantage. Instead of waiting for an answer to a letter or e-mail, you can receive a response from a colleague or vendor immediately. However, IM can be a distraction when you need to focus on a project, conversation, or meeting.

3. **Save instant messages for future reference**

   Like e-mail, you can save IMs when you need to reference a conversation with customers or colleagues, for example. You can also send, receive, and save attachments to messages. However, viruses can infect IMs as easily as they do e-mail messages.

QUICK TIP

Make sure you open only attachments you expect to receive or that have been scanned by antivirus software.

4. **Use professional language**

   Personal text messages often use slang, shorthand, "text speak," and emoticons to abbreviate common words or expressions and to reduce the amount of necessary typing. For example, LOL (for *laugh out loud*) is a common shorthand response. However, these techniques are inappropriate and overly casual in professional settings. Your language can be more informal than in a standard business letter, but it should still be clear, complete, and professional.

YOU TRY IT

Research enterprise instant messaging (EIM) and consumer instant messaging (CIM). Open the WC5-TechWork.docx document and follow the steps in the worksheet. When you are finished, submit the document to your instructor as requested.

FIGURE 5-14: Instant messaging on mobile devices

Oleksiy Mark/Photos.com

Sally Felton/Photos.com

TABLE 5-4: Instant messaging do's and don'ts

IM element	do	don't
Etiquette	• Write simple, short, clear messages • Update your status throughout the day • Ask others if they are available to chat • Use IM for brief, informational messages	• **Don't** make statements you wouldn't make in public • **Don't** use a misleading or unprofessional screen name • **Don't** exchange instant messages during meetings or phone calls • **Don't** use jargon, especially when communicating with customers
Security and Privacy	• Keep in mind that instant messages can be saved • Avoid transferring files because they can contain viruses	• **Don't** use IM to share confidential information such as passwords • **Don't** make statements that could damage the reputation of your employer or yourself
Professionalism	• Keep your work contacts seperate from your personal contacts • Follow your employers guidelines about IM at work • Check your spelling and grammar before sending a message	• **Don't** combine a social chat with a professional chat, especially with a customer • **Don't** use IM at work, unless your employer allows it for personal use or as part of your job

Practice

Soft Skills Review

Understand professional letter writing.

1. **For what purpose do you write a business letter?**
   - **a.** For routine communication with colleagues
   - **b.** To send a message as quickly as possible
   - **c.** To deliver messages outside of an organization
   - **d.** To write to a close friend
2. **In which of the following circumstances is a business letter *not* the best choice?**
   - **a.** You need to create a permanent record
   - **b.** You need to deny a written request
   - **c.** You want to contact someone you don't know
   - **d.** You want to organize a meeting

Write business letters.

1. **What should you do before you write a business letter?**
   - **a.** Identify the goal of the letter
   - **b.** Write the complimentary close
   - **c.** Call the letter recipient
   - **d.** Format the letter
2. **The block style is:**
   - **a.** more appropriate for personal notes
   - **b.** the standard form for business letters
   - **c.** a format that omits the salutation and signature
   - **d.** appropriate for casual messages

Use salutations.

1. **Why should you start a business letter with a salutation?**
   - **a.** To sound formal and serious
   - **b.** To avoid delivering bad news directly
   - **c.** To personalize the letter with handwritten text
   - **d.** To open with a friendly, proper greeting
2. **When do you usually need to include job titles, rank, or titles of honor in a salutation?**
   - **a.** When writing particularly formal letters
   - **b.** When writing complaint letters
   - **c.** When responding to complaint letters
   - **d.** Only for goodwill messages

Close business letters.

1. **What is important about the closing paragraph of a business letter?**
   - **a.** It sets the tone of the rest of the letter
   - **b.** It explains the purpose of the letter
   - **c.** It can affect the reader's willingness to respond to your request
   - **d.** It presents the main idea
2. **Which one of the following should you *not* include in the closing?**
   - **a.** Deadline
   - **b.** Reason for request
   - **c.** Contact information
   - **d.** Direct command, such as "Respond as soon as possible."

Write routine letters.

1. **You use the simplified letter format for:**
   - **a.** direct, informal letters
   - **b.** goodwill letters of sympathy
   - **c.** formal invitations
   - **d.** mixed messages
2. **How should you start a letter written in the simplified letter format?**
   - **a.** With a clear statement of your offer
   - **b.** With a joke or anecdote
   - **c.** With an expression of gratitude
   - **d.** With an apology

Answer request letters.

1. **When should you respond to a request using an indirect approach?**
   - **a.** If you are responding favorably
   - **b.** If you know the reader personally
   - **c.** If your reader might react negatively to your response
   - **d.** If you are using the simplified letter format
2. **How should you start a letter written using the indirect approach?**
   - **a.** By immediately denying the request
   - **b.** By establishing goodwill
   - **c.** By listing facts
   - **d.** By summarizing the problem

Write persuasive letters.

1. **Which of the following is *not* a goal of a persuasive letter?**
   - **a.** To change the reader's opinion
   - **b.** To express appreciation
   - **c.** To convince the reader to take action
   - **d.** To have the reader authorize a request
2. **What is an effective way to open a persuasive letter?**
   - **a.** Introduce your request
   - **b.** Answer potential questions
   - **c.** Ask a question that captures the reader's attention
   - **d.** Motivate action by requesting a specific response

Write for goodwill.

1. **What kinds of messages are included in goodwill communication?**
   - **a.** Appreciation
   - **b.** Persuasion
   - **c.** Bad news
   - **d.** Routine business
2. **Goodwill messages should:**
   - **a.** clarify requests for information
   - **b.** follow the block format
   - **c.** explain and justify your claims
   - **d.** focus on the reader, not on you

Technology @ work: Instant messaging.

1. **How can instant messages be considered the opposite of business letters?**
   - **a.** They are short, informal, and impermanent
   - **b.** Their purpose is to entertain
   - **c.** They have a corporate audience only
   - **d.** They are not intended to establish goodwill
2. **Why should you avoid typical IM techniques such as slang and shorthand?**
   - **a.** No one understands them
   - **b.** They focus on the writer, not the reader
   - **c.** They are inappropriate and overly casual in professional settings
   - **d.** They are entertaining

Critical Thinking Questions

1. **A supplier sends you an expensive gift with a note that thanks you for "bending the rules" to his benefit. Is the gift a legitimate business courtesy or a bribe? How do you respond in either case?**
2. **Do you think persuasive writing techniques involve deception? Find examples of deceptive persuasive writing and analyze how they attempt to persuade readers.**
3. **A customer writes you a letter complaining about a colleague. How do you handle your response?**
4. **Your supervisor hands you a stack of letters and asks you to respond them. One of the letters is from a customer complaining about your supervisor's inappropriate conduct during a sales call. How do you respond to the letter? How do you handle the situation with your supervisor?**
5. **You are responding to a complaint from a customer who is angry because you made a mistake. Should you blame the error on a computer problem or explain that someone else is responsible? Or should you accept the blame, even if it means losing this customer? What if it means losing your job?**

Independent Challenge 1

You work in the Marketing Department of a small Web design company named Overland Designs. Marshall Aronson, the director of marketing, hands you a letter from a customer who is requesting information about Overland Design's services. Figure 5-15 shows the customer letter. Marshall asks you to write a letter in response.

FIGURE 5-15

J&L Enterprises
1586 S. Pine Street
Chicago, IL 60620
(612) 555-9078

January 12, 2011

Director of Marketing
Overland Designs
910 Michigan Avenue
Chicago, IL 60202

Dear Director of Marketing:

I am the owner of a sports equipment manufacturing company, and I would like to set up a Web site to attract and service customers. Please let me know the answers to the following questions:

- What types of Web site design services do you offer?
- Can you provide graphic design services?
- What types of clients do you have?
- How can we start to work together?

Please also send me any examples of your work or other promotional materials.

Sincerely,

Carl Lopez

Carl Lopez
President

Used with permission from Microsoft Corporation

a. Open the **WC5-IC1.docx** document and follow the steps in the worksheet.
b. Proofread the document carefully to fix any grammar or formatting errors.
c. Submit the document to your instructor as requested.

Independent Challenge 2

You are the manager of the flagship Four Winds Apparel store in Minneapolis, Minnesota. Four Winds Apparel specializes in affordable active wear for men, women, and children and has three other stores in the Minneapolis-St. Paul area. Allison Crandall, the Four Winds regional manager, is working with an English-speaking supplier in France. She asks you to format and finish a letter she started requesting information about the French apparel. You need to revise and format the letter.

a. Open the **WC5-IC2.docx** document and follow the steps in the worksheet.
b. Proofread the document carefully to fix any grammar or formatting errors.
c. Submit the document to your instructor as requested.

Real Life Independent Challenge

This Independent Challenge requires an Internet connection.

You are applying for a summer internship in Washington, D.C., and need to send a letter to someone who can act as a reference, such as an instructor or former employer.

a. Using your favorite search engine, search for internship programs in Washington, D.C., such as those in government, media, communications, or the arts. Find a page that describes the eligibility requirements and application procedures.

b. Read about the eligibility requirements and application procedures.

c. Write a letter to someone who can act as a reference for the internship, such as an instructor or employer. Be sure to include the following elements:

- Clearly stated subject
- Direct opening sentence
- Well-organized message body
- Professional formatting
- Appropriate closing statement

d. Proofread the message carefully to fix any grammar or formatting errors.

e. Save the letter and provide it in the format specified by your instructor.

Team Challenge

This Independent Challenge requires an Internet connection.

You work for Farley Worldwide, a company specializing in information services, and have been promoted recently. You travel overseas with a small group and help your client companies install computers and software. You are planning a trip to Beijing, China, and need to set up hotel accommodations and arrangements for travel in Beijing.

a. Using your favorite search engine, search for information about the proper letter format to use when writing to English-speaking Chinese professionals in Beijing. Note the addresses of the Web sites that provide the most useful information.

b. Meet as a team to assign the following tasks:

- Research hotels in Beijing
- Research transportation in Beijing
- Research restaurants in Beijing

c. As a team, decide on a hotel. Also compile a list of transportation alternatives and restaurants near the hotel.

d. Individually, write a letter to the appropriate hotel staff member inquiring about rooms for your team, cost per night, additional charges, and use of a conference room. Include any other details that seem appropriate based on your research.

e. Save the letter and provide it in the format specified by your instructor.

Be the Critic

Review the poorly written letter shown in Figure 5-16. Create an e-mail message that lists the weaknesses of the letter and makes specific suggestions for improvement. Send the critique to your instructor.

FIGURE 5-16

AllCity Electronics

151 Appleton Avenue
Milwaukee, WI 53215
(414) 555-1600

Dear Mr. Edward Lavine,

I received your complaint about the issues that you claim have occurred recently. Keep in mind that electronics equipment is delicate, and that dropping music players or submerging them in water is considered abuse.

Our Customer Satisfaction Team will be reviewing the information you have sent us. If there is a valid reason for your complaint, the Team will conduct a full investigation as deemed appropriate to resolve this matter.

At the conclusion of our investigation, you will be contacted with our findings.

Glossary

Analytical report A type of report that presents data, analysis, and a conclusion by providing different options, identifying pros and cons for alternatives, and including specific recommendations.

Aspect ratio The ratio of the width to the height in an image.

Block style A set of standard conventions for writing business letters.

Blog An interactive online journal. Short for *Weblog*.

Business letter A professional communication tool for delivering messages outside of an organization.

Chart A visual representation of numeric information. Also called a graph.

Chronological résumé A type of résumé that presents your work experience and education sorted by date. Also called a reverse-chronological résumé.

Conjunctions Connector words including *for, and, nor, but, or, yet,* and *so* (FANBOYS).

Cover letter A short, personalized letter you send with your résumé to indicate your interest in an employment opportunity. Also called a letter of application.

Documentation message A type of message that provides a reminder of an upcoming task or restates an earlier message to avoid misunderstanding. Also called a confirmation, to-file, or incident message, confirms events, ideas, discussions, agreements, changes, or instructions.

E-mail message Communication composed on and sent with electronic mail technology.

End matter One or more sections that follow the conclusion in a report or other long document.

Executive summary A short synopsis of the important ideas, observations, problems, and conclusions contained in your report.

External proposal A type of proposal designed to sell products or services to customers, and usually written in response to a request.

Functional résumé A type of résumé that highlights your skills and abilities instead of your work history. Also called a skills résumé.

Goodwill communication Communication including messages of appreciation, recognition, condolence, and apology.

Header The beginning part of a memo that lists basic information about the document. Most memo headers include at least four lines, similar to an e-mail message: Date, To, From, and Subject (or Re).

Independent clause A group of words that has a subject and a verb and can stand alone as a sentence.

Indirect approach A way to organize a message, especially one that delivers bad news, by revealing the message in stages.

Informational report A type of report that presents information in a clear, objective format, and is appropriate when you want to provide a written summary of a subject for your reader.

Instant messaging (IM) A technology that involves communication between two people who type text messages to one another using a computer, mobile phone, or other device connected to the Internet.

Internal proposal A type of proposal that recommends how to solve problems within an organization.

Interview A meeting between a job applicant and the hiring manager in which they discuss the job opportunity and the applicant's qualifications.

Invisible Web Web sites that popular search engines cannot access, such as university libraries and online almanacs.

Letter of transmittal A cover letter or memo that provides a personalized introduction to a report.

Memo A hard, or printed, copy of a document written for people within a single organization.

Online collaboration tool Web-based software designed to help groups work together to achieve their goals, such as completing a project, designing a new product, or writing a long report or proposal.

Paragraph A group of sentences that collectively presents or describes a single topic or idea.

Paraphrase To use your own words to state or explain someone else's ideas.

Persuasion The process of convincing others to change their beliefs or actions.

Predicate In grammar, a verb that tells the reader what the subject is, what the subject is doing, or what is happening to the subject.

Primary source A form of firsthand experience, such as interviews and observations.

Product proposal A type of proposal that suggests your readers buy a product or service. Also called a commodity proposal.

Professional networking site A Web site you use to connect with employers and colleagues using a variety of online methods, such as e-mail and instant messages.

Proposal A written document designed to persuade and inform. A proposal provides information about a product, service, or idea and tries to convince the reader to adopt the recommended solution.

Punctuation marks In writing, a set of symbols that reflects pauses and grammatical structure so readers can interpret text.

Ragged-right alignment Aligning the text along the left margin, which adds white space at the end of each line of text and helps readers locate the beginnings of new lines. Also called left justification.

Report A written document designed to communicate information about a particular subject. Reports are written objectively, though some can include analysis or recommendations.

Request for proposal (RFP) A document that specifies the requirements of a proposal.

Request message A type of e-mail message or memo that asks for information or action from someone else.

Résumé A one- or two-page summary of your education, employment history, skills, and accomplishments.

Secondary source A written document describing a topic or experience, such as an article, book, or Web page.

Simplified letter format An alternative to the block style, a type of letter format that is direct and informal, suitable for routine letters sent as mass mail, such as sales letters and announcements sent to customers, shareholders, suppliers, or employees.

Solution proposal A type of proposal that suggests ideas, services, or complex solutions, and begins by describing a problem and then defines how you propose to solve it. Also called a service proposal.

Style The tone, formality, and voice of your sentences.

Subject In grammar, the person, place, or thing that a sentence is talking about.

White space Areas on a page without text or graphics.

Wiki A Web site that many users can contribute to by creating and editing the content.

Index

A

academic papers vs. reports, Written Communication 51
acceptance letters, Written Communication 88–89
accepting job offers, Written Communication 88–89
adding tables, figures to documents, Written Communication 38–39
addresses
on business letters, Written Communication 100
on cover letters, Written Communication 76–77
e-mail, Written Communication 6–7
on memos, Written Communication 8–9
affirmative writing, Written Communication 28
alignment, ragged-right, **Written Communication 34**
American Psychological Association (APA) citation format, Written Communication 64
analytical reports, **Written Communication 50**
answering request letters, Written Communication 108–109
appendices, in reports, Written Communication 58–59
application follow-up messages, Written Communication 86–87
approval pages in reports, Written Communication 58
aspect ratio, **Written Communication 38**
audience
determining blog, Written Communication 42
for internal, external proposals, Written Communication 50–51
knowing your, Written Communication 26

B

bad-news messages
do's and don'ts (table), Written Communication 15
writing, Written Communication 14–15
bar charts, Written Communication 36
Barlow, Janelle, Written Communication 113
Blind carbon copy (Bcc) field, Written Communication 6
block style, **Written Communication 100**
blogs
described, **Written Communication 42**
vs. other media, Written Communication 3
brackets ([]), using, Written Communication 32
Brosix, Written Communication 114
business communications
e-mail messages. *See* e-mail messages
memos. *See* memos
reports. *See* reports
writing business letters, Written Communication 98–102
business letters, **Written Communication 98**
closing, Written Communication 104–105
examples of, Written Communication 99

C

CareerBuilder.com, Written Communication 81
Cc (carbon copy) field, Written Communication 6, Written Communication 7
charts, **Written Communication 36**, Written Communication 37
Chicago style citation format, Written Communication 64
chronological résumés, Written Communication 83
citing sources in reports, proposals, Written Communication 64–65
closing
business letters, Written Communication 104–105
signature block, Written Communication 6
statement, e-mail, Written Communication 4, Written Communication 5
collaboration
online collaboration tools, Written Communication 66–67
using wikis, Written Communication 18, Written Communication 20
colons (:)
do's and don'ts (table), Written Communication 33
using, Written Communication 32
column charts, Written Communication 36, Written Communication 37
commas (,)
do's and don'ts (table), Written Communication 33
using, Written Communication 32
comments policies for blogs, Written Communication 42
***Complaint Is a Gift, A* (Barlow and Mollet)**, Written Communication 113
complaints, responding to, Written Communication 113
conclusions in paragraphs, Written Communication 31
conjunctions, **Written Communication 32**
Conroy, Martin, Written Communication 99
contacts, organizing, Written Communication 114
cover letters, Written Communication 74, **Written Communication 76**
do's and don'ts (table), Written Communication 77
writing, Written Communication 76–77

creating
See also writing
bad-news messages, Written Communication 14–15
blogs, Written Communication 42–43
documentation messages, Written Communication 16–17
effective paragraphs, Written Communication 30–31
e-mail messages, Written Communication 4–7
Google account, Written Communication 66–67
request messages, Written Communication 10–13
response messages, Written Communication 12–13

D

dashes (—), using, Written Communication 32
dates, memo format, Written Communication 8
deadlines
in message closing, Written Communication 11
on request messages, Written Communication 10
declining job offers, Written Communication 88–89
direct approach, Written Communication 12, Written Communication 16
documentation messages, **Written Communication 16**, Written Communication 17
documenting your communications, Written Communication 98–99
documents
See also specific type
adding tables and figures, Written Communication 38–39
in Google Docs, Written Communication 66–67
illustrating data, Written Communication 36–37
laying out, Written Communication 34–35
revising, Written Communication 40–41
spell- and grammar-checking, Written Communication 40

E

editing
blogs, Written Communication 43
documents, Written Communication 40–41
Edmondson, David J., Written Communication 81
education summary on résumés, Written Communication 78, Written Communication 79
ellipses (...), using, Written Communication 32
e-mail
addresses, Written Communication 6–7
avoiding overload, Written Communication 17
messages. *See* e-mail messages
vs. other media, Written Communication 35
writing vs. texting, Written Communication 33
e-mail messages, **Written Communication 2**
appropriate uses (table), Written Communication 3
composing, Written Communication 4–5
creating professional, Written Communication 6–7
do's and don'ts (table), Written Communication 5, Written Communication 7
example, Written Communication 3
getting past spam filters, Written Communication 4
response e-mail etiquette, Written Communication 13
when to use, Written Communication 2
emoticons, Written Communication 114
employment
follow-up messages, sending, Written Communication 86–87
job searches, Written Communication 74–75
letters of reference, requesting, Written Communication 84–85
résumés. *See* résumés
Enclosure (Enc), Written Communication 104
end matter, **Written Communication 58**, Written Communication 59
e-portfolios, Written Communication 85
etiquette, response e-mail, Written Communication 13
executive summary, **Written Communication 54**
external reports, **Written Communication 50**

F

face-to-face meetings
vs. other media, Written Communication 35
when appropriate, Written Communication 3
fax vs. other media, Written Communication 35
figures
adding to documents, Written Communication 38–39
do's and don'ts (table), Written Communication 39
filters, e-mail, Written Communication 4
FindLaw, Written Communication 57
flow charts, Written Communication 36
fonts, choosing appropriate, Written Communication 34
formatting
business letters, Written Communication 100–101
citations, sources, Written Communication 64–65
e-mail message opening, message body, Written Communication 7
format for external audiences, Written Communication 60
paragraphs, Written Communication 31
résumés, Written Communication 80–83
short report, Written Communication 60–61
tables, figures in documents, Written Communication 39
functional résumés, **Written Communication 82**, Written Communication 83

G

Gates, Bill, Written Communication 9
goodwill communication, **Written Communication 112**
Google Docs, Written Communication 66–67

grammar
checking your documents, Written Communication 40
and 'plain English,' Written Communication 41

H

Haefner, Rosemary, Written Communication 81
Hakia search engine, Written Communication 59
handwritten notes, Written Communication 112
headers, memo, **Written Communication 8**
headings
report, Written Communication 52, Written Communication 56
résumé, Written Communication 79
hierarchy charts, Written Communication 36, Written Communication 37

I

illustrations
adding to documents, Written Communication 38–39
tables of, Written Communication 58
indirect approach, Written Communication 14
Infomine, Written Communication 57
informational reports, **Written Communication 50**
instant messaging (IM)
do's and don'ts (table), Written Communication 115
vs. other media, Written Communication 35
overview of, Written Communication 114
internal reports, **Written Communication 50**
Internet, searching for jobs on, Written Communication 75
interviews
described, **Written Communication 74**
follow-up messages, sending, Written Communication 86–87
invisible Web, **Written Communication 57**

J

job offers, accepting or rejecting, Written Communication 88–89
job searches
See also employment
accepting or rejecting offers, Written Communication 88–89
LinkedIn results (fig.), Written Communication 91
résumés. *See* résumés
steps in, Written Communication 74–75

K

Kartoo search tool, Written Communication 59
keywords
and research, Written Communication 57
using in résumés, Written Communication 82

L

labels for figures, tables, Written Communication 38
layout of documents, Written Communication 34–35
letter of transmittal, **Written Communication 54**
letterhead, Written Communication 100
letters
See also memos
answering request, Written Communication 108–109
business. *See* business letters
format for external audiences, Written Communication 60
job acceptance, rejection, Written Communication 88–89
vs. other media, Written Communication 3
when to use, Written Communication 3
writing cover, Written Communication 76–77
writing for goodwill, Written Communication 112–113
writing persuasive, Written Communication 110–111
writing routine, Written Communication 106–107
letters of reference, requesting, Written Communication 84–85
line charts, Written Communication 36, Written Communication 37
LinkedIn, Written Communication 90–91
Lonchar, Kenneth, Written Communication 81

M

mass mail, Written Communication 106
meetings
face-to-face, vs. other media, Written Communication 3
face-to-face, when appropriate, Written Communication 3
request messages for, Written Communication 10
memos, **Written Communication 2**, Written Communication 60
appropriate uses (table), Written Communication 3
creating, Written Communication 8–9
do's and don'ts (table), Written Communication 9
example, Written Communication 3
format for internal audiences, Written Communication 60
headers, Written Communication 8, Written Communication 9
vs. other media, Written Communication 3
message body, e-mail, Written Communication 3, Written Communication 4
do's and don'ts (table), Written Communication 5
formatting, Written Communication 7
messages
sending follow-up, Written Communication 86–87
writing bad-news, Written Communication 14–15
writing documentation, Written Communication 16–17
writing request, Written Communication 10–11
writing response, Written Communication 12–13
Microsoft Office Outlook, scheduling meetings, Written Communication 10
Modern Language Association (MLA) citation format, Written Communication 64
Mollet, Claus, Written Communication 113

N

networking, person-to-person, Written Communication 90–91

notations, in business letters, Written Communication 104

O

Occupational Outlook Handbook (2008–2009), Written Communication 82

online collaboration tools, Written Communication 66–67

opening
- e-mail messages, Written Communication 4
- request messages, Written Communication 11

organization charts, Written Communication 36, Written Communication 37

outlines, Written Communication 52, Written Communication 53

P

paragraphs
- choosing fonts, Written Communication 34
- developing do's and don'ts (table), Written Communication 31
- developing effective, Written Communication 30
- five-paragraph format for reports, Written Communication 60–61

paraphrasing, Written Communication 64

parentheses (()), using, Written Communication 32

periods (.), using, Written Communication 32

persuasion, **Written Communication 110**

persuasive letters, writing, Written Communication 110–111

phone calls
- vs. other media, Written Communication 35
- when to use, Written Communication 98

pie charts, Written Communication 36, Written Communication 37

Pike, Alan, Written Communication 51

plagiarism, Written Communication 57–58

planning
- reports, proposals, Written Communication 52–53
- résumés, Written Communication 78–79

positioning illustrations, Written Communication 38

predicate (sentence), **Written Communication 28**

primary sources, **Written Communication 57**

printing on letterhead, Written Communication 3

process charts, Written Communication 36, Written Communication 37

product proposals, **Written Communication 62**, Written Communication 63

professional networking site, **Written Communication 90**

pronouns, using, Written Communication 30, Written Communication 31

proofreading
- bad-news messages, Written Communication 14
- do's and don'ts (table), Written Communication 40

proposals, **Written Communication 50**
- do's and don'ts (table), Written Communication 63
- planning, Written Communication 52–53
- writing, Written Communication 50–51, Written Communication 62–63

punctuation, using, Written Communication 32–33

punctuation marks, **Written Communication 32**

Q

question marks (?), using, Written Communication 32

quotations, citations, plagiarism, Written Communication 57–58

R

ragged-right alignment, **Written Communication 34**

readers, knowing your, Written Communication 26–27

reference, requesting letters of, Written Communication 84–85

reference lists, Written Communication 58–59

rejecting job offers, Written Communication 88–89

rejection follow-up messages, Written Communication 86

rejection letters, Written Communication 88–89

Reply to All feature, Written Communication 13

reports, **Written Communication 50**
- vs. academic papers, Written Communication 51
- planning, Written Communication 52–53
- writing, Written Communication 50–51
- writing beginning of, Written Communication 54–55
- writing body of, Written Communication 56–57
- writing end matter, Written Communication 58–59
- writing short, Written Communication 60–61

request for proposal (RFP), **Written Communication 62**

request letters
- answering, Written Communication 108–109
- writing, Written Communication 110–111

request messages
- described, **Written Communication 10**
- writing, Written Communication 10–11, Written Communication 12–13

requesting letters of reference, Written Communication 84–85

research, Web tools for Web, Written Communication 59

resizing illustrations, Written Communication 38

responding to e-mail, Written Communication 13

response letters, Written Communication 108–109

response messages, Written Communication 12–13

résumés, **Written Communication 78**
- developing targeted, Written Communication 74
- do's and don'ts (table), Written Communication 79, Written Communication 81
- planning, Written Communication 78–79

writing chronological, Written Communication 80–81, Written Communication 83
writing functional, Written Communication 82–83
revising
blogs, Written Communication 43
documents generally, Written Communication 40–41
Rosenfield, James R., Written Communication 99

S

sales letters, Written Communication 106
salutations
on business letters, Written Communication 100–101
do's and don'ts (table), Written Communication 103
e-mail, Written Communication 6, Written Communication 7
using, Written Communication 102–103
searching for jobs, Written Communication 74–75
secondary sources, **Written Communication 57**
section, in reports, Written Communication 52, Written Communication 56
semicolons (;), using, Written Communication 32
sentences
do's and don'ts (table), Written Communication 29
writing good, Written Communication 28–29
signature block
do's and don'ts (table), Written Communication 105
in e-mail closing, Written Communication 6
Simonyi, Charles, Written Communication 9
simplified letter format, **Written Communication 106**
skills résumés, Written Communication 82
Small Business Association blog, Written Communication 42, Written Communication 43
social networking sites, using for job searches, Written Communication 75
solution proposals, **Written Communication 62**, Written Communication 63
sources, citing in reports, proposals, Written Communication 64–65
Southwest Airlines, Written Communication 113
spam and e-mail filters, Written Communication 4
spell-checking your documents, Written Communication 40
style, **Written Communication 28**
block, Written Communication 100
blogs, Written Communication 42
subheadings, Written Communication 52
subject (sentence), **Written Communication 28**
subject line
answering request letters, Written Communication 108
described, Written Communication 4
do's and don'ts (table), Written Communication 5
e-mail messages, Written Communication 3
response letter do's and don'ts, Written Communication 109
subtopics, Written Communication 52

T

table of contents for reports, Written Communication 54–55
tables
adding to documents, Written Communication 38–39
do's and don'ts (table), Written Communication 39
tables of figures, illustrations, Written Communication 58
Taylor, Fred, Written Communication 113
telephone calls
vs. other media, Written Communication 35
when to use, Written Communication 98
thank-you messages, Written Communication 86
title pages of reports, Written Communication 54–55, Written Communication 60
titles, in salutations, Written Communication 103
topic sentences, Written Communication 31
Traiman, Susan, Written Communication 33

U

USA.gov, Written Communication 42
user accounts
Google Docs, Written Communication 66–67
using wikis, Written Communication 18

V

verbs
placing close to subjects, Written Communication 28
sentence do's and don'ts (table), Written Communication 29
video
vs. other media, Written Communication 3
résumés, Written Communication 85
videoconferencing vs. other media, Written Communication 35
voice mail vs. other media, Written Communication 35

W

Wall Street Journal, Written Communication 99
Web, invisible, **Written Communication 57**
Web sites
See also specific site
professional networking site, Written Communication 90
Web tools, Written Communication 59
Weblogs, Written Communication 42
white space
using effectively, Written Communication 34
using on résumés, Written Communication 80
Wikipedia, Written Communication 18, Written Communication 19
wikis
described, **Written Communication 18**
overview of, Written Communication 18–19
writing
See also creating
blogs, Written Communication 42–43
business letters, Written Communication 98–102

chronological résumés, Written Communication 80–81
clarifying communication, Written Communication 26–27
cover letters, Written Communication 76–77
developing effective paragraphs, Written Communication 30–31
do's and don'ts (table), Written Communication 27
functional résumés, Written Communication 82–83
good sentences, Written Communication 28–29
goodwill communications, Written Communication 112–113
internationally, Written Communication 102
laying out documents, Written Communication 34–35
persuasive letters, Written Communication 110–111
proofreading, Written Communication 40–41
proposals, Written Communication 50–51, Written Communication 62–63
punctuation, Written Communication 32–33
reports, Written Communication 50–61
request letters, Written Communication 110–111
routine letters, Written Communication 106–107
sentence do's and don'ts (table), Written Communication 29
vs. texting, IM, e-mail, Written Communication 33

Z

Zotero Web tool, Written Communication 59